The Denatured Novel

Books by ALBERT VAN NOSTRAND

LITERARY CRITICISM IN AMERICA (ed.)

THE CONSCIOUS VOICE (ed. with C. H. Watts)

THE
DENATURED NOVEL

by

Albert Van Nostrand

THE **BOBBS-MERRILL** COMPANY, INC.
A SUBSIDIARY OF HOWARD W. SAMS & CO., INC.
Publishers • INDIANAPOLIS • NEW YORK

Portions of this book have appeared in: *American Quarterly* (Summer, 1956), and *The English Journal* (January, 1959, and February, 1959). Passages quoted herein from *I Wanted to Write*, by Kenneth Roberts, copyright 1949 by Kenneth Roberts and Anna M. Roberts, are reprinted by permission of Doubleday & Co., Inc.; from *From Main Street to Stockholm: Letters of Sinclair Lewis*, selected by Harrison Smith, copyright, 1952, by Melville H. Cane and Pincus Berner, executors of the estate of Sinclair Lewis, are used by permission of Harcourt, Brace & Co., Inc.; from *North of Grand Central*, by John P. Marquand, by permission of the publisher, Little, Brown & Co.; from *Past All Dishonor*, by James M. Cain, by permission of the publisher, Alfred A. Knopf, Inc.; from *Hollywood: The Dream Factory*, by Hortense Powdermaker, by permission of the author.

For

NANCY WILLARD VAN NOSTRAND

ACKNOWLEDGMENTS

A GRANT from the John Simon Guggenheim Memorial Foundation made this book possible. With this grant, during a sabbatical leave from teaching, I was able to devote my time and energies for an entire year to the systematic development of an idea. For this I thank the Trustees of the Guggenheim Foundation, and its Secretary General, Henry Allen Moe.

The idea of the denatured novel encompasses both literary theory and economic cause, and my research has had to be broad as well as intense. To this end, many persons have shared with me their knowledge, their opinions—often their disagreements—and their speculations. I particularly remember the help of Joseph Barnes, Knox Burger, William Charvat, Alan Collins, Saxe Commins, Paul S. Eriksson, Hugh MacNair Kahler, Freeman Lewis, William Miller, Charles Neider, John M. Pickering and Victor Weybright. Through various stages of manuscript, the idea of the book became more precise as a result of the demanding responses of Jess B. Bessinger, Jr., Peter H. Davison, Henry Klinger, Louise Lawrence, Robert Ricman, Judith Rothschild and Aaron Sussman.

During six years of research and writing I have also, necessarily, been a student, and I have been blessed with wise teachers. I owe a great debt to Howard Mumford Jones, a teacher who understands the whole endeavor of publishing, and to Monroe Stearns, an editor who is first a teacher.

My thanks are not intended to assign responsibility for the judgments in this book. The judgments are mine. But all of these persons have helped me to evaluate a significant subject for the community to share—which is the aim of scholarship; and for their help I am grateful.

—ALBERT VAN NOSTRAND

Brown University

CONTENTS

The Denatured Novel

Chapter I

Art and Artifact

BEFORE the history of the American novel began, fiction was already a commercial product in the Colonies. The novel was a form of entertainment already fortified with theories of art when it was imported into the Colonies in the eighteenth century, and it became domesticated in the new republic because a great many persons who were willing to buy its entertainment also wanted a certain record of themselves and a certain assurance of their possibilities. Accommodating the entertainment to the practical need for this self-assurance quickly became a business matter. Since popular tastes were crystallized before professional writing was possible in this nation, the American domestication of the novel necessarily involved the abrasions of art and commodity.

There never was any doubt about the commercial patronage of the new literature, but there were plenty of misgivings. The Reverend Samuel Miller summed these up, in 1803, in A *Brief Retrospect of the Eighteenth Century*, concluding his two-volume survey on a note of alarm. "Booksellers have become the great patrons of literature," he warned. The "SPIRIT OF TRADE" prevailed and authors now wrote "in accommodation to the public taste, however depraved, with a view to the most advantageous sale." These were the auspices of the American novel.

But, in a legal sense, the domestication of fiction did not occur until 1891, when Congress finally passed the first International Copyright Act, which forced American publishers to pay foreign authors for the privilege—and profit—of reprinting and selling their books in the

United States. Tardy and in many ways inadequate though it was, the Copyright Act was the best compromise that a few publishers, trade journalists and legislators could achieve after a half-century of lobbying.

The purpose of the Congress had been to protect American book manufacturers. So far as the legislators were concerned, literature was something of a by-product. But the new Copyright Act inevitably had literary consequences. By prohibiting piracy, the law made it equitable for the first time for American authors to be paid for their efforts. Since piracy had involved the reprinting of British novels, the law effectively decreed a domestic market for American novels.

The new market for fiction after 1891 inherited the old contradiction. The venerable literary form still had to satisfy the fashions in entertainment, which meant gratifying certain popular beliefs, but this old contradiction of manufacturing art took on a new economic urgency. An expanding market for literature brought rising costs, so in order to sell what they manufactured, publishers engaged vigorously in promotion.

The merchandising of literature was both the symptom and the result of the changes which occurred in publishing during the 1890's, and made the industry substantially what it is today. These economic changes, which resulted in the new fashion of marketing, were efforts to solve the industry's compelling problem of over-production. Suddenly, publishers had a staggering quantity of books, with no assurance of their getting to their prospective purchasers.

Back in 1804, the year after Samuel Miller had concluded his backward glance, A *Catalogue of All the Books Printed in the United States* listed a total of 1,338 titles. But in 1901, ten years after the Copyright Act, there were more than 150,000 titles in print in the United States, to which publishers were adding about 8,000 new titles a year. But the industry had no system of distribution which could keep pace with this volume. What the Reverend Miller had called the "unprecedented multiplication of books," nearly a century before, had by now gone beyond even the publishers.

By 1891, publishers had abandoned the practice of auctions, by which they had always sold their wares to the trade, in favor of a net-price system of wholesaling and retailing. But they soon discovered that they still had no control over the price of a book or the promotion of it to a putative customer. After John Wanamaker's department store had proved how successfully books could be sold as sidelines to other consumer products, dry-goods outlets, bazaars, and even drug stores followed suit, with the result that the industry's trade paper, *Publishers' Weekly*, expressed dismay over the indignity of this "bazaar spirit" in the book trade, and feared for its effects on literature.

Books suffered far worse than indignity by this kind of selling. The easiest way for the retailer to make money was to stock only a few titles and to sell them in volume, a practice that concentrated the consumer's attention on only a fraction of the titles publishers had made available. It penalized the great majority of books, and aggravated the problem of over-production.

With this sort of merchandising the department stores could under-sell the bookstores which had to maintain more expensive inventories. No reprisal was possible. When the American Publishers' Association obtained court injunctions against the R. H. Macy Co., in 1901, and began a long war of attrition, Macy filed suit for damages against this monopoly, and won. The Supreme Court decision of this case, in 1914, protected that practice of bookselling which denied an outlet to most of the books published.

Ironically the entire trade's active promotion of books during the 1890's accomplished only the same limiting emphasis. Publishers began to advertise their books, and circulate review copies to magazines and newspapers, in hopes of gathering opinions which they could publicize; new journals carried the advertising and supplied the publicity. The most influential of these were the *Bookman*, founded in 1895, and the weekly Book Supplement of *The New York Times*, which appeared a year later; but these could select only a few of the titles for special attention and merely listed the others.

A cataloging system of one of these journals, in fact, soon became the booktrade's favorite and most limiting promotional device: the best-seller list. At the back of its first issue *Bookman* listed retailers' reports of the six books currently leading in sales in sixteen selected cities; and in November 1897 the same magazine compiled the first national survey of "Best Selling Books." To all intents the trade endorsed this summary bookkeeping in 1911, when *Publishers' Weekly* printed its first annual "Best Selling Consensus." And this channeling encouraged the folly of best-sellerism.

What *Publishers' Weekly* called the "bazaar spirit" affected the entire book trade. Subsequently the sales value of literary property—in the cataloging, retailing and advertising of books—was systematically exploited to form public opinion. Best-sellerism affected even the editorial part of publishing. The domestication of literature by the International Copyright Act had enabled the book trade to publish American novels, but what the trade promoted was not an art form but an artifact.

Meanwhile, domestication of another sort in the preferences of American readers and book buyers had already developed. Popular opinion favored English novels of adventure and sentimentality. The first novel published in the Colonies was Benjamin Franklin's reprint of Samuel Richardson's *Pamela; or, Virtue Rewarded,* in 1744; and English novels were imported in considerable quantity even during and after the Revolution. British literary opinion fashioned some of the taste for the novels of Richardson and Laurence Sterne (then Scott, and later Dickens, Bulwer and Thackeray). But the word was really, and literally, spread by American booksellers who enterprisingly reprinted every novel they could possibly steal from the British publishers.

American writers complained that the demand for this fiction stunted native literary development. James Fenimore Cooper's two-volume description of his homeland for European readers, *Notions of the Americans* (1828), contains only a few paragraphs about American writing, and these begin dismally: "As respects American authorship, there is not much to be said." Cooper's book only emphasizes the discrepancy between America's literary dependence and its political independence, for which the author blamed the absence of international copyright and the piracy of the American booksellers.

Cooper's contemporary, John Neal, also complained about the copyright situation, but he went further: ". . . if we would write for nothing," Neal interrupted his novel, *Randolph* (1823) to say, "and *give* the copyright of a novel, for instance, to a publisher, it would still be a perilous adventure to him." He was sure no literary form wielded so much influence on society as the novel, but novel writing in America had been relinquished by men of genius and given over to women and children.

The taste of American book readers, Neal charged, was dictated by British book reviewers. He mocked the public which had waited twenty years to read the novels of Charles Brockden Brown, "till he had undergone an apotheosis at London." Poe and William Gilmore Simms and a dozen other writers lamented this same sad state of affairs, but to no effect. Until the middle of the nineteenth century novels which exploited the inherited taste for English romances were what American publishers wanted.

Virtually every historical account of early American fiction begins with an inventory of the curses and benedictions over the novel, of its evils and its virtues. Fiction was suspect so long as the Neo-Classical fashion of distinguishing between entertainment and instruction held sway, as well as the Puritan fashion of deploring this sort of entertainment. But the moralists might as well have been talking to themselves; the booksellers kept right on grinding out their sentimental—and wicked—novels.

Profit and pietism, in fact, kept each other's company. The nineteenth-century magazines contained the same wicked fiction their editorials denounced. The advertisements of booksellers protested that novels were not their primary stock in trade, but they could scarcely stock enough of them to meet the demand. Even in the novels themselves sentimental heroines were forbidden to read novels. All told, the reader could wallow in fiction's pleasurable vices and save his face at the same time.

The charges against fiction usually specify its wickedness (novels were blatant lies) and its wastefulness. To the charge of lying, the titles of the novels themselves replied. Two of the earliest of these notorious fictions spoke for dozens of others: Susanna Rowson's *Charlotte Temple; A Tale of Truth* (1791; 1794), and Hannah Foster's *The Coquette: a Novel Founded on Fact* (1797). A shrewder shot at a wider target was Isaac Mitchell's *The Asylum, or Alonzo and Melissa, an American Tale Founded on Fact* (1811).

And the novels carried other armament. A rebuttal to the charge of fiction's immorality usually appeared in a preface, sometimes called an "Advertisement" or a "Foreword," an "Introduction," "A Note to the Reader," "From the Author to the Reader," "Introductory Epistle" or "A Word in Advance." Occasionally a novel would protest its innocence in several of these at once, in which the author would deny that fiction was delinquent, and would suggest that the novel could better teach by departing from fact.

But the author did not come right out and say it. Rather, he implied it in so many words. When Nathaniel Hawthorne prefaced *The Marble Fawn* (1860) by saying that "the author proposed to himself merely to write a fanciful story, evolving a thoughtful moral," he summarized far more than his own preface to *The House of The Seven Gables* (1851). No fewer than twenty-one of James Fenimore Cooper's prefaces make the same backhanded gesture, implying that inventiveness has something to do with the didactic ideal. The tone of Cooper's "Forward" to *The Crater* (1848) sounds as though he had been invited to say it: "Whatever may be thought of the authenticity of its incidents, we hope this book will not be found to be totally without a moral."

James K. Paulding's prefaces were bolder, just as his novels themselves were more fantastic. In *Westward Ho!* (1832) he asserts: "The great aim of the author has been to combine an important moral, with the interest of a series of incidents . . . as he knows or imagines exist, or have existed." But no matter what kind of novel the reader had in front of him, he was bound to feel at home in the preface. Edward Bellamy apologized for *Looking Backward* (1886), saying, "The author sought to alleviate the instructive quality of the book, by casting it in the form of a romantic narrative." These fainthearted prefaces bear some vague relation to the classical concept on which so many Renaissance and Neo-Classical poets had defended their art—the concept of virtue as the union of the beautiful and the good—but the classical "virtue" came out merely as wholesome amusement.

American novelists were far more willing to refute the charge that fiction was a waste of time, for here they were sure of themselves. Novels were useful, no doubt about it. They were educational and hu-

manitarian, and hence of practical value. The preface to Charles Brockden Brown's *Wieland* (1798) points out that the novel instructs, by
illustrating "some important branches of the moral constitution of
man"; and Brown appeals the merits of his quasi-science to "physicians
and to men conversant with the latent springs and occasional perver-
sions of the human mind."

Brown's preface to *Arthur Mervyn* (1799-1800) declares his wish to
instruct his readers in the medical and political aspects of the historic
Philadelphia plague, and also to encourage an active interest in social
conditions and, therefore, a sympathy for the less fortunate. What
could be more practical? Historical novelists were even more comfortable with this sort of claim. After all, they taught history, and could
alert their readers to the mistakes of the past.

The humanitarian responsibility was so clear that even the lack of a
"cause" could not stay it. When that arch-journeyman Timothy Shay
Arthur was caught without a specific reform in mind, he nevertheless
knew his place, and explained that *Steps Towards Heaven* (1858), a
book of lay sermons, taught "no special theology. . . . It has no aim but
to assist men to grow better, and thence happier."

These self-conscious prefaces excuse their novels in a manner suggesting that the authors had some civic duty to perform. By and large,
they conveyed what was already taken for granted, and as the nineteenth century wore on the numbers of novels containing prefaces de
clined from five out of every six or seven, to one out of every four or
five. The preface to the American novel had virtually ceased before
Henry James put it to the use of poetics.

There is a reasonable suspicion that these messages were not always
heartfelt. John Neal's preface to *Logan, a Family History* (1822) begins, "I hate prefaces." In any case, by the time Edward Eggleston
wrote, in his preface to *The End of the World* (1872), that "Prefaces
are most unnecessary and useless prependages, since nobody reads
them," the trend was apparent. The popular novel had outgrown the
need for the precaution of sanctifying what readers wanted anyway.

After the 1890's the apologetic preface got a face-lifting. When publishers began to use dust jackets to protect books, they discovered that
the jackets themselves could carry a message to the readers. The text

on the inside flap of the paper cover, in fact, was more efficient than the preface. Unsigned, because it was written at the publisher's direction, it could sanctify the novel without any taint of false modesty on the part of the author. It could speak with authority as it lied about how the book would improve the reader and about the fun he was going to have in the process. But the dust jacket blurb came later.

Meanwhile, the monotone of the prefaces echoed some remarkable similarities among the novels themselves. The resemblance of these novels to one another is explained by the fact that a commercially successful book creates a market for others like it. Just as simple as that! Every publisher follows the leader, even if the leader turns out to be a book on his own list. Nineteenth-century publishers did not labor to point out this fact; the general feeling was that they belonged to a "profession" whose dignity was paramount. If a publisher had to make money he was expected at least not to talk about it.

But decorum began to change during the 1890's, and "legitimate profit" became an acceptable subject. In his 1938 Bowker Lecture on publishing, Frederick Crofts regarded this tendency to follow the leader as an obvious public fact. Publishers are always trying to reproduce the appeal of previously successful books. "An innovation in format, in unusual locale, or an original approach or presentation which results in a best seller is promptly duplicated." This is so, he said, because "a publishing house is not an eleemosynary institution, and is entitled to profit from any definite indication of the public's immediate interest."

In America during the early years of the nineteenth century, the commercial success of native novels depended on their prominently duplicating their English predecessors. John Neal spoke out on this matter too, in his preface to *The Down-Easters* (1833). "To judge by our novel-writers," he said, "we have cottages and skylarks in our country; pheasants and nightingales, first families, a youth of a 'gentle blood' and a virtuous *peasantry*; moss-grown churches, curfews and ivy-mantled towers"; and, he added, hardhearted fathers, runaway lovers and cruel stepmothers: "anything and everything, in short which goes to the ground-work of a third-rate English or Scotch novel."

Poe elaborately classified this imitative substance in a book review he wrote for the *Southern Literary Messenger*, in May, 1835. He emphasized the "succession of dynasties reigning over the regions of romance," each characterized by a popular author (the Radcliffe dynasty, the Edgeworth dynasty, and the Scott dynasty) and "each like the family of the Caesars, passing from good to bad, and from bad to worse, until each has run out." When Poe wrote this, Sir Walter Scott was the novelist who had most influenced American readers.

Scott's novels established a demand for comparable fiction which would celebrate the beginnings of the new nation. In this connection the novels of Cooper, Kennedy, Simms, Daniel Pierce Thompson and James K. Paulding were presented. But Scott's adoring public also supported his imitators without discriminating between the original and the gross copies. The American booksales of the British mannerist, G. P. R. James, for instance, exceeded even Scott's. His five-dozen novels, more or less, flooded American bookstores in the 1860's.

James, of course, wrote more than Scott. But the trick was in writing more like Scott than Scott wrote, and just such a mannerism explains how the preferences of most American book buyers are satisfied. The pathology of this literary cancer was conducted by one of the ablest of American critics, E. P. Whipple, in *North American Review* (April 1844), who made it clear that James was no "maker" in the old significance of that term. He was a literary mechanic working up the same raw material into the same shapes. Whipple had a wealth of metaphors to show the poverty of James' fiction. "For the last ten years, he has been repeating his own repetitions, and echoing his own echoes. His first novel was a shot that went through the target, and he has ever since been assiduously firing through the hole." James could accomplish this precision only by forsaking the individuality of his characters, and presenting idealized heroes and heroines and unmitigated villains, "walking essays on character."

James followed the plot around, "catechism in hand," delivering a homily wherever needed, Whipple said; and his novels showed it. "Characters should be exhibited, not didactically, but dramatically. We demand human beings—not embodied antitheses, or personified qualities, thoughts or passions." Fundamentally, therefore, the imitation was not at all like the original. "In truth, no two writers have less in common, in the essentials of their art, than Scott and James."

Whipple continued his surgery of James's fiction by asking how James could succeed. What did James sell that his customers wanted? He sold the image of a world where good will finally triumph, but only after its feverish, exciting enslavement to evil. "The world to which we are introduced is not a free, common world, where there are chances in favor both of vice and virtue; but a fenced park, full of man-traps and spring-guns. A sort of iron necessity conducts everything. We do not feel ourselves safe until we come to the conclusion. A sort of feverish, unhealthy excitement is the feeling we experience as we read." Together, the happy ending and the premeditated jeopardy denied the possibility of real characters, but the characters were not important, except for the assurance of their ultimate goal. The real attractions were the "man-traps" and the "spring-guns."

James's novels reconstructed the materials of Scott's novels, but James put a greater emphasis on the jeopardy of the hero and heroine and designed a more explicit attention to their travails. By this calculated exaggeration his novels were his own, not Scott's. They happened to be like Scott's, only more so. His was an old trick—the mannerist borrows some prominent characteristics of a predecessor and reinvolves them in a new scheme in such a way as to exaggerate them. But because it is a new scheme, the exaggerated characteristics have no necessity. And this distortion, many times repeated by many authors, explains the process of popular literature.

What the publishing industry has accomplished is a greater efficiency in this eclecticism. The result of its efforts is always a cluster of new books, reflecting the heat of one that has already made good, like a constellation around the sun. The warm qualities of popular fiction radiate from elements that never change. Always the novels that have made good with American readers have in some way involved the family scene, the jeopardy of the toiling heroine, and the strain of religiosity. The combination of these elements is what Frank Luther Mott, in his *Golden Multitudes* (1947), has called the Home-And-Jesus formula.

This formula had a great deal to do with the unprecedented sale of novels in the 1850's. It began when George Palmer Putnam's mother told him to publish Susan Warner's novel, *The Wide, Wide World* (1850), a story about the moral travails of an orphan which was so notoriously successful that publishers lovingly cultivated all the matriarchal novels they could find, and sold hundreds of thousands of the books of Mrs. E. D. E. N. Southworth; of Maria Cummins and Mary J. Holmes; of Marion Harland, Ann Stephens and Marion McIntosh.

There was no coincidence about the gender of all these authors, nor in the genetic similarity of their books—a fact which Hawthorne noted as he railed about the whole situation. "America is now wholly given over to a d—d mob of scribbling women, and I shall have no chance of success while the public taste is occupied with their trash—and should be ashamed of myself if I did succeed." Hawthorne wrote this in a letter to his publisher, William Ticknor, in 1855, while his own books languished on booksellers' shelves. "What is the mystery of these innumerable editions of the *Lamplighter*, and other books neither better nor worse?" he wanted to know, adding: "worse they could not be, and better they need not be, when they sell by the 100,000."

Hawthorne could have discovered from any one of these books the mystery of the others. They dramatized the difficulties which beset love, marriage and home; they were about the consequence of temptation, with plenty of temptation. They all affirmed that human nature is intuitively good, that loyalty and courage will win out, that a girl *can* improve herself in society, and that truth will rise again in the happy home. In a chapter entitled "Home Influence" of *The Popular Book* (1950), James Hart suggests the lineage of these novels by describing some of their other characteristics, or what Frederick Crofts would have called certain prominent duplications: "From Bulwer came the drawing-room scene, purified and Americanized; from Dickens, the pathetic bride, the orphaned child and the kindly eccentric character; from Charlotte Brontë, a watered version of the Jane Eyre-Rochester relation; from Mrs. Gaskell, the sense of quiet rural life."

But the real stamina of these novels lay in the religion of Good Works which they avowed. Humanitarianism, truly a domesticated virtue in this nation, marks another, later cluster of pious novels which appeared after the publication of Mrs. Humphry Ward's *Robert Elsmere* (1888). This pastiche recounts a tale of a young minister who braces up his flagging religious dogma by entering into social work in urban slums. It was promptly pirated in the United States, and vigorously reviewed in the press and in the pulpit; and the author estimated the American sales at a half-million copies six months after the first American reprint.

The newly organized American branch of the Salvation Army gave a timely appeal to this version of the problem of what Jesus would do if He were here, and the booktrade had a marketable subject. In *A Singular Life* (1894) Elizabeth Stuart Phelps Ward wrote about a man who left the Church to live as Jesus had, and to do Good Works. Edward Everett Hale's *If Jesus Came to Boston* (1895) debated the merits of humanitarianism with William T. Stead's *If Christ Came to Chicago* (1894). But the novel which reached by far the most people was Charles Sheldon's *In His Steps* (1896) which abridged all the doubts and preoccupations of *Robert Elsmere* in favor of a program for administrating humanitarian reform. The simple, practical program of a whole church full of Sheldon's characters was irresistible. After its serialization in a religious weekly, *In His Steps* appeared in book form. Then, after a defect in its copyright was discovered in 1899, the book was reprinted by many presses which sold millions of copies.

There was no doubt about the appeal of Sheldon's book, because there was no doubt in it. By expanding one man's humanitarian desire into a public-works program, Sheldon managed to enlarge upon *Robert Elsmere* about as far as possible. Subsequent derivations of Mrs. Ward's novel exploited some of its other characteristics. For instance, the athletic vigor with which the hero performs his newly discovered social obligations became a specialty of Harold Bell Wright's novels.

These clustered novels all served the practical purpose of ethical, humanitarian education. They catechized the doctrine of Salvation-by-Works, a religious heresy in Europe, but turned by the American Puritans into orthodoxy. Within two generations of their arrival in the New World, they had domesticated Calvinism, taming the terrifying doctrine of predestination with a theology based upon a contract between man and God. Thereafter, they made sure, man's behavior in this world would count.

The legalistic Puritans had found plenty of precedent, for the Bible is full of covenants to prove their case. But as this Covenant Theology became popularized during the eighteenth century, it spread beyond the Puritan churches. As more and more people practiced the old heresy, Good Works became synonymous with Salvation. All by himself, it seemed, man could avoid the fires of Hell.

This simplistic belief inspired countless social reforms—always in the name of Christianity—during the nineteenth century. Ultimately, in the name of Jesus and *In His Steps*, it even replaced Christianity. And there were other ironies in this fire. From the beginning, the American domestication had made Calvinism comfortably secular. It was no trouble at all, as Benjamin Franklin proved, to merge the problem of Salvation with the achievement of success in mundane matters. What a coincidence that the author of *Poor Richard's Almanac*, that compendium of piety and profit, also took up the cause of *Pamela, or, Virtue Rewarded!* The attainment of Salvation through material success is the particular pursuit of happiness that Americans have always been anxious to read about.

Books that gratify this gross inspiration are known in the publishing industry as "Blue-Sky" books, and they succeed commercially whenever the authors themselves believe in it. The knack in commercial publishing, of course, is to exploit—and to establish if need be—the coincidence of a writer's personal beliefs with the reigning public attitude. And if the publisher believes in it too, so much the better. His belief will affect the promotion of the book and probably its contents.

The profit in practical religion, by a publisher who believed in it, was superbly demonstrated by the publishing house of Thomas Young Crowell. Beginning in the 1870's for nearly forty years the Crowell lists were studded with inspirational books with clusters of titles which prominently duplicated one another. T. Irving Crowell's biography of his father, *Thomas Young Crowell* (1926), explains how some of these clusters happened.

The elder publisher fashioned at least five successful books from the personal vision he shared with Mrs. Sarah Knowles Bolton. In the fall of 1874 when Crowell read Mrs. Bolton's magazine article, "Poor Boys Who Became Famous," he invited her to write a book to go with this title, and she composed short biographies of twenty-eight famous men. "She skillfully traced the secret of their success, and pointed out that without work and will no great things can be achieved." Signs of the enormous sales of this book showed up on the publisher's later lists, which included *Lives of Girls Who Became Famous, Famous American Authors, Famous American Statesmen,* and *Famous Men of Science*—all written by Mrs. Bolton.

Then Crowell received an unsolicited manuscript entitled "What Is Worth While," and the booklet he published from this manuscript soon grew into the "What Is Worth While" series, written by a half-dozen authors. One of these, Dr. Orison S. Marden, repeated himself for several publishers with *Pushing to the Front, or Success under Difficulties* (1894), *Architects of Fate* (1895) and *The Secret Achievement* (1898).

Here is precedent for the contemporary breeding of those happy-solemn tracts which imitate Dale Carnegie and the Reverend Norman Vincent Peale. But there is more to this evidence. Crowell had no interest in novels, or as his biography puts it, "in ephemeral books" or in *"belles lettres."* "He preferred solid books and was chiefly interested in those that would inspire or be useful for reference, so that one editor was led to say that he 'never issued a book that one is not better for having read.' " The condescension to *"belles lettres,"* and the scores of all books that were not practical had, of course, forced writers to construct all those prefaces to nineteenth-century novels. The suspicion still lingered.

Crowell's attitude was no exception. Little, Brown's anniversary volume, *One Hundred Years of Publishing: 1837-1937,* gravely quotes the policy of the first partners of that house: "Their publications in general literature have been, for the most part, of a grave, solid and substantial character, such as works in theology, history, politics, political economy and biography"; but they had no wish to print novels or to meddle "with those lighter and more ephemeral publications that come with the leaves of spring and go with the leaves of autumn."

Little, Brown repealed this prohibition after 1890, and such was the profit in pietism that when the firm published Henry Sienkiewicz's *Quo Vadis?*, in 1897, it launched the biggest and most intensive promotional campaign for a novel that *Publishers' Weekly* could remember. In that same year a *PW* editorial made one of that journal's most memorable understatements about publishing when it remarked: "We fear it is becoming a trade." After Little, Brown's *Quo Vadis?* campaign, intensive publicity became a familiar device in bookselling. By 1920, when D. Appleton announced to the trade that it was now sponsoring the novels of Harold Bell Wright, it had to shout to be heard over the general promotion.

The "Bazaar Spirit," the competitive promotion of literature, is the most recent stage in the American domestication of the novel, causing a sense of compromise, an astonished awareness of something lost by the process of commercializing. In one form or another for the past seventy years, the editorials in *Publishers' Weekly* have repeatedly asked the question "Is Bookselling Dead?" And for every one of these editorials the *Readers Guide* to more general magazines lists dozens of articles which ask the same question about the novel. These articles assess fiction in terms of "cultural values"—gained or lost—and generally weigh so much air.

There is a certain significance in the repeated doom-calling by which these commentators announce their subject: "Will the Novel Disappear?" (*North American Review*, September 1902); "Is the Novel Being Superseded?" (*Current Literature*, September 1906); "Does the Present-Day Fiction Make for Immorality?" (*Current Literature*, April 1907); "Is Present-Day Fiction Quite Ephemeral?" (*Lippincott's Magazine*, March 1909); "The Passing of the Novel," (*Independent*, December 22, 1910); "Are the American Novelists Deteriorating?" (*Ladies' Home Journal*, September 1911).

It was no passing problem, for apparently the plight persists: "The Break-up of the Novel," (*Yale Review*, January 1923); "The Fate of the Novel," (*Living Age*, December 12, 1925); "Are Novels Worth

Reading?" (*Nation*, February 13, 1935); and "Is the Novel Done For?" (*Harper*, December 1942). Judging from these funerations, "The Slump in American Writing" (*American Mercury*, February 1940) has been continuous. Although most of these essayists think the novel will survive (even the few who hope it won't), they are all worrying over it. More than that, they share an attitude about the novel which makes this whole argument monumentally irrelevant.

These essayists characteristically assume the novel's responsibility to "cultural values," which is what all those nineteenth-century prefaces assumed. The "immorality of the modern novel"—to borrow a frequent phrase from these articles—seems always to be eroding the national mind. This, of course, is always presented as an urgent matter, even though the novel's degeneracy was apparently a foregone conclusion 150 years ago.

In this long, morose debate both the attack and the rebuttal have assumed that fiction is some sort of public utility. Certainly, this nation has domesticated the novel by making just such excuses for it, by pondering its usefulness to individual deportment or collective reform. And the question of whether the novel (like any other public utility) should also serve "commercial interests" has intensified the debate.

But the novel has always been popular, which is to say commercial, because it can always illustrate profusely the drama of moral choice and consequence. The legacy of moralism for the past two centuries in America has pretty thoroughly obscured the nature of fiction. It has obscured the reflexive property of the novel form which really is moral. Fiction is a special way of knowing. It records the human individual as no other expression can. What happens to it is indeed urgent.

Whatever has happened or will happen to the novel, after all, is mainly relevant to the form itself. What fiction *does* derives from what fiction *is*. Whether the novel has succumbed to commercialism —as, of course, it almost always has—ought at least to be assessed in terms of fiction's intrinsic qualities: on the grounds of why it is, and how it is, instead of merely its alleged obligation to public service.

Chapter II

How to Denature a Novel

THE public excuse for the novel is that it is useful. As long as it appears to teach something practical it is perfectly all right for one to indulge in its entertainment, but the real reason for the novel's popularity is its gratification of the deep human desire to merge oneself with the world. The novel finds the terms of the merger. For some reason, however, this profound personal need has never been publicly convincing in America. It is easier to get away with the polite excuse.

The justification of the novel had already been made in the eighteenth century, by the time Americans began to import this product from England. The works of Aphra Behn and Defoe, of Fielding and Richardson and Smollett, and the responses of British reviewers to these works, had already fashioned the theory of the novel as a form of instructive entertainment. It had a purpose, after all. But in America it was emphatically necessary to spell out this purpose, to rationalize entertainment on the grounds of practicality. The alternatives were clear from the beginning: A novel either served some ethical or educational purpose, or it was wasteful. The prefaces to the nineteenth-century novels undertook this face-saving task, but they were only symptoms of the assurance the novels themselves were expected to provide.

This either/or reasoning had been long established by the time publishers began promoting books in the 1890's. If a novel wasn't "serious" it was "popular"—or worse, "commercial." Although "popular" and "commercial" meant roughly the same, the American prejudice that a novel must serve something outside itself has made "commercial" a more comfortably derogatory term. Book promotion has merely gone along with these concepts, in that publishers have accepted the American contradiction of the inherited theory that entertainment *can* be intrinsically instructive.

The novelists themselves had separated entertainment and instruction, using the one to disguise the other, and this divided purpose had existed for a long while. James Fenimore Cooper, the first American to make a profession of writing novels, had devised a simple expedient, in his Leather Stocking Tales, which apparently suited everybody: a chapter for the reader, then a chapter for Cooper. The violent action would move the characters around for awhile, then they would all sit down and have a serious talk.

Cooper was not the only one with a divided purpose. Neal and Simms, even Charles Brockden Brown, were all trying to adapt an inherited form of entertainment to their own sober celebrations of the new American republic and the possibilities it held for the individual. As often as not, they disguised their philosophical indulgences within stories which had nothing to do with their opinions, using the form in spite of itself, as Melville later did in *Pierre* (1852), and as Hawthorne tried to do in *The Scarlet Letter* (1850) with his disarming essay about the Customs House. By the end of the century, with the notable exception of William Dean Howells, the authors who wrote about fiction had firmly polarized the concepts of "serious" and "commercial" literature.

Frank Norris repeatedly distinguished between literary fiction and popular fiction. Literary fiction he equated with art, which he called "serious" and "honest"; popular fiction he called "copyism," and said it was written by timid businessmen. He insisted that art and commodity excluded one another. Hamlin Garland thought the same. The distinction between "serious" and "commercial" literature, in fact, continues unchanged from the commentaries of Garland and Norris through Theodore Dreiser and F. Scott Fitzgerald to James T. Farrell and John Marquand. Just as the earlier nineteenth-century apologists had found "serious" fiction ethically useful, so these later novelists have pronounced "popular" fiction to be merely a commercial device.

The trouble is that each of these terms alleges several things at once about the intention of authors and the tastes of readers, but the terms do not really distinguish anything about the fiction iself. One fact is certain: a "serious" novel is not a "commercial" novel which did not sell very well. The novel form is popular and always has been, and novels that are published are necessarily commercial. Therefore, the term "serious" has some special distinction, but most people have never been able to agree on what this distinction is.

As for distinguishing between the tastes of readers, the terms "serious" and "popular" cause more confusion than they settle, particularly when they are assigned on the basis of book sales. Sales records in book publishing are notoriously individual, inaccurate and incomplete. The book trade never has had a record of book sales which matches books published. This is just a statistician's dream. Only recently, in fact, could the book trade match these two unknowns by subject category.

Most publishing houses have always been privately owned and not required to make their book sales public. Even if they were required to (and even if they had the information), it would now take a mechanical brain to order the confusion of "limited," "trade," and reprint editions. A publisher will announce a book's sales only to his own advantage. Even then his public affidavit is a merchandising tool—intentionally approximate, the better to impress you. "Seven Big Printings in Just Three Months!" the ad will say; "Now in its Fortieth Thousand"; "Destined to be One of the Top Best Sellers." The fact that it is "destined to be" should make you pause.

When an editor can say of a book, "It was quite a best seller," clearly the term is tired. "Best seller," in fact, has been so misused since the *Bookman* first coined it sixty-five years ago that it more often expresses a hope than a fact. Since retailers often list slow stock as "best selling" in order to move it off their shelves, the term is a poor gauge of popularity.

In common usage "popular fiction" condescends, implying that the public somehow makes a book worse by buying it in quantity. This condescension belittles the best-selling novels of Harold Bell Wright, Gene Stratton Porter, or Mickey Spillane. But what about the best-selling novels of Harold Frederic, Thornton Wilder, Sinclair Lewis or

Ernest Hemingway? In the same way the term "serious fiction" usually confuses the work itself with its author's reputation.

Take *War and Peace*, for instance, which everybody agrees is a "serious" novel. If you want to say this in a "literary" way, no one will argue. Its world is abundant. It carelessly piles up incidents so as to dramatize the whole sweep of history, yet it offers an extraordinary sense of pertinent detail. During a dozen years in a nation's life it considers the significant circumstances of a society falling apart and the significant problem of discovering whether an individual can afford merely to survive. No one would disagree with these claims for *War and Peace*. But it happens they are all borrowed from reviews of *Gone with the Wind*, a "popular" novel if there ever was one.

Nobody could ever guess the vast difference between these novels by reading book reviews. Many generations have decided that *War and Peace* is one of the great novels of all time, while *Gone with the Wind* has already passed into limbo twenty-five years after its publication. This simple fact of public response is a timely reminder of the loose language of most book reviews. No one even mentions *Gone with the Wind* any more, except everybody in the book trade. This is another part of the problem. The way books are defined in the book trade has nothing to do with their literary qualities. The literary scholar and the bookman talk shop together about as ineffectively as a botanist and a florist discussing flowers.

Communication between the two is difficult at best, but some important concepts require the language of both the scholar and the bookman. The denatured novel, for example. In order for anyone to talk about the denatured novel it is first necessary for him to be clear about the novel and its nature. But in what language? The bookman's terms, like the scholar's, are often not intended for public communication.

Like every other business the book trade has its "inside" words. There is no public equivalent, for instance, for the noun "one-shot." A "one-shot" is a book that is marketed—sometimes even written—to exploit a timely interest. The promotion of the book, therefore, will be based on the decision to print a large first edition. A one-shot is journalistic; it depends on news value and opportunism. If two of a man's plays were to make a huge profit on Broadway and cause a lot of talk about him shortly after he had died, as in the case of Eugene O'Neill, you might expect a lot of one-shots about him.

If this celebrity were not a playwright but a general or an athlete or a politician, the shot would be louder. But this is a relatively precise term. I once heard a salesman refer to a meretricious novel as "a piece of pork"; an editor at another house called it "sheer hamburger." It is somehow symptomatic of the scholar's semantic problem that in Publishers' Row "pork" and "hamburger" are the same.

The trade has no official vocabulary. It has had instead, since the 1890's, a public parlance and a great many private ones. An editor uses one vocabulary when he talks to an author about a book and quite another when he presents that book to his sales department. They are two versions of the public vocabulary—the marketese with which he sells his books. This is a language of classifications which implies merit without having to specify any reasons for the merit.

The terms "serious" and "popular" belong to the trade's public parlance, but they denote no formulas. Nor do they suggest any judgment of performance. If they have turned up favorably in book reviews, the publisher will always pass them along in his ads, but to him "serious" and "popular" are merely classifications of a market. In bookselling they are accessories after the artifact. Their familiarity makes them useful in describing both the novel and its denaturing. Anyway, since commercial publishing is responsible for denaturing the novel, its own marketing terms might better describe the process.

The book trade's functional view of fiction is that fiction is merchandise. Another functional view, which the book trade inherited and has had to accommodate, is that fiction must be practical; in America this means that fiction must contain useful information and serve the cause of ethics. For different reasons, therefore, the book trade and the American public have sold the novel short. They always try to denature it.

But the novel, being fiction, need not live down to this condescension. On the contrary, no mere functional view of fiction can take it all in. Fiction is more than utilitarian. We do not *use* fiction, we *need* it. It is everyone's continuing preoccupation. Being small and fallible, every human being compensates with fiction, inventing a world that will acknowledge him according to his own desires. He spends his life keeping that world in repair.

Fiction is the fashioning of an occasion appropriate to one's deepest need, which is to justify oneself. It is a kind of knowledge we cannot come by in any other way. No one can state his awful dereliction, so he curses or prays, or both, and builds a fiction. He realizes a cast of characters and a narrative. What his characters are and what they do and feel represent all their author did not know he knew.

Fiction is a bizarre exaggeration of mere actuality. The author must exaggerate in order to communicate at all; otherwise his fiction would not be necessary—or believable. But it still must satisfy one's knowledge of the way things happen or one's feeling that they could not have been otherwise, given what one knows or learns about the characters. Therefore, a kind of necessity or inevitability rules it, in that the action follows given conditions, and nothing else could have happened.

Since these conditions lie partly in the nature of the character, the inevitability depends partly on him. Cinderella, for example, has no significance apart from the circumstances she helped to produce, or their resolution which justifies her nature. Like any actual person, therefore, the character in a novel is a circumstantial being. His existence is an acute metaphor of the human condition, for unless he participates in the affairs which contain him—unless he acts—the fictional character has no life at all. He must have efficacy, or we will have none of him.

The necessity of fiction, therefore, lies in its believable commentary on more than itself. In our own lives we cope with things-as-they-are by assigning them value according to the way they impinge on us. From our involvements we derive our "values": that is, our convictions, our dogmas, our ideals which have shown stamina in the course of still other involvements. Certain of these ideals with particular stamina seem to be absolute values. But since we derive them only from our own experience, most of what we call values are fragmentary and are likely to be at odds. Our just deserts are often contradicted, and this is why we need fiction.

Our recognition of conflict in actual experience is itself a reordering (an evaluation) of actuality. Through the liable character, the kind of knowledge fiction yields is the nature of one's relativity to everything else. Just as fiction in general is one kind of knowledge about relativity, so the novel in particular is one way of knowing. (A lyric poem or an epic or a drama are other ways.) A novel is a long narrative fiction which appraises at the same time that it represents the mutual involvement of characters.

The essence of the novel lies in the way it represents; in the way it repeats and amplifies its substance to appraise it. It repeats and amplifies a particular metaphor. All fiction represents by metaphor, by analogy to things known; and the substance of all narrative fiction is the metaphor of conflict. The novel's particularity is its appraisal of characters by a various repetition of conflict.

The metaphor of conflict—the encounter—convenes opposing forces (emotions, traits, and values, persons and circumstances, or all of these) in such a way as to localize one's feelings. Conflict tries the persons and their values by their actions. Cinderella meekly dressing her step-sisters' hair dramatizes the first condition of the beatitude which that tale represents.

Action characterizes the heroine of another fiction, *The Scarlet Letter*, quite otherwise but just as surely. Hester Prynne first appears leaving the jail defiantly displaying to the townspeople the scarlet letter on her bosom. Each of these heroines reveals herself by what she does, because the gesture of each responds to her involvement. It makes no difference whether the heroine runs away from the dance, like Cinderella; or faces the music, like Hester Prynne. The action always responds to something.

The metaphor of conflict reveals and evaluates because it establishes the cause of action. This is why we know more about fictional *personae* than about persons. In actuality we only vaguely realize most of the relationships involving us. But conflict organizes actual confusion. It clarifies cause, creates the necessity of choice, and therefore makes action a response.

Fiction has a capacity for conjecture and discovery about human beings beyond the actual and customary extent of one's knowledge.

Even more, it stresses what it clarifies. The need for resolution inheres in any complication, and by emphasizing complication the metaphor of conflict accentuates the need to resolve. Thus, in most versions of "Cinderella" the palace ball, which poses the girl's irreconcilable conditions, occurs for three nights.

But "Cinderella" is only a tale. A novel differs from it by the breadth and depth its length allows. With a plurality of characters the novel repeats the fact of involvement. It proceeds by addition or by accretion. It gathers analogues to its subject so as to represent an emerging conflict by means of many relevant and contiguous encounters.

The novel's accretion is not just quantitative. Its process can be described by a singular verb: the novel *intricates* its conflicts, so that one reinforces the others. It is a system of repeated conflicts which variously echo one another; each new encounter evaluates the others. This is the way in which the novel appraises as it represents.

This developing of involvement is a way of making the most of the least material. In painting, for example, a basic fact of composition is that the parts repeat one another, not literally but with variations. In music, sequential treatment repeats a motif elsewhere on the scale, or by another voice or instrument. The most familiar form of repetition in orchestral scores is the theme-and-variations, although its most intense use is probably in the fugue, which counterpoints its parts. And so in fiction: the novel builds a system of comparisons; its conflicts test opposing values and also, by analogy, one another. Like parallelism in painting or sequential treatment in music, the dynamics of a novel exceeds mere restatement for its own sake, but uses it variously to develop an idea. And appraisal inheres in development.

This developing involvement occurs in *The Scarlet Letter*. The novel dramatizes sin and confession in a God-centered world. Hester Prynne has already borne a child to the Reverend Dimmesdale when her husband, Chillingworth, appears on the scene, and the sins which the novel dramatizes are committed after the adultery. Dimmesdale fears to admit his paternity; Chillingworth vows to punish him by torture; and Hester complies with Chillingworth's trespass.

Each character experiences the crisis of confession in a way that variously repeats the others. Hester's private confession to Dimmesdale of her compliance in his torture begets Dimmesdale's confession to the world. But the shock kills him, and so Chillingworth is denied the opportunity to shrive himself. Chillingworth's failure to confess most certainly damns him.

The dialogues which render these encounters (between Hester and her child, between husband and lover, between Hester and her husband and then her lover) gradually reorder the early encounter between Hester and her community into a conflict between pride and humility in everyone concerned. What gradually emerges is the empirical proof of the human dereliction. But because this is fiction the representation cannot be stated. When Hawthorne tried to state it he failed.

In his conclusion he selected a moral and exhorted the reader to "Be true! Be true! Be true! Show freely to the world, if not your worst, yet some trait whereby the worst may be inferred." But however relevant his message, its statement terminates the possibilities of the fiction. It scarcely matches, or even connotes, the dynamics of the book.

Mere accurate statement fails to match the amplitude of any fiction, no matter what the fiction's intricacy. This is equally true of a much simpler novel, Margaret Mitchell's *Gone with the Wind* (1936). In this book the warring elements of an entire society convene precisely in the heroine's struggle to find both love and security within the narrow limits of respectability. The novel contains a truism which seems to stitch it all up. One of Scarlett's many counselors, a *grande dame* on a neighboring plantation, tells her, "It's a very bad thing for a woman to face the worst that can happen to her, because after she's faced the worst she can't ever really fear anything again." But this calculable wisdom cannot sum up *Gone with the Wind* any more than Hawthorne's exhortation to be true compends *The Scarlet Letter*.

There is more to say about these novels than that they are both fiction. They are superficially similar but profoundly different, and this fact reveals a lot about the nature—and the denaturing—of the novel. The similarities are obvious. Each heroine has been cast out of her community: one, for adultery; the other, for stealing husbands and for breaking most of the lesser rules for a lady; and both are punished. Both novels are didactic, as all novels are, but *Gone with the Wind*, the popular novel, is far more doctrinaire.

Despite Hawthorne's tiresome moralizing in *The Scarlet Letter*, the moral issue of *Gone with the Wind* is clearly more explicit. We know exactly where the heroine stands at all times—and where she ought to stand. No fuzzy equivocations mar Scarlett O'Hara's indictment; her retribution is tidy and immediately satisfying.

The difference between these novels lies in the moral involvement of *The Scarlet Letter* and the moral posture of *Gone with the Wind*. Hester's violation of Dimmesdale's soul makes her suffer the fears of the damned. But Scarlett O'Hara, who has violated many individuals in her attempt to get another woman's husband, suffers merely the frustration of never getting what she wants. What seems like her just deserts in *Gone with the Wind* is really only an expedient—like the prosecution of a gangster for income-tax evasion.

One novel develops an involvement comparable to the unresolved complexity of the world. The other novel evades complexity and simplifies its subject. In *The Scarlet Letter* Hester's apprehension over the nature of her illegitimate child leads her to interpret the child's incessant questions about Dimmesdale and Chillingworth as God's own ministrations. Hester's inference of divine revelation is what finally discovers the analogies in all of the conflicts of the novel. But in *Gone with the Wind* there is no such developing involvement. Its heroine's conflict is merely—but repeatedly—asserted. In *Gone with the Wind* there is a much clearer conflict between a heroine's instinctive desires and her inhibitions. Her society will not countenance her only means of acquiring the man she wants. But the dialogues between the heroine and the other characters, which render this conflict, never get anywhere. Scarlett repeatedly rejects everyone's advice. The trouble is that everyone's mind, including hers, is already made up. Nothing changes except the scene.

The simplistic treatment and the moral posture go together in popular fiction, and they have nothing to do with the agony of appraisal. Nothing ever changes in *Gone with the Wind* because the heroine's ideal of happiness is unobtainable. But the dream of it is durable. As long as there are new events to sustain it, the dream goes on and on. That is why so many millions of people have sat up all night with it, indulging in the heroine's miseries, anticipating her success. The goal in *The Scarlet Letter*, however, is not happiness but salvation and the awful crisis of self-appraisal.

Hawthorne's novel is a re-creation of the values of the seventeenth-century Puritan community two hundred years after the fact. According to the doctrine of this community salvation is far more possible than happiness on earth. Like the dream of happiness, it is also based on human failure, but achieving Grace requires at least a life of continuous and agonizing doubt. This takes work of the sort that denies happiness—one reason why the quest for salvation often degenerates into a misguided pursuit of happiness.

If Hawthorne had really wanted to match the success of that "d—d mob of scribbling women" he complained of, *The Scarlet Letter* would have needed a thorough revision. He had an enchanting situation: his heroine had a husband at home and a lover-at-large (this caused the book to be banned in Russia and the film to be bowdlerized in the United States, so he was on the right track), but he spoiled it. Hester had already had her lover, thereby removing the delicious frustration on which the popular heroine's dream of happiness thrives.

What small popular appeal remained after that error Hawthorne also ruined: Hester was not at all concerned about the security of her home or about becoming acceptable to the community. She was, in fact, accepted long before the book was over. Meanwhile, the author made it obvious that the real subject of his novel was the awful crises of human dereliction. As far as book sales were concerned, Hawthorne botched it.

This is merely another way of saying that *Gone with the Wind*, the popular novel, offers an utterly simplistic view of the human condition. It has stylized the metaphor of conflict. It has made the conflict tidy, explicit and literally repetitive. This is how to denature the novel: attenuate or thin out the system of analogous conflicts. The terms "serious" and "popular" fiction bear on this fact. The "popular" novel is usually a denatured one.

Ideally the novel accumulates thought and action in such a manner as to exploit analogies to a conflict, and so appraises as it represents. Addition of any new analogous substance necessarily moves attention from one point to another and forces comparison of some sort. This psychological movement is peculiar to each fiction (and different, for instance, in *The Scarlet Letter* and *Gone with the Wind*). The simpler, stylized comparison always marks the popular novel.

Narrative is what moves the attention. Bookmen in the trade refer to "story," which means that quality resulting from a stress upon the narrative. The "story quality" exercises the desire to resolve things. It exploits and satisfies a sense of destination: the universal feeling for that consummate end toward which events tend to move. With this sense everybody transforms his own actual experience. Thus, the "story quality"—the emphasis on narrative—readily distinguishes one novel from another. It distinguishes *Moll Flanders*, for instance, from *Pamela*; from *Madame Bovary* or *Sister Carrie*; from *Marjorie Morningstar*; from *The Scarlet Letter* or *Gone with the Wind*—in fact, each of these from the others.

This is an aesthetic, not a historical, matter. Two novels by one writer can differently exploit the narrative. Henry James's *The Ambassadors*, for example, which appraises Lambert Strether's growing realization of certain circumstances, shows almost no concern for resolving the situation in which he finds himself. But James's *The American* has a strong sense of story: of the need to improve the unfortunate state of Christopher Newman's courtship; so strong, in fact, that James's conclusion in terms other than the story's anticipation becomes an anti-climax.

The specious clarity of *Gone with the Wind*, repeatedly resolving the same conflict, is the result of this story quality. The way a writer exploits this emphasis on resolution, in fact, controls the scope and therefore the meaning of his fiction. Two novels might appear in all other respects to be extraordinarily similar, but their differing emphases on the resolution of the same conflict will make their entire subjects different.

Two such novels are *The Plutocrat* (1927), by Booth Tarkington, and *Dodsworth* (1929), by Sinclair Lewis. They were contemporary and both were best sellers. They share the subject of the American abroad; they both endeavor to define the American's qualities, which they commonly assess by European standards of behavior. Each novel characterizes its American hero—Earl J. Tinker in Tarkington's, Sam Dodsworth in Lewis'—by comparing him with his opposite, and so demonstrating assumed national traits in a tabloid fashion.

These novels even arrive at approximately the same estimation of the heroes. Sam Dodsworth, in fact, explicitly admires his predecessor, Earl Tinker. All in all, their similarity might at first suggest an extraordinary coincidence in literary history. Yet Lewis' novel presents a symposium of irreconcilable attitudes, and Tarkington's novel resolves the debate.

The difference between the novels is not philosophical but formal. Tarkington's novel develops a conflict in terms of Earl J. Tinker's journey across North Africa, with each episode disclosing some new realization about Tinker by witnesses who come to scoff and stay to praise. The money this Rotarian showers on the province of Algeria somehow validates his innocent, outlandish opinions about the culture of the Roman Empire. Tinker inspects ancient sewer systems and reconstructs the Roman culture in terms of Saturday-night shopping, bond issues for war monuments, and public utilities. He resembles first a careless barbarian, then the Roman himself, and finally a formidable priest of civic religion. This contradiction between what Tinker unhappily seems to be and what he ultimately turns out to be, prods attention.

Tinker's low estate in the opinion of more pretentious Americans, at the start of the novel, obviously needs correction, but Lewis' novel omits the discrepancy between what seems and what is. Dodsworth's journey from Zenith, U.S.A., to the Old World causes the reassessment of two cultures, each in the other's terms. But the fact of the matter—the mutual differences between Americans and Europeans—prevails because each apologist argues from only a limited understanding of the other's culture. Dodsworth comes to realize this, but nothing needs to be resolved. His final realization is quite consistent with the situation in which he started. It merely explains the antipathies which have obviously existed throughout Dodsworth's journey.

Tarkington and Lewis wrote a great deal of apparently similar fiction, in that both worked with large, obvious subjects: the complacency of the small-town mind, the mores of business, and the confusion of ethical ideals in America. Tarkington anticipated Lewis in all of these ideas, just as *The Plutocrat* preceded *Dodsworth*, but they wrote from completely different views of their common experience. In his best novels Lewis developed these static ideas, with many analogies, into resonant fiction. When he tried (as he did once or twice) to pare down a novel to a narrative which had to arrive somewhere, he wrote a flat, dull novel. Lewis never could write a story like Tarkington's. Nor did Tarkington ever win the Nobel Prize.

The story quality, as in *The Plutocrat*, conveys the sense of becoming. It does so by violating one's natural inclination for order, by disturbing the stability of any given situation. The habit of representing disturbance by the metaphor of conflict is a token of our relative view of things which impinge on us, which makes fiction necessary in the first place. So, in the merely relative view, whenever one's convictions are forcefully contradicted they lose their comforting surety until such time as they can again prevail.

The humiliations forced on the virtuous Cinderella are intolerable; so are the ignorant opinions which contradict Booth Tarkington's Earl Tinker. Something must be done about it. Likewise, the ignominy which the townspeople heap on Hester Prynne contradicts her admirable self-sufficiency and honest devotion to her child; and the mores of Scarlett O'Hara's world suddenly seem to deny her preservation. But the only way to relieve the discomfort these given conditions cause is to project them into an action which will prove them wrong. One needs to complete the story in order to gratify his wishes for the way things ought to be.

To some degree this reaching sense conveys all of fiction. But the story quality, exciting the need for stability, is a simplifying force. It tends to ignore variation or development, to override the complexity in any arrangement of conditions. The degree to which the narrative presides over the fiction that contains it is what distinguishes a resonant novel from a denatured one. An author can exploit this sense of becoming merely for its own sake, as in most denatured novels, or he can use it as the means of development, the means of intricating any material into some reflexive structure. The sense of becoming can be diverted into a resonant system of analogies, which is the essence of the novel form.

The comparison between *The Plutocrat* and *Dodsworth* is no special case. The distinction between a dominant narrative and a resonant system of analogies discriminates among all novels that seem otherwise to be similar. A well-established category of merchandise in bookselling, for example, is the religious novel (the historical novel with a Biblical subject); and the peculiar nature of the invented substance in religious novels clarifies this distinction.

The New Testament usually furnishes the conflict, which they all dramatize, between the Christian way and the human way. Three novels about the last teachings and the death of Christ illustrate how differently the same historical evidence can be fictionalized. *The Nazarene* (1939), by Scholem Asch, is a resonant system of analogies whose subject is the human dilemma. *The Big Fisherman* (1949) by Lloyd Douglas, and *The Silver Chalice* (1952) by Thomas Costain are dominating narratives which solve the dilemma.

The Nazarene is the most fantastic and the most believable. Its action moves back and forth between Israel in the year of the Crucifixion and a modern European city, whose inhabitants recall the historical events. The modern characters are reincarnations of a Roman soldier and of a Jew who took part in the original drama and is now engaged in translating a manuscript of the Gospel according to Judas Iscariot. The reincarnation amplifies the terms of the original conflict and perpetuates the old dilemma. Hence the novel's illusion of a continuum. Nothing is resolved, but everything is realized.

The Big Fisherman is more cautious than *The Nazarene*, more authentic in its details, but it fails the illusion of reality because the dominating narrative insists on a conclusion. The novel tells of Simon Peter's relationship with Jesus, but the narrative which dramatizes Peter's dilemma is a love story involving an Arabian princess who has become a Christian. The whole book hangs on the problem of her winning the reluctant prince on her own terms—and, of course, she does.

In the same way a love story dominates Costain's religious novel. *The*

Silver Chalice sets out to dramatize the irreconcilability of self and Christ through the struggle of the disciples to preserve the cup of the Last Supper from the Jewish High Priest. But the invented substance takes over this idea. It concerns a blundering young man who cannot make up his mind about Christianity, a conflict dramatized by his love for two women. Early in the novel this unfortunate person declares his love to the wrong woman and then marries the right one without loving her, and this intolerable beginning naturally precipitates an end. His discovery that he loves his wife (hundreds of pages later) is so final, in fact, that it pre-empts the struggle of the disciples with which the novel started.

The difference between *The Nazarene* and these other two versions of the human dilemma is the difference between a resonant novel and a dominating narrative, or the difference between a round fiction and two flat ones. The flat ones are denatured. All three are competent, but the two that feature the narrative are simpler and more limiting. This distinction is basic; it goes beyond the novel form. In all of the fine arts, in fact, the reaching sense dominates what for one reason or another is called "popular" expression.

It happens that the terms "serious" and "popular" art in this formal sense convey an even more explicit distinction in other art forms, as for instance, the distinction between illustration and painting. The illustration promises a destination. It reorganizes the actual subject so as to urge attention forward to a particular destination. In advertising design the destination is a product or a specific idea. The illustrations of fiction, in books and magazines, likewise anticipate the climax of a story.

Illustration on magazine covers often suggests a whole story in this way. Norman Rockwell's covers for the *Saturday Evening Post*, for instance, illustrate the pregnant moment—that point in time when some significance is about to become obvious to the persons in the scene: the view, from above a sand lot, of the home-run ball speeding toward a window, just before the players become fugitives; or the precise moment when the girl discovers her brother reading her diary.

The significance of such scenes is not the predictability but the inevitability of a climax. Rube Goldberg makes fun of this inevitability.

When he illustrates his contrivance to water a buttonhole flower, involving eighteen mechanical operations and the conditioned reflex of a small seal, the viewer patiently follows the directions of the diagram from steps "A" through "S," or whatever, conditioned by the fact that the end will come. His is a kind of shaggy-dog art, which exploits the desire for completion and then offers an anti-climax. The humor depends on the ludicrous discrepancy between effort and accomplishment, but no one would laugh at this without a prior agreement of the end in view.

A painting, unlike an illustration, exploits the sense of becoming to create a different subject. It tells no story; it concerns itself, its parts and their mutual relationship. A painting represents space and planes of energy. Its subject is the amplification and development or contradiction of a curve, or of light or darkness, or buoyancy, or brilliance or weight.

The idea of pure painting, or non-illustrative art, is not very old—a hundred years, more or less; it did not develop until there were public galleries to encourage it. But even within this short time the medium has become its own emphatic subject. The styles of painting in the dozen years which bracketed World War I show the preoccupation. Duchamp's notorious "Nude Descending a Staircase," like all the others which upset the visitors to the Armory Show of 1913, is really about itself. Cubism, Futurism and Orphism were attempts in different ways to evolve the same illusion—the simultaneity of experiences which actually occur during elapsed time.

By correlating several states of being, the painting itself becomes the subject. Picasso's "Girl Before a Mirror," whose mirrored image distorts an already deformed original, has the movement of a continuum. The eye's unending shuttle between distortion and distortion-squared exploits the sense of becoming and makes the viewer collaborate in realizing a new, resonant subject. With similar intent Balla composed in one painting many separate stages in the continuous movement of the "Dog on a Leash." The painting itself is the totality of experience; this is why in Duchamp's painting it does not matter that the nude descending a staircase never gets there.

The contemporary vogue of abstract expressionism, which denies all representation, merely emphasizes the vast difference between illustration and painting. A certain painting and a certain illustration may derive from a common subject. The illustration renders an awareness of that subject; but the painting renders awareness of the medium and the means which dramatize it. If the illustration succeeds, the subject from which it derives comes alive; if the painting succeeds, the medium itself becomes vital.

The same formal significance also distinguishes among musical compositions. The standard juke-box song, for example, (conventionally thirty-two bars divided into four sections, three of which state the same melody) is a skeletal sonata form; but it emphasizes the melody, and shortens the developmental section to the length of each of the three melodic statements. Consciously or not, everyone acknowledges this stylization when referring to popular "tunes." The accompanying lyrics develop a story congenial to the melody and, like the melody, exploit a sense of arrival.

This stress on melody actually emphasizes the movement of becoming, for it is the property of any melody—any succession of tones—to move toward stability. The ear responds to the four active tones in the octave scale by anticipating their resolution to the nearest inactive tone. Consequently, certain pulls and tensions inhere in any melody. The melody of a popular tune, which normally complies with the expected resolution of active tones, is relatively predictable.

What is called "serious" music, on the other hand, characteristically delays these resolutions, continuing to pull and play on the tensions of the active tones. This suggests a preoccupation with the medium itself, with the relationships between the tones. The essence of jazz, for instance, is developmental and harmonic, not melodic. By virtue of each instrument playing against the rest, the jazz composition continuously refrains from resolution. But the music called "swing" is a stylization of jazz. It simplifies the developmental quality and emphasizes the melody—much as Tin Pan Alley modifies the sonata form.

As for the novel form, the narrative capitalizes on the need of an end to things. Unburdened by interference, it correlates the universal desire to correct the present by projecting it into the future. But any development along the way which delays the resolution of the narrative frustrates the reader's sense of futurity. The novelist who wants to explore the nature of the conflict itself rather than its resolution, therefore, is at odds with most of his readers.

This has always been the great contradiction in the form itself. The novel builds a system of analogous conflicts. It is a means of forcing the reader to a larger awareness of a subject. But to accomplish this it must work with a conflict the reader naturally wants resolved. This contradiction explains why James Fenimore Cooper made his novels tell two stories at once. It explains why *The Plutocrat* is more immediately satisfying than *Dodsworth*, and why *The Scarlet Letter* was not so popular as Hawthorne could have wished.

It explains why *Gone with The Wind* and *The Big Fisherman* and *The Silver Chalice* are tabloid versions of experience. The fact that they are caricatures explains their popularity. They are one kind of compromise between the novel form and the commercial auspices of the artifact itself.

The book trade has always encouraged the stylization of the novel, the thinning out of analogous conflicts to get on with the story. The reasons are all a matter of economic incentive. In the present day these reasons are complex, but they all lie in the kind of product various marketers of fiction (the magazine, the reprinter and the film studio) demand of the trade publisher. And the publisher has always managed to convey his desires to an author.

Even after it is completed a novel can be stylized for profit. It can be edited or abridged or adapted to another medium and popularized in the process. The original can be simplified: the narrative made to dominate and the analogies thinned out, so as to shift the emphasis from an experience to its resolution. This is how to denature a novel.

This is also the process by which most contemporary novels are bred. Many times repeated, under the auspices of commercial publication, stylizing causes a peculiar continuity of the novel form. What repeatedly happens is that many novels stylize a few that have made a lot of money.

Stylizing begins with the economic fact that a commercially successful book creates a market for others like it. By this fact the economics of book publishing continually modifies literary theory. But book publishing has its own complexities, which in many strange ways—and often for the wrong reasons—have shaped the contemporary novel.

Chapter III

The Clay Feet of Polk & Franklin

Any similarity between this publisher and any persons living or dead is purely coincidental, because everyone knows publishers are not real.

"ACCORDING to legend, book publishers move in mysterious ways. If not clairvoyant, we are at least marvelously intuitive, as we select, define, and propagate the word." So Lewis Gaynor, president of the publishing house of Polk & Franklin, sketched the opening of the forthcoming Bowker Lecture on book publishing. Gaynor had decided to call his lecture "Book Publishing: The Insular Industry."

"One reason for this legend," he continued, "is the crazy-quilt nature of the book industry. It is a congeries of small, diverse, independent entities, so diffuse that the solution of one economic problem causes a worse one somewhere else. The book trade proceeds by exceptions. Most publishers operate as retailers; manufacturers occasionally become publishers; the economic importance of retailers is not bookselling; and we all spend our advertising allotments to impress our colleagues in the trade. No wonder the myth of the publisher's intuition!"

This is Gaynor's disenchanted view. A year ago when he accepted the invitation to add to that distinguished series of annual lectures, he had no idea he would make such a frightening statement—in public, at least. But the more he has thought about the industry's problems the

48

more clearly he has seen that they are exactly like his own. Except for the Polk & Franklin books that are sold by direct-by-mail methods, Gaynor has no idea who reads what he publishes or why customers buy what they do. Polk & Franklin is, in fact, the "most average" publishing house in the industry. The story of this firm explains the economic attrition of literature.

I

THE NOBLE IMAGE

Gaynor has cause to think as he does about this jackpot business. During the past twelve months P&F has made an enormous profit on a Deluxe ("limited") Edition of the "Song of Solomon," profusely illustrated, handsomely boxed, and retailing for $17.50. But Gaynor lost his shirt on the best history of the French and Indian War he had ever read. The house has also lost heavily on a fine sensitive novel by a sensitive young novelist. Also, an expensive book about elephant guns has had to be remaindered—sold at a fraction of its cost to a mail-order house.

The editor of the novel and the book about elephant guns has, of course, been fired. He ought to have known better. He has listened to an agent's sweet-talk in the hope that the agent might someday send him some really salable manuscripts. But this editor's mistake did not explain why practically no one bought the really great book about the French and Indian War, which Gaynor had personally promoted.

In the first draft of his lecture Gaynor sneered at the myth of the publisher's intuition, by quoting O. H. Cheney's *Economic Survey of the Book Industry* (1931). This definitive study of the American book trade begins by asserting that "the industry is organized around causes and effects about as related as dice throws," and for this reason publishers themselves have come to believe in their mythical intuition.

"The book industry," Gaynor quoted, "is generally believed to have no rules, only exceptions. That is why so many actions in the industry are not only not planned or controlled, but they are not even motivated. Many are hardly intuitive, nothing but tropisms."

On second thought Gaynor crossed this passage out. No need to flaunt the fact. The book trade already knew it, and the layman might get the wrong idea. After all, book publishing has always been a personal venture, as a genealogy of publishing houses in the United States would prove. It would show the persistence with which firms have split apart like amoebas into new and whole organisms. Although publishers may now know statistically more about their operations than they knew thirty years ago, most of the old vagaries persist, intensified by steadily rising costs. The organization of Polk & Franklin testifies to this.

This firm acquired its present personality after the crisis which began in its trade book department* in 1948 and finally led to a change in management. In that year the entire industry produced 9,897 books, and Polk & Franklin accounted for one per cent of the business. It was only one of about 1,100 publishers reporting to the Bureau of the Census in 1948; but to an industry in which a few publishers issue most of the books P&F was important.

In 1948 a few more than three hundred publishers produced eighty-five per cent of the total of new books or editions, and only fifteen publishers produced more than one hundred. Polk & Franklin's 106 titles placed the house modestly among the leaders. In the past fourteen years it has kept pace with the industry's increased production; in 1958 P&F published 134 titles.

The public image of Polk & Franklin carries dignity. The firm has always published distinguished books of history and economics, and to these the works of a dozen well-known English and American novelists were added in the early thirties, when it absorbed the list of another firm. These additions have attracted other novelists, one of whom the trade regards as a candidate for the Nobel Prize. Five Pulitzer Prizes have already gone to Polk & Franklin authors. The works of the two contemporary poets on its backlist have received academic approval; and the National Book Award to one, followed by two honorary degrees, has eased the awful strain of a losing venture.

The backlist, as Gaynor likes to point out, is rich and varied. Many

---

* "Trade book" is the publishing industry's name for a book sold primarily to a retail book store, or wholesaler, for resale to the public, in contrast to a textbook, or a "direct-mail" book—that is, one designed to be sold direct to the purchaser by mail solicitation.

motives have built it: the desire to make money, to attract more good authors, to exploit a timely interest, to publish enduring books, to establish a certain image of the house in the trade. Were any of its editors to make a public statement, however, he would say that Polk & Franklin has always tried to publish the best book in any given category. This statement carries a faint odor of respectability. It also makes "best" a relative word, and accommodates those inspirational novels which continue to sell year after year without benefit of advertising. (P&F's unauthorized edition of Charles Sheldon's *In His Steps* still sells five hundred copies a year.)

Polk & Franklin is proud of its literary reputation. When the house advertises an "unconventional" novel—to use one of the trade's ambiguous terms—the retailer can expect a serious formal experiment, not a prurient story. Although institutional advertising notoriously fails to sell books, this company has for years purchased space in the literary supplements during the first week in July, to inform people that reading is worthwhile. Its letters to authors explaining the rejection of a manuscript invariably cite that manuscript's literary inadequacy instead of its poor sales potential.

Although P&F has made its reputation publishing general books through the trade, its trade department's sixty titles a year comprise less than half its titles and only a quarter of its volume. After World War II the firm established a college text department, and a juvenile list within its trade department. The company has always operated a mail-order enterprise. Not many persons know the proportionate income from these departments, for Polk & Franklin, with stock held by one family, issues no public statement of profit and loss; but it is no secret that P&F's bread-and-butter is its mail-order department.

Direct-mail publishing, a way of making books to order, is the industry's most flagrant example of the synthetic book. The publisher assembles a mailing list of persons with known interests; he then manufactures the contents of a book to gratify those interests and sends a description of it to the names he has collected. It always sells and the expense is minimal. The publisher can even use—and often does use—his mailing list to solicit instructions for the next book.

The mail-order business at P&F is mainly nourished by the Franklin

Library of Practical Living. This venture makes it possible for the firm to lose a certain amount of money in its trade department and still show a corporate profit. The importance of the Franklin Library (there has never been a Franklin in the firm) has always been affirmed by its founder, the elder Horace Polk.

Issued in celebration of the company's twenty-fifth anniversary in 1922, Polk's autobiography explains how his publishing venture began. These personal reminiscences of Polk's own success would be at home in the Franklin Library. Having worked his way through college, Polk took over the management of his uncle's dress-pattern magazine; and through this connection the young man learned the virtues of hard work and frugal living (he earned eight dollars a week). He found in his work still other unique opportunities. When the magazine's printer went bankrupt with an issue on the press, Horace Polk received as payment for his duress the unbound sheets for an edition of *Poor Richard's Almanac*. Some of these he bound and tried to sell through the subscription list of his magazine, but with small success.

Polk persisted, however, and made what turned out to be a brilliant decision. He enclosed the rest of the sheets in a letter to each of his subscribers, asking how she would like to have this book brought up-to-date. The return mail was so encouraging that he hired a lay preacher to write a manuscript to order. Polk entitled this manuscript *The Complete Home Treasury of Successful Planning for Health and Happiness in Your Life*. He cleaned up with it.

The young publisher then set about acquiring a list. He purchased two other books: a home nursing manual, which he titled *The Plain Man's Pathway to Health*, and a cook book with a large mailing list already compiled for it. He larded the recipes in *Bridget's Food of Life* with inspirational messages. All three volumes, uniformly bound in sky-blue, sold as fast as the expanding mailing list could accommodate. Other ventures, like the garden manuals Polk occasionally developed, prospered by mail order also. Later Polk established a book club to furnish his subscribers with similar products at a slight discount automatically. But through the years the Franklin Library showed the greatest stamina.

Contemporary mail-order titles (devoted to practical philosophy and religion, to public manners, and to simplified psychology) sell about 600,000 copies a year. The archetypes are still around. Five times revised, now illustrated with quaint woodcuts, the cook book has sold 3,000,000 copies. The home-nursing book has been restyled as a loose-leaf manual with subscription supplements. *The Complete Home Treasury of Successful Planning for Health and Happiness in Your Life* is still one of the book club's membership premiums. When the young members of the editorial staff scorn the founder's enterprise as "Polk's Practical Piety," they are likely to be chastised.

The trade department came to Polk & Franklin in the early thirties, when it absorbed the firm of Worth and Loesser, whose list included a popular history of American military victories and a best-selling report of prohibition and organized vice—both edited by Worth. Then Worth retired, and Loesser, a literary man, became the editor of Polk & Franklin's newly acquired trade department. Loesser brought with him the works of a French novelist and three British writers. He also brought a passionate interest in American writing, and largely because of his efforts during the next twenty-five years, P&F now has a backlist of distinguished fiction.

The fiction list also followed other personal interests. Since the 1930's Polk & Franklin has published sea stories because of Lewis Gaynor's enthusiasm. This began while he was the company's sales manager. Gaynor had maintained a house in Maine, made his own lobster pots, and cruised off-shore. One day an agent had a hunch and sent to Gaynor the manuscript of a novel with a Down-East setting. Gaynor immediately became a reader—and buyer—of fiction. For the past fifteen years historical novels, particularly about New England seaports, have been prominent on the list. Gaynor has even ventured once or twice with novels about Indians, a subject he hopes will permit him to cash in on the new interest in domestic archeology.

Gaynor sees this development of a list of fiction reinforced by regional and scientific interests as an example of sound marketing. "Everyone knows there are not enough book readers," he says. "I learned that years ago from Horace Polk. He taught me what to do about it. He made me read Brander Matthews on the fallacy of trying to please 'the taste of the public'—as if there were only one public, with one taste." Gaynor's standard speech to retail associations, entitled "The Big 'M' in Marketing," develops this argument.

Any competent book, he maintains, will find its small and usually insignificant public or market: regular readers devoted to a given subject, plus a few additional gift purchasers. But the problem in selling—and building—a book is to get beyond this limited market, to find many small groups of readers who might one way or another respond to it. "Call this congregation of many groups the book's Market—with a capital 'M'. Every book should be an overlap, to capitalize on its possible interest to many markets." He explains that the publisher may break even on his initial cost by the sale of the book to its small and known market, but the book will prosper only as its sales exploit the interest of many marginal groups.

This philosophy of marketing—of learning a book's basic readership, then tailoring it for sales beyond that readership—accounts for the so-called "house book" at P&F, conceived by an editor and jobbed out for writing. Three or four house books, primarily non-fiction, are continually in process at Polk & Franklin. But whatever reassurance they provide in calculating cost and profit, their timely nature usually limits their period of sale. The house book is a one-shot.

At the opposite extreme, unsolicited manuscripts, which offer the least assurance, deluge the publisher. Polk & Franklin receives about 2,500 unsolicited manuscripts a year, virtually all of which it rejects. Editorial assistants empty the slush box after each morning's mail, returning the impossible manuscripts to their authors and forwarding the few promising ones to an editor for a second reading. Occasionally one gets on the agenda of the weekly editorial meeting, and possibly one a year will be published. But Polk & Franklin dares not forego this expensive procedure which might sometime yield another *Gone with the Wind*. Most publishable manuscripts come from literary agents, from published authors, and from ideas conceived in the firm. Considering all their sources of supply, the editors of Polk & Franklin say "no" ten or twelve times a day and "yes" about once a week.

One editor's personal convictions usually determine the firm's decision to publish any given manuscript. This conviction must concern more than sales. Shortly before his retirement, Horace Polk installed in every office in the company a framed copy of a statement by one of the trade's leading advertising agencies. "People Are More Alike than Anybody," says the copy. "A publisher who prints a book because he likes it usually finds that many people agree with him." And it continues: "A publisher who doesn't like a book but prints it anyway often discovers that most people agree with him." Lewis Gaynor has encouraged this idealism in his own way. Every editor at P&F knows that he had better not make more than one mistake a year.

The editor must temper his enthusiasm for a manuscript by considering the sales records of others like it. Gaynor calls it "exploring a book's possibilities." Since no editor has all the facts—since his own recollections include only the past fifty or sixty manuscripts he has read—he must test his convictions against the devil's advocates whom he meets each week at the trade department's editorial conference: other editors, and the heads of the production, sales, advertising, publicity, and business-management departments, who pass judgment on manuscripts, on ideas for books, and on books-in-process.

II

RANDOM HARVEST

It was in one of these weekly conferences late in 1948, when Gaynor was still sales manager, that all the trouble in the trade department started, although no one knew it at the time. According to the minutes of this meeting, discussion centered on two books: a war novel and an autobiography. The novel came from one of Loesser's authors who submitted two chapters and an outline of a war story. It was his second novel. The first, although well-reviewed, had sold only 4,700 copies, but P&F had recovered its costs by selling the reprint rights for a paperbound edition. Even though the house held an option on this new manuscript at the original terms, calling for no advance to the author, publishing it would be risky.

The other manuscript, the autobiography of a country banker, had been submitted by an agent. One of the younger editors at Polk & Franklin reported: "Its earthy observations and brash episodes of small-town living are very contagious, but the manuscript needs thorough revision." George Tasker, another editor, had helpfully summed it up: "You mean it stinks but it's great."

After a fruitful discussion of dirty books, the group considered the problem of how best to collaborate with the author. One way was to return the manuscript to the author for rewriting (for which the agent would first demand a contract for eventual publication); another way was to purchase the idea and have the book ghost-written; or, somewhere between, to offer the author a contract that would provide for the house to be reimbursed out of the author's royalties for the extensive editorial revision planned by the firm.

(Had this particular manuscript first been submitted to George Tasker, it would have come before this group as a finished product. Through an agent, Tasker has frequently signed an author of an ailing manuscript to a contract, whereby Tasker rewrites the book for a share of the author's royalties and then presents the manuscript to P&F. Since an editor must one way or another provide his publisher with marketable books, everyone prospers by such an arrangement. Tasker has a knack with house books, or what might be called a pure notion of book sales. He has even offered to compile and edit a *Treasury of Filthy Religious Wood-Cuts* to prove that P&F could profit enormously by tapping the immense reservoir of illiterate book-buyers.)

Of fourteen books the group discussed, according to the minutes of this meeting, seven were rejected and five were tabled for lack of information, although in the case of three of these it was decided that "Mr. Gaynor's sales force will get a market check," meaning a positive endorsement from a few large booksellers on the decision to publish.

As for the novel, Loesser was directed to canvass the possibilities of a reprint edition and of a movie sale. The minutes continue: "Mr. Loesser will also discuss with the author's agent the possibilities of sharing first-serial rights." This, of course, the agent would refuse if he knew his business, but P&F wanted a talking point for any compromise that might occur. They would need every break to recover costs on this book. As for the banker's autobiography, its editor was "directed to negotiate a contract for publication, which reimburses Polk and Franklin for editorial work."

The meeting adjourned after the business manager "asked the production department to present at the next conference budgets based on estimated sales of the war novel and of the autobiography." This last entry would startle anyone but a publisher. Each book would have a budget before it had a complete manuscript. This budget was intended to influence all editorial changes.

A book's budget is a way of establishing the number of copies that must be sold in order for the publisher's investment to be recovered. This "get-out" figure is arrived at by dividing the edition's manufacturing and advertising costs (expressed in thousands of dollars) by the publisher's net receipt per copy (expressed in pennies), which is what remains after the direct costs of discounts, distribution, royalties, advertising and general overhead have been deducted from its sale price. Dividing the fixed or heavy costs by the net income per copy yields the number of copies which the publisher must sell to break even.

But the costs in this budget, which determine the "break-even" number of copies, are themselves projections of an estimated number of copies to be manufactured in the first place. In short, the budget begins by assuming part of what it proves. It is merely an educated guess about where to write-off the product. This necessarily elliptical logic doubtless occurs before the manufacture and sale of any consumer product, but at Polk & Franklin the products are books; in these two instances, moreover, books scarcely begun before they must submit to a budget.

P&F accepted both of these fragmentary manuscripts, gambling on an estimated sale of each to its own basic market plus other groups of possible purchasers. What the publisher accepted was really only the beginning of an idea, the rest of which would grow and take shape according to specifications in the budget. Although each manuscript originated with its author, the books themselves originated with the publisher who had, in effect, to conceive them in space. Gaynor always explained to a new editor that planning a book was like designing a house from the roof down. He failed to explain the author's problem in completing such a manuscript, which is more like building a house from the roof up.

Nothing seemed to be amiss. The minutes of editorial meetings through the spring of 1949 revealed progress on both books. As expected, Loesser could get no income from magazine rights to the novel, although two paperback publishers—Monster Books and Cleavage Press—had expressed interest. With this possibility of bargaining, P&F could probably count on a $15,000 advance against paperback sales, half of which would belong to the author. Accordingly, the business manager approved a budget based on a break-even sale of 7,500 copies of a $4.00 novel.

A large package would have to help justify this high retail price. After the success of *The Naked and the Dead* the year before, the literary fashion in war novels called for length and great detail. Loesser would consult with his author about building into the story several episodes not presently in the manuscript. One of these, the firm agreed, should be the American liberation of a brothel. This would give point to another new episode, when the hero would return to the scene of said liberation.

Since the book's sale seemed largely unpredictable, the advertising to the trade would represent it as a "quality" novel—a distinguished work which Polk & Franklin was "proud to publish." Now it was time to name the book—or rename it. The author's title, *Toe Hold in Elysium*, simply would not do. As Gaynor said, they wanted a quality novel, not a precious one. The narrative told of a landing operation in the Mediterranean, Loesser explained. George Tasker, who had read most of the manuscript, said that if a precise title was wanted, it ought to be called *Honest, I Was Really There.* But the minutes state merely: "After some discussion, the meeting decided on *Red Beach Assault.* Mr. Loesser will explain the change in title to the author."

The other book, the banker's autobiography, also progressed. It would be tailored to fit a 350-page package retailing at $4.50. The banker had a success story to tell, and since he also had a way with homespun maxims, the edition might possibly find a second sale in the Franklin Book Club. On the strength of this the production department requested manufacturers' estimates of the cost of producing 20,000 copies.

With general agreement the autobiography was titled *They Bank on Me.* The editor penciled a memo to the art department, suggesting a folksy book jacket; and from several designs he chose a village scene in the style of a cross-stitch sampler, with the title set in Olde Almanacke type. By July each book had a production schedule for publication in the spring of 1950. Under its editor's direction the autobiography proceeded more smoothly than the novel. With the final manuscript ready in September, both its dummy and jacket were prepared for the December sales meeting. The manuscript of the novel arrived late in November. By this time the designer and the copy editor had already prepared its jacket.

Production of dust jackets signaled the start of the advertising campaigns for both books. Each book's budget provided for an advertising appropriation based on an estimate of its sales to retail booksellers and to jobbers in advance of publication—as low an appropriation as feasible, considering the estimated life of the book. Polk & Franklin normally spends ten per cent of the gross receipts from advance sales on advertising the list as a whole, unequally apportioned to individual titles. Each book must earn its basic share of this kitty: ten per cent of the net receipts of its own advance sale. A percentage of the difference between net and gross receipts builds a reserve fund to which the house can charge extra advertising as needed.

Accordingly, *They Bank on Me* and *Red Beach Assault* each had a basic allotment. The autobiography, with an advance sale of 15,000 copies, at a net of $2.70 per book yielded $4,050. The novel's advance sale of 5,000 copies yielded an advertising budget of only $1,200. But gambling on Loesser's enthusiasm (an expensive luxury, as it turned out) P&F increased its appropriation by another $1,200 from the reserve fund. Following publication, each title would have to earn its advertising by current sales.

These advertising appropriations at Polk & Franklin proceeded from two principles of book selling. One principle is that a book sells primarily by its own contagion, for which advertising offers no substitute. One reader tells another, a process which may take months or years for the book to find its market. Advertising can speed this process, once it begins, but consumer advertising must follow book sales. Advertising can anticipate the book only by announcing it, and then only to the trade.

The purpose of this trade advertising is to impress on everyone connected with the book, from author to retailer, how much the publisher believes in his product. He also promises that everybody can make a lot of money on it. Ads in *Publishers' Weekly* are part of this campaign. But P&F also has a carefully updated mailing list of key persons in the trade who receive advance copies of the book. These persons also receive a personal letter from the president of the company, which is to say one of seven different form letters written in the sales department, expressing the president's profound faith in this splendid new book. If bookmen believe all this enough to start talking about the book, the publisher has spent his money well.

At Polk & Franklin they call the second principle of bookselling "the infallibility of the advance sale": an overstatement of the publisher's belief in the reliability of the pre-publication sale to jobbers and retailers as an indication of its ultimate market. Books' budgets are estimates; but even an estimate must begin somewhere. More important, this advance "sale" influences subsequent editorial decisions. In view of a book's sales record a year later, its advance sale will help estimate the possibilities of any similar manuscript in the future.

The advance sale is at least calculable—or was, until ten years ago, when retailers demanded the privilege of returning unsold books, by a system similar to magazine distribution. Considering that a "sale" is not necessarily a sale, the degree to which publishers rely on the consignment of their products to establish their costs would frighten most manufacturers. In fact, Gaynor has lately given up trying to play this guessing game with retailers, and is now experimenting with the scheme of sending them assortments of books, like variety cereal packages.

The advance sale has traditionally become important because of seasonal marketing—and crowding—of books. Every P&F title released through the trade appears on one of two lists a year. The fall list, aimed at Christmas buying, begins with publishing dates in August and with books already presented to jobbers and retailers in June. The spring list, with publishing dates beginning in February, has already been presented to the trade in January. At Polk & Franklin semi-annual sales meetings precede these July and January deadlines.

These sales meetings represent both cause and symptom of Polk &

Franklin's frantic seasonal preparations for merchandising books. On these occasions the house calls in its travelers who sell to the retail trade, for a two-day conference to acquaint them with the new list. Polk & Franklin's travelers have always formed the infantry in its sales campaigns. With their advance sales to retailers they consolidate the publisher's trade advertising. But since their jobs largely depend on their customers' confidence, the salesmen also represent the retailers to the publisher. The traveler must be shrewd enough to know—without benefit of reading—the nature of a given book, why it has been published, and how the publisher plans to sell it.

The presentation aimed at answering these questions comes from the editor. From the moment of the book's conception, it has been his job to define its qualities and to translate them into selling terms. This representation of a book usually requires a further translation into sales quotas by P&F's sales manager. With thirty new books at every sales meeting, time and attention are limited. Since an average presentation lasts only eight minutes, the editor needs some shorthand method to reduce the book to a negotiable status, so he expediently classifies it.

Classifying a new book according to its subject or its theme offers the advantage of making its appeal measurable by the sales of past books presumed to be more or less like it. But this is the only advantage. To the degree that it succeeds in that compromise, classification moves everyone's attention away from the book's individuality, away from that quality which makes the book vital. Categorizing books contradicts the industry's maxim that every book is an exception. An editor at Polk & Franklin may spend months nurturing a book's peculiarity, some precious eccentricity of its author, but at the sales meeting the only way he can express its freshness and its difference is by homologizing it.

Tom Loesser always used to chafe at this need for classification. Any worthwhile book, he would say, projects a personality, and should not be tolled off as merely one of a category. While still a young man, Loesser was privileged to know the late Maxwell Perkins and to share some of the fascination and the pain of that editor's celebrated mission. Perkins had received an amorphous, much-rejected manuscript fortuitously entitled "O Lost," and had made its author discipline it into *Look Homeward, Angel*. In the process of making his emotions articulate in some more manageable form, Maxwell Perkins had projected the singularity of Thomas Wolfe.

Loesser always believed in the lesson he had learned from Max Perkins. The editor must represent the book at every stage of its production: consultation, copy editing, manufacture, jacket design, advertising and selling. Yet, in the last analysis, he must amplify the author's intentions in the most commercially feasible way. This contradiction always disturbed Loesser. "Novelists don't write categories," he would say. "The question is not *what* is a pot boiler but *who* is a pot boiler. A man writes as he is. If he has the soul of a pot boiler, he will write pot boilers."

When Loesser spoke like this he spoke like Henry James. But James never sold many books. Anyway, book promotion has always worked the other way around. A publisher will emphasize a book's similarity to others so that he can then show how it exceeds these others in the qualities they presumably share. Sooner or later the salesman must sell the book, having judged it on his own terms. His terms are the sales of previous books like it.

Loesser's notes for Polk & Franklin's sales meeting in the winter of 1950 yielded on this point. He later said they had made him retch, and Gaynor had agreed. After a typed synopsis of *Red Beach Assault*, Loesser penciled these notes:

1. As you can see, novel concerns Italian campaign in World War II.
2. Has a love story, like *A Farewell to Arms*, only it takes place in Sicily.
3. Soldier-hero is not running away. It is more positive. He goes off to the enemy like the last episode of *The Gallery*.
4. A landing at Anzio and suspense of a limited, bitter campaign— like *A Walk in the Sun*.
5. Soldier has no idea where he fits into the sense of what is going on around him, like *The Red Badge of Courage*.
6. Promotion: we will give this shock advertising, like *The Naked and the Dead*.
7. But our pitch is that it is first and foremost a quality novel.
8. Will be a paperback edition.

9. Movie rights have already been sold, possible tie-in with Hollywood's advertising. We think can get a *Life* article on World War
II films and how this one will be different.

Shot-gun salesmanship also marked the presentation of *They Bank
on Me*. Gaynor remembered thinking that this young editor had
learned fast.

You remember impact of *Country Lawyer* and *Country Doctor*.
WARM books!! This banker has watched over his town in the same
way, and taken care of its people for fifty years.
This book will break down image of a bank as a big, impersonal in-
stitution. Banker has his own personal problems, like Charles Gray in
Point of No Return.
But in this new book, appeal of the man in the bank is really more
like *David Harum*. A kind but shrewd honesty. WARM-HEARTED!!
National Usury Association is behind us on this one. Its journal for
July will lead off with a review of the book. And we will advertise in
Wall Street Journal.
One other important tie-in: the Southern crisis. This bank is in a
Southern town and the big episode (synopsis) is about the banker try-
ing to help the school principal get money for a new building for an
integrated school.
We plan to advertise this book as controversial in the South. This
will go big in East, West, and Northern markets.
The rape and the lynching speak for themselves.
Author is already signed up for a series of appearances on college
campuses. The liberal angle. Publicity Department is already working
on the endorsements.

So the books went to market. Both justified the original estimates,
but with unexpected consequences. Considered an investment in its
author, *Red Beach Assault* performed as intended. Polk & Franklin
sold out the original edition within a year, although scarcely recovering
costs because of the increased advertising budget. The advance sale to
the trade, 4,300 copies, proved slightly less than the estimate. Nevertheless, P&F followed up a half-page ad in *Publishers' Weekly* with a
series of smaller ads before and after publication in the New York
Times and *Herald Tribune* book reviews and in the more literate maga-

zines with a small but national distribution. It was also listed in several of P&F's other ads in these same publications.

When the paperbound edition of the novel, retitled *Beachhead in Hell*, appeared a year after publication, the sales of the hard-cover edition stood at 7,300 copies. Its trade sales stopped at that point, but the paperback went well. Monster Books sold 200,000 copies in the first printing; another 650,000 copies in 1951 tied in with the movie. But no one had made any money except the author. By June of 1952 the reprint sales had barely repaid Monster Books for its $12,000 advance against royalties. All the milkmaids had done their job, but there was not enough milk to go around.

Well reviewed and carefully published, the war novel was a *succès d'estime*, a fact which curiously nullified P&F's investment. All had gone according to plan, but the author did not see it this way. He attributed the difference between the favorable reviews and the small sales to the lack of advertising. P&F's capital risk and its negotiations with the subsidiary marketers which had enabled the publication in the first place made no impression on him. Then, on the strength of this novel another publisher offered the author a ridiculously large advance for a volume of his short stories, and he immediately challenged P&F with the offer. This was an outright trespass. Everyone knew it, including the agent who had promoted it.

Tasker reminded everyone that this was exactly the sort of raid P&F pulled off whenever it could. Nevertheless, Polk & Franklin was on the spot. The other publisher obviously planned to steal the author by publishing the short stories at a loss. Expensive luxuries, short-story volumes yield only small sales (2,000 copies in this case would be good). Having published this author's works with as yet no profit, Loesser urged him to continue work on his third novel, even offered him a $1,000 advance; but P&F "regretfully" turned down the short stories. The refusal to lose more money finally cost the house the author in whom it had invested.

They Bank on Me brought surprises too. Advance sales had totaled 10,000 copies, slightly higher than expected. Fortunately a trucker's strike had prevented P&F from supplying the printer with enough paper for the first run, and so a second printing before publication had been necessary. Then came the break which made the book. A large manufacturing company ordered 7,000 copies—at a jobber's discount —to be delivered in time for distribution as a Christmas bonus for its employees. This company's president, like the banker a self-made man, had noted the strong preachments in the book about the beauties of living happily with less money, and desired to bestow this comfort on his employees.

Timing was perfect. Polk & Franklin printed the copies and immediately took full-page newspaper ads to announce the third printing within a week after publication. The book, in fact, did sell the 7,200 copies within the first month; and, still on the strength of its Christmas-bonus order, Polk & Franklin gambled on another printing ahead of sales and another series of ads proudly announcing "Four Big Printings in Five Weeks." The lure worked. The book began to sell. Enough retailers who had overstocked it reported the book a best seller to give it a place on two best-seller lists. Cleavage Press offered P&F $25,000 for reprint rights. The book sold steadily in the trade edition, and with the help of Christmas buying P&F got rid of 35,000 copies. The remaining books became selections in the Franklin Library.

III

THE REVOLUTION

Polk & Franklin published these two books at a time of rapid changes in book markets, when it was becoming evident that trade publishers had no business publishing fiction. For one thing, over-production had returned with the peace-time economy. During World War II, when the rationing of metal and paper had severely limited the manufacture of books, publishers had enjoyed a seller's market; any book would sell. During the war years the industry had produced an annual average of 7,800 trade titles. In 1947 the total jumped to nearly 9,200, then to 11,000 by 1950. But customers for these books had failed to materialize.

A more specific change had drastically affected the sale of fiction. This was the tremendous increase in the number of inexpensive paperbound reprints. The adjusted Census of Manufacturers indicated a sale of 95,500,000 paperbacks in 1947, slightly less than a fifth of all books published in the United States. By 1952 sales had risen to 270,-000,000 copies, more than a third of the annual total production. And between these years fiction comprised nearly ninety per cent of the paperback titles. Clearly, more book buyers wanted their novels in paperback.

Simultaneously during the early post-war years manufacturing conditions all but prohibited the profitable publication of novels in trade editions. Before the War, as late as 1941, a trade publisher could break even on the sale of 2,500 copies of a novel, and since fiction had always been his most speculative product he could afford to publish many titles each season in hopes of one sales winner. But the scarcity of paper persisted for several years after the war. Book publishers could not compete with the magazines, which were able to buy paper in large quantities, or with newspaper syndicates able to purchase mills and contract for their entire output in pulp.

The rising cost of labor also worked against small editions. Make-ready time on short printing runs became too expensive, so book manufacturers gave priority to large editions. Delays were costly to the publishers. In the early post-war years all costs had increased at Polk & Franklin, but the firm clamped down where it could on the cost of advertising and the cost of royalties. As a consequence of these economies, in the case of the war novel at least, Polk & Franklin lost an author.

Rising costs and changing readership had determined most of the editorial decisions at P&F in the publication of these two books; and their respective sales helped cause a palace revolution in the firm. As an investment the *Red Beach Assault* had failed; the departure of its author nullified much of the prestige its publication had brought to the house. But, as a one-shot, the autobiography had succeeded. With better luck than the novel and with shrewd merchandising this piece of editorial carpentry had paid off, earning the house almost $85,000 from trade sales and another $12,500 in reprint royalties. Because all books tend to attract others like them to a publisher's list, P&F could expect more of each kind. Some policy had to be set.

Everyone at Polk & Franklin recognized these books as belonging to different breeds, but neither book was an extremity of its kind. The novel was promising but not first-rate. The autobiography was merchandise but not worthless. Tom Loesser justified publishing both. "We want a varied list," he said, "the best of all kinds of books." He argued that this was the only sound compromise a publisher interested in quality could make. Since a book's sales did not correspond to the book's quality in this imperfect world, then competent merchandise would have to pay the way for good literature.

Some of the facts have justified Loesser's argument. For better or worse, a publisher's bookkeeping characteristically charges all the cost of a book against the trade sales of its first edition, making it look like a poor investment. Any income the book earns from a magazine, a reprint, a book-club selection or a film is entered in a separate account for "subsidiary" income. The income in this second account the publisher considers as profit, overlooking the fact that his original investment (his trade edition) helped earn this subsidiary income and therefore merits credit for a share of it.

This arbitrary partition between ledger pages often determines editorial decisions. According to Loesser's thinking, one book had to support another. This was the way the publisher could justify "the worthwhile book of limited appeal." But Gaynor saw it differently. The only way to justify a loss was to blame the editor, and axe him. The guillotine always works.

Loesser had patiently tried to argue his compromise by analogy. "The auto manufacturer doesn't expect the same dollar-return from the carburetor and the clutch plate and the hub cap. He sells a composite. Each of the parts costs him more or less than average, yet the whole product needs all its parts."

For awhile Gaynor argued with him. "According to your analogy, the manufacturer could afford a better clutch plate by making a cheaper carburetor. But you don't want to admit it, because if you did, then you couldn't rationalize publishing junk."

The times favored Gaynor. P&F steadily lost money after 1948, and the sons and daughters—and the new in-laws—of the Polk family finally persuaded the president to step aside. Upon the retirement of

Horace Polk, Jr., to a newly created chairmanship of the board, in January 1950, Lewis Gaynor was appointed president of Polk & Franklin. Within a month the business manager became vice-president, and the advertising manager took over the sales department. Two of the five trade editors were fired, and replaced by younger men from the production department. Loesser was persuaded to head Polk & Franklin's new textbook department; and his successor, with a title of executive editor, was hired from Monster Books.

The consequences of this palace revolution presently appeared. A series of memoranda from the president to all department heads firmly defined a new editorial policy for the trade department. "We believe in making substantial profits on books of which we can be proud," the first memo began, "but we are not content with marginal profits." Simply stated, the intent staggered Loesser: every book must make a substantial profit. "To guide your thinking along these lines," the memo continued, "we will aim at a total minimum sale of $25,000 net for each title over a reasonable period of time." The memo suggested three years as "reasonable."

This was sound policy. A book's pricing formula would depend not on the number of sales needed to break even but on a stipulated revenue to be earned by any means whatever. A book priced at $3.50 and returning $2.00 net to the publisher would have to sell 12,500 copies in order to meet its obligation to the firm; or for every thousand sales less than its quota it would have to earn for the publisher $2,000 of subsidiary income. This policy would eliminate the marginal book. Although the president did not bother to explain it, this policy would censor future lists at Polk & Franklin before they could even be assembled. This censorship would take its heaviest toll among novels.

The effective book selling period of novels (from three to five months) is shorter than for other books. Novels would, therefore, have less time in the market to achieve the stipulated minimum sale. Unless its author's name had sales appeal, or unless it could provide enough subsidiary income to make up the difference between its actual sales and its quota, a novel henceforth would have small chance of acceptance at Polk & Franklin.

Subsequent memoranda elaborated this policy. One of them, entitled "Our Biggest Liability," explained why the expense of marginal books exceeded even their estimated costs. "The book with the limited market will usually be over-printed to meet our pricing formula, over-advertised because it is over-printed, and over-sold in terms of its true market. Unsold copies returned to us for credit cause a loss in every department that must touch the book." Another memo, entitled "Conservative Terms," informed the editors that advances and high royalties to authors were no longer automatic. "Polk & Franklin," it said, "is not a charitable institution."

In view of these changes, Thomas Loesser's final transaction in the trade department caused him unusual distress. Before the revolution he had received the manuscript of a Western novel. It was about a rancher but offbeat, what the trade would call a "serious" cowboy story. It was a character-study of a man who turned out to be his own worst enemy. Loesser had originally liked the outline and had invited the author to submit more copy. Now, the first five chapters and a précis of the rest looked promising. The story began conventionally with a stampede and a narrow escape and even ended in a chase, but with a difference. It all occurred in the man's mind; and Loesser recognized the quality by which the trade would label this novel as "serious." The story concerned less the events than the perception of these events; it was cerebral.

It was a splendid book and worth publishing, but Loesser knew it would never make its quota under the new system without the aid of subsidiary income. Since its marketing category disqualified it as a Western no reprinter would even consider it until he could see a completed manuscript. Meanwhile, the author had run out of money and needed an advance in order to finish the book.

But the change in command intervened. When the new executive editor was briefed on these data, he did not need to read the manuscript. He dictated a letter of regret to the author, censuring "the novel's aesthetic failing." He faintly applauded "the descriptive quality," but pointed out that "in the last analysis the characters are not quite believable in this context."

IV

THE INSULAR INDUSTRY

Loesser was not the only lonely man at Polk & Franklin. Its new president had distresses of his own. Lewis Gaynor had put his house in order only by exchanging compromises, but he felt he had to curb over-production—too many copies of too many titles—which (except for the war years) had plagued the firm as long as he could remember. Horace Polk's impeccable logic had taught him the consequences of over-production; and he had reduced the arithmetic of publishing to what he called Polk's Law: "Thou shalt not oversell."

Gaynor still recalls those two books Polk & Franklin published while he was sales manager: the war novel and the autobiography. Probably neither one should have been published, although for different reasons. The house had published one for its literary merit and the other for profit, but neither had profited Polk & Franklin's list. The novel had cost the house an author, and the autobiography had certainly not attracted any worthwhile manuscripts.

Gaynor recalls these events as he prepares his lecture on the sad state of the publishing industry. One trouble, he has decided, is that most publishers know so little about their own business that they have to pretend to be intuitive. For years the trade has ignored the statistics of its own operations. Nor can a publisher readily find out what he needs to know. The trade's partial and private bookkeeping denies the discovery of even fundamental statistical knowledge.

Separately recorded as they are, even the two most elementary facts about the industry—the number of titles annually published and the number of copies sold—are mutually irrelevant. The annual inventory of new titles in *Publishers' Weekly* and the periodic tabulation of sales in the United States Census of Manufactures classify information according to different subject headings. The integration of textbook, trade and mail-order publishing within a single publishing house has compounded this problem of finding relevant statistics.

These are only symptoms of the real problem, Gaynor concedes— which is the trade's ignorance of book readers in this country. The publisher might make an educated guess about the number or geographical location of book buyers for any given title. But about readers, he knows almost nothing. For years he has ducked the responsibility of finding out.

Gaynor lays no claim to scholarship, but he does have a historical sense; and his marginal notes in Cheney's *Survey of the Book Industry*, in a chapter called "Readers or Book Buyers," indicate that he has found the problem. "We are beginning to realize that the processes of the book industry do not form a straight line from author to reader," Cheney states. "They form a sort of continuous circle within a circle in which the reader does (or rather, should) influence every branch of the industry, including even the author and the critic."

The industry has been so concerned with the book that it has forgotten the reader. But the influence of the reader on the book must sooner or later be understood by the publisher and bookseller—and the result must inevitably affect the nature of books published, their format and their price, their theme and style——and, it is hoped, merchandising methods.

Gaynor has underlined it. *"The industry has been so concerned with the book that it has forgotten the reader."*

The inevitable guesswork by which publishers build their lists Cheney facetiously calls the "spawning theory of publishing," in a chapter called "The Book, the Buyer and the Critic." The whole business is based on guesswork. "The good publisher is the one who guesses wrong least."

Logically, therefore, it appears to be the duty of the publisher to guess as often as possible—the longer the lists, the more the good guesses. The spawning theory of publishing cannot, if it carries its logic to a conclusion, reject any manuscript which contains even traces of merit or theoretical sales possibilities—it might turn out to be a good seller.

Cheney explains the relationship between too many books and their short life in the market place. The excessive lists of titles seasonably issued mean that each book gets inadequate promotion and selling time. "Books are cannibals," the *Survey* states, "and the competition between books is a contributing cause to every major problem of the industry." Crowding too many titles into short periods of market time taxes the bookseller's capital and his display space. It also taxes the care and attention of everyone who touches the book—publisher, jobber, retailer, and book reviewer—necessarily causing the neglect of some titles in favor of others. "Of the total number of trade books available," says Cheney, "not sixty per cent receive even fair merchandising attention." The ideal remedy would be to publish fewer titles. But who would know which titles to cut out?

That is why the vision of the publishers sitting around a table and deciding to cut down their lists is almost equal, in stirring the hollow laugh, to a disarmament conference. But the picture is lugubrious compared with the one of each publisher, surrounded by his staff, doing the actual cutting down.

Despite seventy years of marketing, book publishing is still an insular industry. The argument of Gaynor's lecture is simple. The economic organization of the American book trade, still patterned on its nineteenth-century origins, includes hundreds of small business units, each handling many (and many of the same) products in limited quantities. The sale of these books (and often the books themselves) depends on the variable desires and predilections—or the "taste"—of thousands of groups of people; but none of these business entities has ever had the means to afford a thorough and systematic exploration of book markets. Anyway, nobody has ever analyzed public taste, except in retrospect.

Unable to find or to create any useful opinion-makers among the nation's book buyers, these individual enterprises have consequently looked to one another to define taste. By a process of trial and error, the publisher produces as many books as possible, testing the appeal of his products to other business entities within the trade, even as they pass these products along to the ultimate buyers. The rising costs of operating a business, and the high price of experimenting, have rein-forced this tendency to look within the trade for means of measuring the appeal of books.

Gaynor's forthcoming lecture is all about this inversion of the book trade, and he illustrates his argument by describing three conditions: the plight of the retail bookseller, the ridiculousness of the publisher's advertising, and the problem of book-club distribution. Gaynor's argu-ment is so impressive and so discouraging that he himself sees more frightening implications than he expected.

Retail bookselling, Gaynor's lecture points out, offers as timely a subject now as it did in 1872, when Frederick Leypoldt founded *Pub-lishers' Weekly*. In that year the United States, with a population of 40,000 people, had about 3,000 book stores. Today, with a national population more than four times larger, there are *fewer* than 3,000 retail book stores in the United States.

Even this startling comparison falls short of the facts. Polk & Frank-lin's mailing list, for instance, includes only 2,100 stores whose gross receipts come primarily from books; and only twelve per cent of the names on P&F's list—stores located in New York City, Philadelphia, New England, Chicago, St. Louis and scattered West Coast cities—stock more than 2,000 current titles. (Gaynor does not express his pri-vate opinion that P&F cannot rely on any more than fifty of these stores for aggressive and intelligent marketing of current and backlist books.)

Although the reprint publishers have discovered 100,000 new outlets, including cigar stores, bus terminals and supermarkets, most retail sell-ing of original hard-cover books is confined to a very few bookstores. The plight of the rest—of the average booksellers—has its effect on the entire trade. Gaynor emphasizes this with some of Jacques Barzun's observations in *The New Leader* (May 13, 1957), about the bookstore as a bottleneck—"a plugged-up medicine dropper."

The bookseller is caught between the rent of his poky shop, the high cost of shipping and accounting, and the vagueness of the public mind —the mind which would forget the name Lucky Strike in a week if unprompted by ads. In this literal and figurative box, a bookseller would be a fool to stock anything but best-sellers and college diction-aires. Which means that the trade's effort at marketing concentrates on persuading him that some new work will be a best-seller.

Surely, the bookseller offers no vital communication between the publisher and the public he seeks. Readers dependent on the retail trade often never see or hear of books they might otherwise buy, yet the myth of "the infallible advance sale" persists. His sales are negli-gible, yet his store has traditionally played a crucial part in the pub-lisher's planning. As an outlet for advance sales, it has long been a kind of laboratory for a book's dry-run. The transactions between pub-lishers' salesmen and the booksellers they visit have usually determined how and to what extent the publisher will advertise his book. To the extent that publishers have heeded the advance sale, they have acceded to the judgment of their salesmen and the booksellers.

As further evidence of the trade's inversion Gaynor cites its methods of advertising, which he compares with other industries. In the national economy advertising has become the primary selling tool, the means of creating desires in order to sell products to satisfy them. The pur-pose of book advertising, accordingly, would seem to be increased sales, but publishers advertise only deviously toward this end. To be sure, every publisher goes through the motions of advertising books to con-sumers, but most of the media cannot reach his markets for prices the publisher can afford.

Publishers buy no time on television or radio. They buy space in less than one per cent of the nation's 1,750 daily newspapers, in about five per cent of the nation's six hundred consumer magazines and in all trade and general book-review journals. But the rising cost of adver-tising space, beyond the increase in book prices, has reduced even this pitiful effort. (Gaynor remembers a memo he sent to Loesser about *Red Beach Assault*: "We can nicely afford a one-inch ad stating 'Com-pliments of a Friend.'") And what the publisher cannot afford he tries to get for nothing through the efforts of his publicity department.

Instead of telling more people about his books, the publisher in-vests in brand advertising of the most inverted sort. He has decided he can sell more books by advertising himself to the trade. He tries to create an image of his list to authors and their agents, to the editors of book reviews, to book clubs, to the story departments of motion picture studios and to other publishers, in order to convince them of his strength and of the sales appeal of the books he sponsors. This, says Gaynor, is the tip-off. His customers are not readers. They are the authors of new manuscripts and the marketers who will sell the books he makes of them. In this sense his advertising moves in a closed system. It is meant first for the trade, which provides and buys titles, then for the consumers who buy books and other furniture, but only casually for readers.

There are some other consequences of this tight little book world. Advertising agencies assign and prepare most of this advertising. But of twenty-seven New York advertising agencies specializing in books, six or eight handle most of the publishers' accounts, a few of them representing at one time as many as twenty different publishers. In any other business this friendly little custom would constitute malpractice, particularly, as in the book trade, if all the agent's accounts wanted to create the same public image.

Even when all the products are supposedly different—one of the book trade's half-truths—the agent must represent each book on its own terms, yet suggest its relevance to the common image of strength, integrity, discriminating taste and sales appeal which every sponsor happens to want for his own. It is rather like playing all the hands in a poker game and playing them all to win. Were advertising books merely a matter of buying space and writing copy, the agency would never earn its fees. But because books belong to publishers' lists, and because building the list and advertising it usually go together, the agency often consults on editorial matters.

Such consultation occurs in those seasons of doubt prior to the publisher's semi-annual sales meetings when, for any of a dozen vexing reasons, the list is not "complete." An author has not finished a manuscript, the possibility of libel has temporarily delayed a book, the discovery of new material necessitates the revision of another, or a novel in galley form may suddenly reveal everything wrong with its story. But the publisher must "fill" his list. "Filling" the list is poor publishing. It ignores the quality of an individual book, but it constantly tempts every publisher.

Remembering his fixed overhead and the uncertain market, he believes he must produce—even over-produce—to compensate for the books now scratched from his list. He recalls rejected manuscripts from literary agents, detours a title or two from the mail-order department, and hurriedly hunts for a juvenile or even a technical book to "balance" the list. Without time to establish an advance sale he scarcely knows these new books, yet he must advertise them. The publisher obviously needs some coordination between list-planning and advertising, so he deputizes his advertising agent.

Chances are, the agent can estimate more accurately than his client any new book's possibilities. Without the pressure of sales quotas he can judge a book more effectively on its own terms. In this seasonal breach of publishing routine the advertising agent becomes more than ever a taste-maker. Even more directly than the publisher's salesmen or the bookseller, he shares the editorial responsibility.

Direct-by-mail advertising is a more reliable means of communicating with the book buyer because it aims at sales rather than customers. Although the results are limited, they are immediate. The responses from a selected mailing list to the announcement of a prospective book are so reliable that the publisher can accurately forecast its sale. By split-run advertising—mailing different announcements of the same book—he can even learn how to increase sales by varying that book. (Gaynor might have added that Polk & Franklin often builds a book to order in this fashion, starting with nothing but a title, a description and a mailing list. But this is beside the point Gaynor means to make.)

Selling books by mail, in the form of the book club, has revolutionized trade-book marketing. But Gaynor calls this merely one more symptom of the trade's inability to communicate with readers. The book club sells a contract which obligates a purchaser to buy books in return for a bargain. The book which a club sells is usually a simultaneous reprint of a trade edition. The large club rents plates from the publisher, manufactures its own books, and pays royalties jointly to author and publisher. Its prime costs are less than the publisher's. Plate rental eliminates most of the expense of composition, and the large distribution a club can guarantee reduces printing and binding costs. The American archetype of this business, the Book-of-the-Month Club, has exploited these factors since its founding in 1926. During its first year, even without dividends and with readers paying postage, this club managed to distribute over 230,000 books to nearly 4,700 buyers. The membership reached 110,000 by 1929 but shrank with the Depression, so the Club inaugurated the book-dividend system in 1931. In its twentieth anniversary year the Book-of-the-Month Club distributed more than 11,000,000 books to about 900,000 members.

On this pattern, many hundreds of book clubs have been founded with nothing but small capital (or credit) and a mailing list. Many have gone bankrupt or been absorbed by others, and new ones continually appear. Among the giants in the field by 1950, the Book-of-the-Month Club and the Literary Guild, and a third, the Dollar Book Club, accounted for eighty per cent of all current book club sales. The book clubs are the publishers' best customers. They pay more than half of all trade publishers' subsidiary income. Their advertising increases the trade sales of books by as much as ten to fifty times.

The effect of book clubs upon publishing has caused a lengthy and unresolved debate. By selling large quantities of relatively few current titles they have exploited best-sellerism; they have made a few authors rich, but they have jeopardized the retail booksellers—in sum, trade publishing as now practiced could not exist without them. But one of their characteristics, says Gaynor, has been too long overlooked. Notwithstanding their enormous sales—even because of them—the book clubs have made even more distinct the difference between the book buyer and the reader.

Gaynor refers to the transaction between the club and its members. The critical, unpublicized fact of all these clubs is the tremendous turnover in membership they have had to sustain. About forty per cent of the Literary Guild's membership accepts the Guild's monthly selections. Offering a more varied selection, the Book-of-the-Month Club manages to sell books to a monthly average of only about twenty-five per cent of its members, and half of its membership changes every year. The significance of this high mortality rate, Gaynor believes, is revealed in book-club advertising.

The clubs advertise a bargain: books at less than retail price plus free book-dividends. The Book-of-the-Month Club spends millions of dollars each year on membership campaigns merely to maintain its *status quo*. But neither the cancellations of membership nor the purchases of books in the first place have much to do with reading.

People will accept almost anything free, even books. Some will continue to buy book bargains until their shelves are full; others—women mostly—even intend to read them. But with astonishing regularity new books arrive, adding to the pile of homework. The self-improvement campaign which once looked so promising begins to pall; with guilt and annoyance the purchaser cancels her subscription. What happens, Gaynor explains, is that book clubs continually oversell their selections, offering give-away books to people who would not normally read them or even buy them. In so doing the clubs contradict the first commandment of the trade: "Thou shalt not oversell."

Changes in book-club memberships within the past ten years have borne this out. By 1950 the Book-of-the-Month Club had lost nearly half the number of subscribers it had four years earlier. Also in 1950 the Reader's Digest Condensed Book Club began with 200,000 members; it now has nearly 2,000,000. Gaynor pauses over this comparison. The Reader's Digest Condensed Book Club, as its name implies, sells a different product.

Ironically for the trade publisher the demand for condensation of original works appears to be based soundly on readers' habits and desires. This is far more secure than the appeal of the give-away clubs. Its success poses some sobering questions about reading in the United States, a subject which suggests exploration if book publishing is to thrive.

The condensed book club offers a better bargain than any other in its promise of entertainment with less effort. It sells books that have been pre-read, with the difficulties of reading thoughtfully removed—a masticated product that is the closest correlation yet discovered between book publishing and American readership. Perhaps the perfect books for this democratic literacy will turn out to be only Tables of Contents.

Gaynor's lecture stops short of asserting the reason for this. By overproducing books which are subject to the discrimination of book marketers the trade publisher has lost control of the whole operation. He has lost control to his customers, and these customers are not readers or even book buyers. They are the book marketers.

V

MASS LITERACY

In the light of the trade's colossal disregard of the Cheney *Survey*, Gaynor can expect no more than a polite acknowledgment of his lecture. *Publishers' Weekly* will applaud him in an editorial statement. But even Polk & Franklin will continue its publication of trade titles for subsidiary markets, its investment in a larger textbook department, and its production of manuals of this-and-that for direct-mail customers (in spite of the fact that Gaynor would rather publish any competent novel than the "Song of Solomon" profusely illustrated).

Basically a distributor of books, the marketer originally had no editorial function. But the markets for fiction have changed in the twentieth century and grown far beyond the bookstore clientele. Marketers have persuaded the trade publisher to change his wares. Gaynor's tactful omission about book clubs comes close to the point. There may in fact be no editorial collusion prior to a club's purchase of a book, but there need be none, so long as the publisher remains aware of the kind of purchases a club has previously made. "Completing" the list is often the trade's euphemism for loading it with candidates for subsidiary markets.

The so-called subsidiary markets now support the trade publisher. By a slip of the bookkeeper's pen "subsidiary" has become "subsidy." Ever since the 1890's, trade publishing has been continuously involved with one or several of them; not groups of individual purchasers, but other media which use fiction. The earliest of these markets were the magazines which existed to carry advertising to national circulations. Then the movies effectively influenced the book trade after the U. S. Supreme Court decreed copyright protection to authors and publishers for filmed adaptations of their books. Most recently the inexpensive paperbacks have revolutionized the sale of fiction.

Gaynor's lecture set out to illustrate the book trade's concentric influence, but it concludes in dismay over the success of appealing to readers who don't want to bother with the effort of reading. Having worked it through, Gaynor now reads his own message with awe. Surely the problem has outgrown Polk & Franklin. Some supra-agency must take over. Gaynor has just decided to do what you might have expected. He has enclosed a pre-print of his lecture in a long letter addressed to a large philanthropic foundation (the Maxwell-Essex Fund) requesting several million dollars for the book trade to study the acute problems of mass literacy.

Chapter IV

Slick Nirvana

POPULAR fiction has always assured the reader about himself and his possibilities—that humanity is naturally good, that the individual counts for something, that he *can* improve and that material success has Divine benediction. When the novel is on the right track with these ideas it can show all the world's wickedness with impunity. Indeed, the assurance of better things to come does not have to be insistent. So long as it is there at all, the reader will magnify it as needed, while enjoying the trials and crises of righteousness.

Fiction that makes a policy of this particular life-assurance will always find readers, so long as it can be distributed to them, which is why the commercial magazines have had so much to do with the development of the American novel. By a plurality of hundreds of millions of readers, Americans have read more fiction in magazines than in books.

Particularly since the 1890's, magazines have financially supported most American writers. That eminent magazinist, William Dean Howells, spoke confidently of this fact in October 1893, in his epochal essay "The Man of Letters as a Man of Business." As he told the readers of *Scribner's Magazine*, "story-telling is now a fairly recognized trade, and the story-teller has a money-standing in the economic world." Authors could now live, he said, "and live prettily enough, by the sale of the serial publication of their writings to the magazines."

Howells included more than just the few or famous writers: "a much larger number of clever people who are as yet known chiefly to the editors, and who may never make themselves public, but who do well at a kind of acceptable work." In fact, Howells announced, "the prosperity of the magazines has given a whole class existence which, as a class, was wholly unknown among us before the Civil War."

Howells was talking about the cumulative effect of many changes. Although installment publishing had occasionally occurred since the eighteenth century, it became popular when *Harper's New Monthly Magazine* made it a policy after 1850. The editor of this same magazine, and a novelist himself, Howells could talk with authority about installment fiction. What made his statement newsworthy was the tremendous growth of the popular magazines after the 1880's, both in numbers and in circulation.

The growth of the magazines coincided with the book trade's organized promotion of literature which followed the new Copyright Act of 1891. In fact, the Federal Government had already (incidentally but immeasurably) assisted popular literature by subsidizing the magazines. An Act of Congress in 1879 which reclassified the mails designated magazines as second-class matter, subject to the privilege of a new and lower mailing rate. When the native market for fiction began to develop, therefore, the magazines were the chief means of reaching it.

In *A History of American Magazines: 1885-1905* (1957) Frank Luther Mott estimated that the number of magazines in the United States increased from 3,500 to 6,000 during the twenty-year period of his study, and that some 7,500 new magazines had been started. There was more to what he called the "Magazine Revolution" than simply growth in numbers. The invention of the halftone process, of adapting the photograph to an engraved printing plate, made lavish illustration commercially possible. This changed the appearance and the entire nature of magazines.

The new ten-cent magazines in the 1890's were handsomely illustrated and printed on slick (coated) paper devised for photo-engraving. Their prosperous appearance amplified their contents. They were timely, favoring contemporary subjects, in fiction and in factual articles, for the entire family. They offered entertainment, education, romance and vicarious excitement to as large a public as possible. They were popular in every sense of the word.

Subsidized by low mailing rates, the publisher could afford to build the circulation of his magazine. If he could guarantee a large subscription list, he had something far more valuable than the income from his subscribers. He had a possible market for anyone with a product to sell. So he became a broker in names, a dealer in consumers, to whom manufacturers—for a price—could advertise their products.

Finley Peter Dunne's spokesman, Mr. Dooley, once commented on the magazines' economic incentive. In *American Magazine* (October 1909) he found fault. There were not enough ads to suit him: "What I object to is whin I pay ten or fifteen cents f'r a magazine expectin' to spind me avenin' improvin' me mind with th' latest thoughts in advertisin' to find more thin a quarther of th' whole book devoted to lithrachoor." Some publisher, he hoped, would be bold enough to devote his magazine entirely to advertising. Since Dunne was both a magazine writer and an editor, his Mr. Dooley carried some weight with his opinion that "Lithrachoor an' business are hooked up together."

Advertising rates depend on the magazine's circulation, so the publisher wants to build and maintain as large a readership as possible. His surest way is to capitalize on established interests among his readers. The editorial content of his magazine is a means to this end—utterly functional.

There are many publics, which is to say many large groups of consumers sharing common interests. Every magazine cultivates some such group; ideally, it is a unique editorial package which consolidates and encourages the habits of its readers. The literature which serves it must remain dependably the same.

To insure his own stability the magazine publisher seeks a variety of publics at the same time, but not for the same magazine. He publishes several at once. For many years the Curtis Publishing Company issued three very different slicks: *Ladies Home Journal* (1883-) a women's service magazine; *Saturday Evening Post* (1821-), a weekly for the men of the family; and a farm magazine, *Country Gentlemen* (1911-1955). The Crowell Corporation (later Crowell-Collier) bought and issued *Woman's Home Companion* (1897-1957); *Farm and Fireside* (1906-1929), which became *Country Home* (1929-1939); and

Collier's (1911-1957), a weekly family magazine to compete with
Curtis' *Saturday Evening Post*. The Hearst publishing enterprise
moved into the magazine field with products similarly compart-
mented: two women's service magazines, *Good Housekeeping* (1885-)
and *Pictorial Review* (1899-1939), and two of more general interest:
Cosmopolitan (1886-) and *Hearst's International* (1901-1925), which
Cosmopolitan later absorbed.

In his attack on the vested interests in literature, *Money Writes!*
(1927), Upton Sinclair decided—in a chapter called "Artificial Selection"—that these chains were all "run exactly like the department
stores and shoe-factory chains, upon the same principles of standardi-
zation and mass production." But the size of a publisher's organization
is incidental to the compartmentalization of his products. He is a
specialist in audiences, because the advertisers must have an accurate
gauge of their markets. For instance, *McCall's* (1897-) and *Redbook*
(1903-) both published by McCall, go to two different groups of
women, differentiated by the amount of the husband's income. The
advertisements in *McCall's*, like those in *Ladies Home Journal*, appeal
to a higher standard of living and reading. *Redbook's* competitor used
to be Crowell-Collier's *American Magazine* (1888-1956), but is now
Hearst's *Cosmopolitan*.

Nothing is left to chance. Condé Nast's *House and Garden* (1901-)
and Hearst's *House Beautiful* (1896-) competitively seek an audience
of similar interests but higher income than Nast's *Better Homes
and Gardens* (1924-). Similarly, Nast's *Vogue* (1892-) represents fashions in women's wear differently than Nast's *Glamour* (1939-) or
Street and Smith's *Mademoiselle* (1935-). And Hearst's *Harper's
Bazaar* (1867-) goes to readers older and richer than readers of *Seventeen* (1944-), published by this same house.

Aimed at a precise audience, the magazine must continue to gratify
it with the same fare. In token of the publishers' strenuous attempts
to stay with the readers, most of the slicks have changed hands or been
absorbed by others. But it is striking that despite the high mortality of
the magazines themselves the literary product has remained constant.

The editorial content of some of the failures, for instance, is representative of the entire slick field over the years, both in quality and in

quantity. *Woman's Home Companion* (1873-1957), for instance, always offered a rich fare in fiction, and counted among its contributors Mary E. Wilkins, Margaret Deland, Sherwood Anderson, Willa Cather, Booth Tarkington, Pearl Buck, Ellen Glasgow, Sinclair Lewis, John Galsworthy and Arnold Bennett. But the staple fare in each issue, beginning in the 1920's, was the serialized novel (usually two) by women who could repeat their performances: Kathleen Norris, Edna Ferber, Dorothy Canfield Fisher, Mary Roberts Rinehart, Faith Baldwin and Taylor Caldwell.

Another magazine which failed, *Pictorial Review* (1899-1939), offered comparable fiction by well-established authors: Edith Wharton, Carl Sandburg, Joseph Conrad, Emil Ludwig, Booth Tarkington, Gertrude Atherton; and characteristically the best of their writing. The pages of *Collier's* (1911-1957) tell a similar story. This magazine sought both British and American novelists, and built its circulation on big names. The roll call of *Collier's* contributors from 1900 through the 1930's correlates remarkably with the authors of best-selling novels.

The life of a slick magazine depends on its rapport with its readers, which doubtless explains why these three magazines lasted as long as they did. And maintaining rapport is a delicate business. Bernard DeVoto, another eminent magazinist, described (in *Saturday Review*, October 9, 1937) some of the demands of this readership. "People do not read the slicks," he said, "to encounter the brutalities, the profundities or the complexities of experience. They read to have their ideas confirmed and their emotions ratified, to have their phantasy life stimulated, and to increase their knowledge of the minor sanctions and rituals of society—but first of all they want to be amused."

No writer can escape the reader's influence—even the established and calculable writer. Temple Bailey's long and profitable career of writing magazine serials ought to make her an expert on what she calls "the idealistic presentation of young love"; yet she long ago developed the habit of writing a serial concurrently with its publication so that the readers' mail could help her determine the plot. For this agility, even in the Depression years, *McCall's* paid her $60,000 a serial.

The syndrome works both ways. The magazine also informs the readers of their own habits and appetites. The editor is a taste-maker, defining and stimulating the habits, desires and impulses of his readers simply by choosing and shaping what they read.

So the editor uses his prerogatives in telling authors what he wants. Even Faith Baldwin insists on this. Contributing to a symposium called *The Writer's Book* (1950), she says, "The writer has something to sell; the editor something to buy. I doubt that it is ever a seller's market in this field. The buyer is in the better position; and writers are a dime a dozen." Consequently, "An editor is prone—even obliged—to tell writers what he believes they should write."

Upton Sinclair put it differently in *Money Writes!* indicating the magazines' "Artificial Selection" of their material. "They know what they are going to want a year from now, and they order their stories as they order their trainloads of paper from the mills; they even order their writers; they will take a young genius and 'make' him, exactly as Lasky or Paramount will turn a manicure girl with pretty pouting lips into a world-famous 'star'."

A more patient explanation of the editor's collaboration with his author is Elmer Davis' Bowker Lecture, "The Economics of Authorship" (1940). Davis wrote: "When a magazine editor has located somebody who has that aptitude, and who can write well enough so that his name has, or can acquire, a circulation value, he has a pearl of great price; and he is going to feed that man ideas, when he no longer has ideas of his own." This goes beyond merely priming the pump. Margaret Culkin Banning, who wrote a serial a year for thirty-five years, makes this clear. In the symposium called *The Writer's Book* she says: "The story which the novelist intends primarily for serial sale and its rewards is too often the child of the editor. The novelist only has it committed to his care to bring up and develop."

The editor's aim and the reader's, although compatible, are not the same. The fiction the editor prints serves the need of his sponsors, the advertisers, to the extent that it must capture and hold as many readers as possible. This is a restraining influence. The fiction may not offend business in general or in particular, or American government of any variety, or any religious, civic or military organization. The fiction may not contradict the mores of the average consumer-reader without punishing the offender. These well-known prohibitions are similar to the ones levied on motion pictures; most of them also apply to the inexpensive paperback books. The prohibitions and the devious ways around them belong not to art but to manufacture.

Slick magazine fiction must entertain several million readers without offending them or straying beyond their interests. It must offer the same fare over and over again without seeming to. These requirements prescribe the editorial content of every mass-circulation magazine. The most familiar evidence of this requisite product and of its effects on the economics of writing is undoubtedly the *Saturday Evening Post*.

The *Post* contains more information about the national personality than any other publication in the world. It is the slick by which all others are measured. The slurs about its middle-brow superficiality, and the response that most of the disparaging writers could not meet the *Post's* standards of publication, are quite familiar. Charge and countercharge are grounded to the man who guided this magazine to its eminence—George Horace Lorimer, the *Post's* boss from 1899-1936.

Lorimer's first editorial page (September 30, 1899) declared the *Post's* homage "to the great mass of intelligent people who make homes and love them, who chose good lives and live them, who seek friends and cherish them, who select the best recreations and enjoy them." The incense is unmistakable. The sweet dream in which "the great mass of intelligent people" would share was already being fabricated.

For nearly forty years the *Post* demonstrated what this patriarch meant. He was a conservative and a nationalist. Like his readers he believed in God, in love and marriage, in college educations, in success, in the conservation of wild life and in the policy of American isolation. He opposed the League of Nations and the New Deal; he fought for restrictive immigration, for free enterprise in business, and for the sanctity of the family. The *Post* amplified all of these convictions. The magazine was an extension of the man.

Lorimer selected all of the material, wrote the editorials, selected the cover and the story illustrations, even censored the ads. He kept his fingers on his writers—and on their pens. He frequently corresponded with them and entertained them in order to check on the progress of their work. Emerson Hough referred to his novel, *The Covered Wagon* (1922), as their "partnership book," in token of Lorimer's proposing it in the first place, helping him to plan it, and consulting in the revision. Occasionally Lorimer even ghosted. When David Graham Phillips was murdered, his unfinished serial, "Grains of Sand" (1911), was running in the *Post*; Lorimer finished the manuscript.

Lorimer paid his authors handsomely, and set the rates for all other slicks to beat; but paternalism went with the pay. He would not bargain over manuscripts or offer contracts, but after an author had published in the *Post*, Lorimer took his loyalty for granted and assumed that the *Post* would have first refusal on the next story. Leaving the *Post* for another magazine—as Irvin S. Cobb did, and Jack London, Ring Lardner and Peter B. Kyne—Lorimer considered a breach of friendship. Such paternalism, along with Lorimer's shrewd sense of fiction and vigorous scouting, secured an imposing list of contributors.

Some of these might surprise you: Stephen Crane, Frank Norris, Theodore Dreiser, James Branch Cabell, Edith Wharton, Willa Cather, Ellen Glasgow, Zona Gale, William Faulkner and Rebecca West. Others you might expect: Margaret Culkin Banning, Katherine Brush, Temple Bailey, Edna Ferber, Fannie Hurst, and Fanny Heaslip Lea and Mary Roberts Rinehart. Yet they all published in the *Post*, and Lorimer made no distinctions.

He had, in fact, a narrow view of the word "literature," saying that only time could decide literary status, and that he did not buy manuscripts for their promise of future distinction. An issue containing a Dreiser story and a serial by Temple Bailey offered no problem at all, as long as each of them was good enough to be published.

The variety, however, was more apparent than real, as indicated by the frequency with which these writers published in the *Post*. A few of them published in it all of the time. This observation bears on the economics of magazine authorship. The more often a writer's work appears in the pages of a magazine, the more it is worth in building that magazine's circulation, for the reader gets in the habit of looking for it. Lorimer paid everyone well, but he paid most to the competent writer who could repeat himself.

The pages of the *Post* during 1934, the last year of Lorimer's presidency (before he became board chairman), show how well he had exploited the value of repetition. During that year each issue, of about a hundred pages, carried two serials, four or five short stories, and four or five articles. Among the contributors Sophie Kerr, Mary Roberts Rinehart, E. Phillips Oppenheimer, Oliver La Farge, I. A. R. Wylie and Kenneth Roberts each published a serial; Margaret Culkin Banning, a serial and two articles. John Marquand published a five-part serial, a six-part serial, and five short stories; Walter D. Edmonds contributed a serial and four short stories. There were also nine stories by Everett Rhodes Castle, six by Booth Tarkington, five by Richard Macaulay, four each by Thomas Beer, Ben Ames Williams, Joseph Hergesheimer, Lucian Cary and Corey Ford, and three by Octavus Roy Cohen, William Faulkner, and Bernard DeVoto.

Magazine publishing thrives on over-production; it contradicts the familiar law of supply and demand. The more a given editorial product appears in the magazine, the more valuable it is. The familiarity of the author's name helps to maintain circulation. In his Bowker Lecture Elmer Davis explained this fact. "If you sell any given magazine ten stories in a year," he said, "you will get more for each story than if you sold them only three stories a year. It may well be that three stories, three good stories, are all you have in you that year; but if your production falls off your price is likely, sooner or later, to fall off too."

The writer's alternative is to force his production beyond what he has to say. "So you write your three good stories; and then you use the tricks of the trade that you have learned and your knowledge of the tastes of the editors of that particular magazine, to knock off seven more stories that are good enough—good enough to sell with the advantage of a name well known to the magazine's readers, even though they might be sent back if they came up from Joe Blotz of Podunk Corners."

The conditions of the industry which encourage this enormous over-production penalize all kinds of writers. "But the most regrettable case of all, which unfortunately is far too common in this country, is that of the man who has something to say, but not much." The magazines' demands for more of the same "make it practically impossible for a writer to retire into dignified silence when he has said all he has to say, or to lie fallow for a while if he is going through a period of sterility."

The predicament of success is a peculiar condition of American authors. For most of them this predicament consists of publishing in the magazines to pay their bills while trying to write, as the saying goes, the Great American Novel. This has urged many commercially successful writers to a pathological hatred of the magazines.

Henry James's tales of writers who struggle between conscience and commerce dramatize a universal condition of the artist. But one way or the other his writers always choose between the alternatives or fail in attempting both. James's stories are not parochial enough to fit the American scene; the really genuine American fable is Jack London's novel, *Martin Eden* (1909), about a writer who ironically succeeds in serving both masters.

Martin Eden wants to write a masterpiece, to correlate all knowledge into the theory of one book; but to keep from starving meanwhile, he grinds out stories for the magazines and newspaper syndicates. So he works out the perfect formula. He finds "that the newspaper storiette should never be tragic, should never end unhappily, and should never contain beauty of language, subtlety of thought, nor real delicacy of sentiment." But it must contain sentiment, "plenty of it, pure and noble . . . 'For-God-my-country-and-the-Czar' and 'I-may-be-poor-but-I-am-honest' brand of sentiment."

This is what will gratify the reader. The mechanical contrivance is simple. "The formula consists of three parts: (1) a pair of lovers are jarred apart; (2) by some deed or event they are united; (3) marriage bells. The third part is an unvarying quantity, but the first and second parts can be varied an infinite number of times."

Eden's problems really begin after he has succeeded in both his endeavors. His masterpiece, a philosophical essay as unpopular as you could imagine, becomes a great commercial success for all the wrong and whimsical reasons. It brings him immense notoriety (there is a fine deadpan satire of his publisher's antics); and the magazines fall all over themselves begging Eden for the reams of hackwork they have already rejected.

This whole experience, however, has broken him. He has rendered his life into his masterpiece and has nothing of his own left to say, and he has outgrown the need to create the dreams of his formula-days. His situation is hopeless; and since he has nothing left to be, Jack London puts him to death. The suicide's failure to resolve anything is only one of the difficulties of this novel. Nevertheless, the condition of Martin Eden-the-writer, which Jack London abstracted from his own life, is a fiction which sounds like a good many biographies.

The writing career of Stephen Vincent Benét was just such a battle with success. For nearly twenty-five years Benét had to depend on the slicks for most of his income. While his agent, Carl Brandt, master-minded a career for him with his Cinderella stories, Benét was always trying to get one story ahead so that he could explore the American past and write poetry about it. He desperately needed the magazines in order to live, and he hated them for it.

Benét's diary and his correspondence record his continuous battle with the magazine editors—"ravens," he called them—over their re-quirements for the "candy-laxative" product: their demands for a happy ending or a less controversial story. Brandt's rationalization, "You can change it in the book," only maddened him more. The irony of Benét's first popular success came close to Martin Eden's. He did manage to write what he wanted, and *John Brown's Body* (1928) be-came a convincing success. Its large trade sale and Book-of-the-Month Club distribution brought Benét money and fame. But the truth of Benét's life was more impossible than London's fiction.

The stock market crash of 1929 sent Benét back to the magazine chain, and only after he published "The Devil and Daniel Webster" (in the *Post* in 1936) did he find some small liberation. It was just a parole, however. His prices were higher, and he could sell a little more of what he wanted to write. His disdain of the magazines lasted until he wrote himself to death.

F. Scott Fitzgerald's disparagement of the slicks is well known. His letters in *The Crack-Up* (1945) show how critical he was of his own work which the slicks published. It was typical of his feelings that he referred Edmund Wilson to the book version of *Tender Is the Night* (1934) rather than the magazine version which "in spots was hastily put together." He had complained to John Peale Bishop that although he was getting $2,000 a story, they grew worse and worse, and his ambition was to be able to ignore the magazines and write novels. Once, when he could afford to, he turned down an offer of $15,000 for the serial rights of *The Great Gatsby* (1925).

Even Booth Tarkington, who sold all the fiction he ever published to the magazines, took the same dim view of them. When his young friend and neighbor, Kenneth Roberts, learned that Lorimer had instructed him to make drastic cuts in his manuscript of *The Lively Lady* (1931) he asked Tarkington's advice and then wrote in his diary: "Consulted Booth; he said at once that I should agree: that magazine publication was a purely temporary affair, forgotten in a matter of weeks. Only the book lives and is remembered."

Roberts included this in his personal record, *I Wanted to Write* (1949), and among these odds and ends of a long career were some of Tarkington's letters which related to this magazine-and-book dilemma. Tarkington was impatient with the novel reader who "seeks to escape from life itself by the reading of romances—a very numerous type." Though she does ask that the characters be plausible enough for her to accept them while she reads, "she doesn't want an interpretation of life."

. . . it may happen that a serious writer writes a book that just by chance satisfies and pleases this enormous class of readers; but it probably won't happen often, since, being serious . . . he can't please them any more than their own lives do, since what he's doing is trying to paint life as truthfully as he can, and not to tell children bedtime stories.

The double standard of magazine fiction and book fiction was so well established in the trade that when John Marquand was ready to publish *The Late George Apley* (1937) his publisher advised him to adopt a pseudonym so as not to injure his profitable reputation in the slicks. This condescending to serious fiction so annoyed Marquand that he determined to set the record straight. "I have never been able to be patient with this sort of literary calcification," he explained. "I have never understood why a sinner is not allowed at least to attempt reformation in the American world of letters."

He wrote this in one of the prefaces in *North of Grand Central* (1956), a trilogy of his first New England novels. After twelve years of writing for the slicks Marquand became tired of their inhibitions, and since he could afford to he began to write to suit himself. With *The Late George Apley* he made a startling discovery:

I found that the task of writing it, though occasionally difficult and discouraging, was far easier than the effort I had previously expended on obviously mediocre serial stories. Yet the result was apparently better than anything I had achieved previously.

The reason for this was so obvious that I should have recognized it years before. For almost the first time in my life I had written about something that I thoroughly understood.

He had not been able to write from his own experience for the magazines; as a professional he had trained himself to write as "an outsider," to offer that deft touch of "reality in the details" to satisfy the casual reader. But his "contrived entertainment" had nothing to do with his own experience, without which an author has nothing worth saying. Without the original experience, "no matter how great may be his skill and brilliance, he is a huckster who is trafficking in the inflated currency of artificiality."

Marquand's discovery about himself casts light on the awful shadow of success in which so many American writers have found themselves. A man must write what he knows and feels, or he cannot believe in what he writes. If the author cannot believe in it, who will? Like any other fiction, slick fiction involves this matter of belief. The ideal slick story is far more than the arrangement of a conflict which resolves satisfactorily.

For enough money almost any professional writer can learn how to use a few conventionally off-beat details to suggest a character, how to make a scene look authenic, or how to hide the evidence of a story's conclusion in the conflict itself. These are the techniques by which an author tells a slick story and gets away with it. But there is more to slick fiction than the correspondence courses can teach. It must convince the reader that what he wants to believe is so.

The slick world is a dream-world with an ideology as old as original sin. In that world the reader is assured of happiness ever after. Most readers of the slicks are women, although women have no monopoly on wishful thinking. Everyone desperately wants to rationalize the miseries of the world, and to believe, even temporarily, in some plausible way of making it all better again. This is the easiest way of vindicating oneself. Any story which makes this heart-warming face-saving gospel seem believable is bound to be popular.

This economic fact is of great importance to magazine publishers. The slick magazine is built on mass circulation, no matter what the social stratum of its audience. To keep it so, the editor will always try to gratify this great common yearning for human nature to be good and for goodness to win.

The trick is to find the writer who believes in it enough to make it convincing. Frank Munsey, the originator of the ten-cent magazine, once exclaimed that good writing is as common as clam shells, but good stories are as rare as statesmanship. If an editor finds a writer who can write this rare story and write it often, money is no object; $60,000 a serial is well worth it.

There are very few competent writers who believe that courage and loyalty will triumph over ignorance and evil, and that virtue will finally get the better of temptation. The triumph of goodness did not happen to be the truth of Scott Fitzgerald's or Stephen Benét's—or even Martin Eden's—experience. So the magazines must find writers who can counterfeit the dream-world convincingly and often.

All the rule books say this cannot be done by patronizing the reader, and they are almost always right. An author cannot borrow a philosophy and make it convincing—except occasionally, with great skill and good luck and a desperate need of money. The bare possibility that a writer may earn what he needs without contaminating himself in the process has made the dream a nightmare to all the Martin Edens.

Sinclair Lewis has spoken for them all. In 1930 he became the first American to win the Nobel Prize for Literature, and no sooner had he won it than he carried to the world his quarrel with the slicks. Of all American writers, he mourned, "We still most revere the writers for the popular magazines who in a hearty and edifying chorus chant . . . the bucolic and Puritanic simplicity of Uncle Sam." This was partly a confessional, for Lewis himself was a thoroughly discontented magazinist.

Even before *Main Street* was published Lewis had worked his way up to $1,000 a story in the *Post*, yet he spoke, with a sense of compromise, of "earning a living by nimble dives into *Saturday Evening Post*." These nimble dives required all his dexterity; as he explained, "I have steadily sought to work out a means of doing as honest work as the powerful negations of the magazine editors would permit." He wrote this to Carl Van Doren in a letter dated November, 1920 (later published in his selected writings, *The Man from Main Street*, 1953).

The pain of Lewis' compromise was acute during the two years in which he finished and published *Main Street*. His letters to his publisher, Alfred Harcourt (in Harrison Smith's *From Main Street to Stockholm*, 1952) record the author's struggle with himself. After Harcourt, Brace announced the novel to the trade in May 1920, advance orders promised an unusual sale; and the excitement of reviewers promised even more in the way of prestige for its author. But Lewis was out of money. While finishing the novel, he had managed to pay his bills by selling stories to the *Post* and to *Harpers*, but as yet without any book royalties he was worse than bankrupt. His future was complicated by the prospect of a *succès d'estime* whose sales, he felt, his magazine writing would only injure. He described his dilemma in a letter to Harcourt (November 30, 1920).

I am, frankly, having a hell of a time in trying at once to turn myself back into the successful S. E. P. writer I was a year ago—and yet do for them nothing but stories so honest that they will in no way get me back into magazine trickiness nor injure the *M St.* furore.

He explained that he had just destroyed a sixty-thousand-word manuscript which he could have sold handsomely to the *Post*, "but which was so shallow, so unreal, so sentimental that (featured as they do feature a serial, even a short one) it would have been very bad for *Main Street*."

God knows I don't expect you to bear the responsibility for this, which may have been foolhardy. I relate it only to prove how vigorously I have been attacking this problem. . . . I'm going, of course, to go on plugging at the *Post*, but I don't believe I shall ever again be the facile *Post* trickster I by God was—for which, doubtless, we shall in the long run be glad.

Lewis' experience with serializing his novels aggravated his either/or attitude about fiction. *Free Air* (1919) had only a modest sale, which he blamed on its manner of publication. The *Post* had run the original serial which Lewis then revised, nearly doubling its length for a book. Lorimer persuaded Lewis to run the new material as a separate serial in the *Post*. When the book failed Lewis decided its prospective buyers had already read it.

He and Alfred Harcourt agreed thereafter to withhold the serial rights to his novels, but neither one lived up to this agreement. Harcourt later sold the magazine rights to *Arrowsmith* (1925) for $50,000; and Lewis wrote a serial for *Collier's* which he persuaded Harcourt to bring out as a book. This was called *Mantrap* (1926). Neither author nor publisher regarded it highly, although Lewis felt called upon to defend it. He wrote to Harcourt (November 10, 1925), "I recall nothing shoddy in it, and as for the critics who insist that I have no right to do anything but social documents, they may all go to hell."

Lewis' lame excuse emphasized *Mantrap*'s curious relation to his other novels of the period. It followed *Main Street* (1920) and *Babbitt* (1922) and preceded *Dodsworth* (1929), all of which it approximates and all of which exceed it. That it was not a "social document," as he put it, is one way of saying that it does not represent Lewis' view of experience.

In fact, *Mantrap* offers no view of experience whatsoever; no presiding idea grows out of its conflict. It is a listless failure. Yet it is mechanically like the three contemporary novels which Lewis never intended to be serialized. A reading of the serial and novels reveals how Lewis tried to accommodate the magazine values in the serial.

Mantrap tells of a mis-marriage between a fur trader at Hudson Bay and a manicurist he has met in Minneapolis. Mantrap Landing, the desolate scene of most of the novel, is inhabited by unfriendly Indians and friendly trappers, both of which jeopardize the virtue of this lonely bride. Their presence threatens her with a fate alleged to be worse than death. She loves her husband, but not enough to live with him faithfully at Mantrap; and he loves her, but not enough to move away from the place.

The marriage falls apart when a bachelor from New York City, who has arrived on a canoe trip, discovers his love for the woman and prudently decides to leave. But she escapes with him; and after an arduous chase across the wilderness the husband catches up with the pair, insisting that he must save his friend from his wife. They sit down and talk it over, but after exploring all possibilities they separate, each returning to the place he started from. Here the serial stops. No one has changed, and the story proves only the dissolution of a marriage which gave no promise in the first place. Nothing is really at stake because there is nothing by which to judge this marriage; the story contains no analogies. All its vigorous talk of a conflict between wilderness and civilization cannot fill the vacancy.

The plot of this serial about the estrangement of a husband and wife is exactly like the plot of *Main Street*, of *Babbitt*, and of *Dodsworth*. The serial and the novels all depend on a scheme of trap and escape. In each, one spouse is trapped by the marriage, and the course of this marriage carries the meaning of the book. Babbitt's estrangement and reconciliation make him finally realize his own littleness in conforming to the mores which contradict what he really wants. Carol Kennicott's marriage makes her realize how in need of reform she herself is. Dodsworth's separation from his wife forces him to reappraise all the material values he has taken for granted.

Mantrap has all of the machinery but none of the significance of these others. Lewis' belittling view of humanity, after all, was not congenial to the dream world of the slicks. But when he tried to write a story without that belittling view he had nothing very convincing to put in its place.

The scheme of trap and escape, so compatible with magazine fiction, continually tempted Lewis. Martin Arrowsmith's first fiancée and his second wife threatened to confine and distort his intellectual ideals. Lewis planned still another novel about the situation of a marriage, whose projection—even though he never wrote the book—seems perfectly clear: "the story of a young couple bucking society in a city about Minneapolis; a story of that never yet adequately described but extremely important phase of American life—middle-class existence in an American cross between town and city. . . ."

He wrote this to Harcourt (October 22, 1919), continuing, "I am planning such a story, with a lot of drama and unexpectedness but also complete reality, as a serial for Sat Even Post, and I may do it before I go on with *Main Street*—which will almost certainly NOT go as a serial." Here was the young writer counting two novels before they were hatched, calculating on the same plot, the same substance, but different values, and doling them out: one for George Horace Lorimer and one for Alfred Harcourt.

Without that genuine belief in the dream world which distinguishes the real magazine serialist, each slick writer must find some way of his own to make the conflict turn out believably but also without offending the readers' platitudes. This was where Lewis had failed. His magazine serial simply offered the logical consequence of what the conflict had promised at the beginning. Lewis had suppressed any adventitious change which might have made things turn out better.

This was his concession to art—avoiding the "magazine trickiness," as he put it. But in serving the magazine he also suppressed any idea the plot might have suggested—as the plot had suggested ideas in his novels. Since Lewis never could write a good story, this compromise was not very convincing.

The story sense, which Lewis lacked, was precisely what enabled Booth Tarkington to succeed in counterfeiting the values of the slick world. Tarkington had strong ideas, as Lewis did, about human pettiness and irresponsibility and the degrading materialism America had come to worship. His convictions did not agree with the platitudes of the dream world, but he managed to make his stories assimilate his attitudes and still appear to turn out all right.

Tarkington made the perfect compromise over and over again, the compromise that most novelists have had to face. He said exactly what he wanted to say and made everybody love it. For nearly fifty years his fiction about American families at home and abroad so epitomized the national culture that he became a celebrity. It was somewhat less apparent, all this while, that he also epitomized the goal of every American novelist, which was to render his own convictions, however sobering, and to be popular at the same time.

Between his first book in 1899 and his death in 1946 Tarkington published thirty-nine volumes of prose fiction, and wrote twenty-one plays for the professional stage. He also wrote six plays for magazine and radio audiences, two volumes of essays, and a book about painting. A fragmentary novel and three short novels were published after he died.

Still, there was more. Six magazine serials remain among his uncollected writings, along with two hundred short stories and as many articles and editorial essays. But he had more than facility and stamina, he had the knack of satisfying the magazines. Every novel and story Tarkington published in book form—all thirty-nine volumes—first appeared in a magazine.

The means of this accomplishment bear looking into, for they were the means of counterfeiting the dream-world. To begin with, Tarkington observed the technical necessities of serial fiction. His novels are simple constructions in the narrative present with seldom a detour into the past. The main conflict is evident in the first episode, and smaller conflicts which amplify it along the way are comfortably divisible into installments. The characters all appear early; they are identified by their responses to the situation in which they are discovered (as in a stage play), and except for the hero or the heroine they remain unchanged. There is nothing to confuse the suspense between installments.

Tarkington took particular care of his conflict by building his novels backward—or so he said. (Any author's statement about "how he did it" is always questionable.) Tarkington once described his method in a publicity questionnaire which the Literary Guild customarily sends out to its authors, although the Guild never publicized this particular discovery. "I make a detailed outline or synopsis before beginning the manuscript of the novel," Tarkington wrote. "This synopsis begins at the end or final scene and goes backward from the opening of the story. I use this method because it produces its own order of action." And this, he explained, "means that you cannot change the course of the story without producing disorder, fumbling and uncertainty."

Unlike the serialist, Temple Bailey, who relied on sharing the desires which her readers wrote to her as she continued her stories, Tarkington would not change a story's resolution. He had to *plan* for it to turn out all right. Despite its dubious function of publicity, Tarkington's statement happens to explain plausibly what went wrong with so many of his novels.

One such failure is *The Lorenzo Bunch* (1936), about neighboring families in an apartment house. The novel was supposed to feature a conflict between a husband and wife, each with a liaison on the other side of town. Early in the story, however, the neighbors in this apartment house begin to come alive and to steal the scene from the hero and heroine. These limited people are so bored by their confined existence that they have resigned their private lives to a kind of communal emotion. Tarkington had something big going here when it came time to resolve the crisis. The synopsis had called for the heroine's panting escape from an extra-marital situation, but meanwhile too many live characters had got involved for any quick solution to be convincing, and Tarkington needed more room than five installments of *McCall's* could accommodate.

Firm, pre-meditated resolutions often jostled Tarkington's novels out of proportion by denying any real development of the characters or any resonance to their involvements. The problem was that in order to express his own attitudes about human shortcomings Tarkington had to tell two stories at once—his own and the magazine's. *Turmoil* (1915), for instance, is about a father trespassing on his sons in order to build an industrial empire for himself, but this gets absorbed into a magazine story about one of the sons. This is typical.

This magazine story is always the same. It is the story of Parsifal or of Jack-and-the-Beanstalk: of the lowly hero who is scorned but who proves himself and then collects the rewards of his courage and virtue. It is the exile and return of Monsieur Beaucaire, of the Gentleman from Indiana, of Bibbs in *Turmoil* and Dan Oliphant in *The Midlander*, (1923), of Tom Vanrevel and Hatcher Ide and Irvie Pease. What each of these Tarkington heroes most resembles is all of the others.

This was Tarkington's permanent sub-story. He was skillful at localizing it and merging it with recognizable conflicts in the American society. In its purest form, uncontaminated by any ideas, Tarkington called it *The Conquest of Canaan* (1905), a fable that explains all of his fiction.

Canaan is a small, conventional Midwestern community in the 1880's, whose citizens measure themselves by money and "position," and who have no room in their hearts for the hero. On one side of town—at the end of a long, comfortable lawn, in a Victorian mansion —lives Judge Martin Pike, a large man who has always "stood for all that was respectable and financial." On the other side of town, along the river front—and near a disreputable dance-hall area called Beaver Beach—young Joe Louden has grown up.

Louden is a lawyer and an outcast in his own town except for the loyal friendship of Ariel Tabor. She has grown up with Joe, and was something of an outcast herself until her uncle's legacy and a trip to Paris bestowed beauty and desirability upon her. When it develops that her trustee, Judge Pike, has embezzled her inheritance, it becomes Joe Louden's formidable chore to rescue what is left of the girl's money. One other obstacle is the presence of Joe's urbane step-brother who went East to college and has now returned to ingratiate himself with Judge Pike.

Here ended the first installment in *Harper's Magazine*, but the reader who wanted to jump at conclusions had to wait for five more installments until Judge Pike was defeated (exposed, in fact, as the owner of the disreputable Beaver Beach); and it took one more installment after that for Joe Louden to head off another suitor and win Ariel Tabor for his own.

The heroine of *The Conquest* is one of Tarkington's permanent fixtures. She stands for health and vitality, tolerance and understanding, and sensitivity. Except for one or two tiny but obvious imperfections she is an abstraction of all positive human qualities; being abstract, she satisfies the need for what the trade calls "reader-identity."

Outside the story this heroine is no more credible than the picture of the girl on the magazine cover, but within it she fulfills a necessary function. The hero is at odds with his world, and someone must understand him and champion whatever cause he may have. Since he is not perfect, yet perfectible, someone must correct his mistakes and furnish him with an ideal. Since he must arrive at a marriageable age anyway, this virtuous woman's love denotes his earthly as well as his spiritual success. She is not a person but a project.

Tarkington later invented a childhood for this typical heroine in *Kate Fennigate* (1943). After burying her alcoholic father and her invalid mother this orphan girl grows up in a household where everyone uses her good intentions and selfishly exploits her. But this strenuous training in virtue pays off, for after Kate has grown up and married she discovers that her acquired patience is really her best asset in subtly managing her husband's life.

The heroine is just one of the caricatures in *Canaan*. Another is the hero's step-brother, who stands for everything the hero is not. This counterpart turns up in most of Tarkington's novels, and like Cinderella's older sisters, he always offers the alternative. Over the years Tarkington worked every possible permutation of the counterpart characters, with heroes and heroines, pleasant and unpleasant.

The counterpart is a technical device with distinct advantages for the slick story. It is quick, it increases the possibility of explicit conflict; and the reader is assured of the virtue of one character by indulging in the unpleasantness of the other. It is also a kind of mirror-writing in which, however, the object and the image reflect only unreality. It is no different in Tarkington's fiction than it was in the novels of G. P. R. James, one hundred years ago; and E. P. Whipple's judgment still stands: "We demand human beings, not embodied antitheses, or personified qualities, thoughts, or passions."

Tarkington contrived a certain efficiency with this device by having his counterparts take sides in the conflict of some larger ideas, which is how he managed to dramatize his own opinions. He also occasionally exploited the possibilities of the character with the split personality. Usually, this double-character has temporarily acquired a new appearance: by an accident (in *The Guest of Quesnay*, 1908) or by education (in *Mirthful Haven*, 1930), or by being spoiled (in *Image of Josephine*, 1945). The new state of affairs is always dreadful until the exiled character begins to discover his old self again. Then he returns to conquer Canaan.

Tarkington made this double-character convincing only twice, in two different books: a farce called *Presenting Lily Mars* (1933), and *Alice Adams* (1921). Lily Mars has a job in a theatrical company and a small part in a play about to open. She is so obsessed with making good that she creates an off-stage role for herself which upsets the entire production. Her double character is convincing enough for the farce, but only in *Alice Adams* does the convention reveal anything about live human beings.

Overcome by her own mediocrity, Alice Adams manages to convince herself that she is somebody else, a Miss Adams with a self-respecting father, with money and clothes and a college education, a girl whose charm and beauty is the toast of her many friends. But even as she carries on this public performance she realizes its imminent failure and tries to evaluate her two selves.

Alice's father also devises an escape from the dead-end of his own life; and he too deceives himself to anyone who will listen. Having stagnated for years as the head of the "sundries" department in a drug company, he dreams of manufacturing a new glue with a formula he long ago discovered. His wife is willing to be deluded. Father and daughter and mother press farther into their own imaginations, each repeating the others' deceptions, each believing in his own. Each comments on the others without knowing it, and the analogy of their lives is the only dreary truth there is.

This is Tarkington's finest novel. It is resonant and vital. It is also an explicit denial of the dream world. The dream is a fake which thrives on fear, which feeds on dignity until there is no dignity left. *Alice Adams* uses the same fixtures as Tarkington's other novels use:

the conventional heroine and the conventional double-character; but this time the conventions themselves are the subject—and subject to judgment.

Alice Adams was the great irony of Tarkington's career. It was the only time he made the dream-world completely real—and then, only by demolishing it. And it was the only time he ever tried. Although he continued to write for twenty-five years after its publication, his later novels were merely more skillful counterfeits than their predecessors. This fact does not square very well with what he once told Kenneth Roberts about the permanence of books and the transience of magazines.

Tarkington wrote, in the Literary Guild's questionnaire: "My books are rather various both in substance and in manner. One of them tried to do and be one thing, and one of them tried to do and be another." But only one of them is really various—and wholly lifelike. What he meant by "variety" can be explained, in the others, by the ingenious transfer of old fixtures to new settings.

The most valid criticism of Tarkington's fiction is that there is too much of it. It belongs to that great bulk which Elmer Davis called "not what somebody wanted to write, but what somebody else wanted to get written." The reason there was too much of it lay in the economics of magazine publishing. Booth Tarkington, the magazinist, epitomizes the paralyzing success of American authorship, for he counterfeited the slick Nirvana so well that he came to believe in it.

Chapter V

Hollywood Pay-Off

THE American motion picture industry, which began in 1896, during the past fifty years has become the trade publisher's largest customer. Within this brief period the movies have eroded the novel form more than anything else in the novel's history.

The film itself and the economic organization of the industry have caused this damage. The film narrative is limiting. It necessarily abridges the complexities of any subject it narrates. It is more susceptible than the novel to clear, uncomplicated attitudes, but American producers have nearly always forced just such clear and uncomplicated attitudes upon it. The size of the industry extends this damage.

The film industry outgrew the penny arcades and shooting galleries of the 1890's so rapidly that by 1939 it grossed annually more than three-fourths, and netted more than ninety per cent, of the income of the entire entertainment field in the United States. By 1925 the film studios were paying prices in six figures for the film rights to novels. By 1931 Cheney's *Economic Survey of the Book Industry* described a new occupational disease called "novelist's nystagmus," which was "caused by keeping one eye on the typewriter and the other on Hollywood."

The same factors which have caused the film industry to give way to television in recent years have even increased purchases of fiction by motion picture studios. The cost of manufacturing and distributing motion pictures rose so high after World War II that most producers merely leased the facilities of a few giant corporations already in business. The possibility of producing a movie on credit and without cap-

106   The Denatured Novel

ital investment has enticed many venturesome people, and some have succeeded. There are 125 so-called independent producers now buying novels for films, none of whom were even in business fifteen years ago.

This bidding for literary property has driven prices sky-high, although the bidding goes highest among the few established corporations. At the moment the record is held by 20th Century-Fox, which commissioned Grace Metalious to write a sequel to her notorious best seller *Peyton Place* (1956) for $265,000. The record is only temporary, however, because high prices have great publicity value.

This was an important transaction for more than just the money involved, because the whole idea of this second novel was instigated not by the author or even the publisher or the reprinter, but by the film company. The amount of money had nothing to do with the sequel itself which did not even exist at the time except as an idea in the producer's mind. The price was established solely on the strength of the publicity which had been generated for *Peyton Place*, and which had helped to sell eight million copies of that novel in all editions and to promote a successful motion picture. Some publicity, it was thought, would doubtless rub off on another novel by the same author, and another picture. So the studio got enough copy for the new scenario, in the approved Hollywood fashion by commissioning the author to write a new manuscript to be called *Return to Peyton Place*.

Although the price was higher than usual, this whole transaction was characteristic. *Publishers' Weekly* was talking about "cinema novels" back in 1917. Today, although the film rights to most novels fetch less than $35,000, Hollywood buys literary property but really pays for its notoriety. The merest possibility of notoriety keeps the film companies always interested in an editorial partnership with authors.

Suppose an author has a manuscript in progress and a contract with a publisher. If a film company were to buy an option on the completed work, all parties would benefit, including the agent who handled it. The film company would get a title and an author's name. The author would have more money to start with, shared equally with the publisher. Everyone would have a surer piece of merchandise, and if the book were finally filmed, the publisher and the producer would profit by promoting the book together.

The film company is not interested solely in an easily adaptable novel, it wants the best novel it can get. This is not a matter of being noble; it is simply good business. When the time comes, a screen writer can translate the book into a film better than its author can. Meanwhile, any book a lot of people will talk about is the property the producer wants most. The motion picture studio will be glad to retain, of course, whatever movie values the novel itself may have.

This enlightened attitude prevails only because all other means of editorial collaboration have usually failed, although there have been a great many experiments, all of them undertaken in the film industry's urgent need for story material. Ever since 1900, when the Frenchman, Georges Melies, filmed the first multi-scene narrative (the sequence of *Cinderella*), the industry has needed more stories than it could get. The motion picture studios have scavenged fiction from the public domain and purchased what they had to, even as they hired gangs of writers to generate more.

Published fiction had a particular appeal to the movie industry long before the idea of coordinated book promotion. In the early days, under threat of organized boycott for filming censorable stories, producers found a reasonable guarantee of respectability in the fact of a novel's prior publication. If a story were questionable, at least the producer could take the position that it was not his fault. If a book had some vintage, so much the better. Thus, by 1913 there had already been four motion pictures based on the Leather Stocking Tales and three on *The Scarlet Letter*.

Adapting published fiction, however, quickly involved the problem of copyrights. A test case of the film studios' liability for the use of literary property, involving finally a Supreme Court decision, changed the whole prospect of trade-book publishing. In 1907 Sidney Olcott produced for Kalem studio a motion picture of Lew Wallace's *Ben-Hur* (1880), and like the novel the film found an immense audience. Still one of the most expensive films ever made, it cost an estimated $6,000,-000. Partly because of its notoriety, Wallace's publisher brought suit.

The case was settled in 1911, with a judgment against Kalem for $50,000. During the litigation other studios began paying token sums for literary property: D. W. Griffith, for instance, paid $100 for the film rights to Helen Hunt Jackson's novel, *Ramona* (1884). But the decision in the *Ben-Hur* case sanctioned new prices for fiction. Since the industry now had to purchase fiction, a studio was wise to buy a novel with proven salability.

Best-selling fiction consequently became valuable property. In 1920 Eleanor Porter sold the film rights to *Pollyanna* (1913) for $80,000; current novels by Rex Beach, Jack London, Ben Ames Williams, Booth Tarkington, Richard Harding Davis and Irving Bacheller brought comparable sums for screenplays. The novel's most valuable asset, of course, was its author's name. This fact led the studios to experiment in editorial collaboration. They began to hire novelists to make their own adaptations.

Occasionally it worked. The film industry's most efficient novelist was Zane Grey, who finally adopted the system of sending the manuscript chapter of a novel to the film studio even before he sent it to his publisher. One result of this efficiency was that Grey sold the film rights to more novels—for something over forty motion pictures—than any other writer has ever sold. Samuel Goldwyn succeeded for awhile in hiring novelists to make their own adaptations. In 1919 he organized, within the Goldwyn Company, Eminent Authors Pictures Incorporated, a group of writers who would direct the screen adaptation of their own fiction: Gertrude Atherton, Mary Roberts Rinehart, Rupert Hughes, Gouverneur Morris, Basil King and Rex Beach. This organization led the way to all kinds of contracts between authors and studios, involving publishing rights to publish present and future works and the author's services for original screenplays.

During the 1920's the writer became the highest-paid worker in the movie industry. Whereas he had once earned $5 to $15 for a story idea, in 1906, he could now earn $1,000 to $2,500 a week in salary or $10,000 to $25,000, for piecework. Meanwhile the studio profited by his name. But most of the contracts worked only in theory. Hiring well-known writers continued through the thirties, but authors and producers alike began to discover diminishing returns.

The trouble was that the studios bought properties and services they could never use. It is customary in the film industry, unlike the book trade, for a writer to submit his work simultaneously to several producers. Buying competitively, the studios not only overstocked their manuscripts but made most of their purchases sight unseen—a routine procedure which would horrify any publisher. Like the purchased novel, the purchased author's services seldom fitted the requirements. Hiring novelists to write scenarios turned out to be a misappropriation of skills, rather like hiring a cabinet maker for carpentry.

Scores of writers have fled from Hollywood and lived to tell about it in sour novels or in angry statements which the magazines are more than happy to publish. Writers have always complained—even Sam Goldwyn's Eminent Authors—that they were hired not to write but to practice some fancied verbal specialty, such as plots or gags or dialogues, and to collaborate with other writers who were also paid not to write. The waste of effort and money over stories that were abandoned was infuriating, but their bitterest complaint was over the ruining of literary property. After the studio improved what he had written the author could scarcely recognize the mess.

Adapting a story to a screenplay in Hollywood is a matter of shrewd improvisation. Writers are paid to reassemble ideas borrowed from screenplays that have already succeeded. This is exactly what has always happened in the book trade. And when the author and screenwriter, Mildred Cram, described this process in the *American Spectator Year Book* (1934), she spoke for all embattled writers in Hollywood. "You are, let us say, writing a scene of seduction. Someone reminds you of the great seduction scene in 'The Guardsman.' Formula Number Eighty. Or someone else calls your attention to the sure-fire seduction in 'Red Dust.'"

They like 'em strong, fundamental, earthy. The anemic heroine is out. Let's write this straight from the shoulder—maybe with a laugh—you know, like that scene in "Farewell to Arms," where she laughed at herself. That was a wow. People loved it!

Presto, your seduction scene is a patchwork of the best seduction scenes! Formulas eighty to nine hundred, inclusive!

Every writer in Hollywood sooner or later discovers that what is "acceptable" in fiction has already been prescribed for him. The only tolerable invention—what he is hired for—is some new twist of a few old and salable ideas. This is so because the screenplay is not an autonomous art form, and never has been; it has always been a by-product of something else. In the whole history of the industry the motion picture itself has served one master after another.

Right from the start the film industry has belonged to the manufacturers of production equipment (cameras and projectors, and later, sound recording and projecting devices). The manufacturer has regarded the motion picture as merely an adjunct to his main line of business. This emphasis began with the industry in 1896, in New York City, in Koster and Bial's Music Hall—by utter chance on Shakespeare's birthday—when a machine known as the Vitascope projected onto a screen a filmstrip lasting about a minute and a half.

The projector was Thomas Armat's improvement of the Kinetescope which Thomas Edison had invented in 1889, partially patented in 1891, and installed in penny arcades. Edison's peep-show had allowed only one viewer at a time to see the filmstrip, but Armat's projector, enabling an audience, made real profit possible. For seven or eight years, Armat, Edison, and several other manufacturers experimented with cameras and with the production of motion pictures, and by 1903 they had established a pattern of control by leasing to exhibitors both their projectors and their films. They maintained this control.

In 1908 four manufacturers—including Edison and Armat—pooled their patents and organized the Motion Picture Patents Company, to restrain competition and to keep the market for themselves. Although this trust was liquidated in the courts in 1917, three years after it had lost most of the market to independent manufacturers, it had forced a characteristic growth on the industry. Controlling the market for motion pictures mean controlling three separate but related operations: production, distribution, and exhibition; and in order to fight the trust, independent producers had to achieve similar control.

The economic development of the industry after 1920 merely concentrated control in fewer and larger corporations, each combining production and distribution facilities with a chain of theaters. This was speeded up after the invention of the talking picture in 1926. By 1929 the silent film was no longer profitable, and the motion picture companies—and their film studios—gradually fell under the dominion of the manufacturers of recording as well as projecting equipment: Western Electric, a subsidiary of the Bell system, and later, R.C.A., which bought a film studio and a chain of theaters in order to market its own patents.

By 1929 there were five major combinations engaged in the production, distribution, and exhibition of films: Warner Brothers, Paramount, Loew's, 20th Century-Fox, and Radio-Keith-Orpheum. Within each of these combinations film production was determined not by the studios but by distributors and exhibitors. After the stock-market crash these major combinations could no longer finance new operations out of earnings, and outside capital (from banks, real estate holders, and motion picture finance companies) exerted new influence on the production of films.

Economic Control of the Motion Picture Industry (1944), by Mae D. Huettig, gets to the significance of this within its first chapter: "The fact that the major producers of film have not been forced to rely exclusively on the excellence of the product itself for profit may contribute to an understanding of many questions concerning the progress of the film as an art form." Every change in the industry has resulted in making this art form a more efficient source of income for capital invested in related properties.

This includes literary properties. Since Armat's invention of the Vitascope, every economic crisis in the industry has increased its demand on the book trade for more fiction. Competition between independent producers and the Motion Picture Patents Company, after 1909, resulted in the feature-length film. Two world wars shut off European competition even as they increased the world market for American motion pictures. The invention of the talkies added major producing companies to the industry, and caused an increase in the production of films. The box-office decline in the early 1930's prompted the double-feature program, offering twice as many reels for the viewer's money. Every major change in the business increased the need for screenplays and the value of literary property.

After World War II independent producers joined the industry in force. Their presence expresses more than a growing need of story material. They typify Hollywood's precarious financial position. They are independent in name only, since their business is entirely answerable to the banks and the distributing companies who control their credit. The so-called independent sets out to produce a film with nothing but a few contracts and a large debt. His creditors have not loaned him a dime without being satisfied that his product will make money.

The values of fiction are box-office values, as far as the screenplay is concerned. The fact that businessmen have always controlled the major companies which the screenplay serves, accounts for some of the weird ideas—the so-called "business values"—which box-office sales are supposed to reflect. One axiom is that the film serves one vast public which it must please at all costs. Another axiom, until the independent producers (artists mostly) proved otherwise, was that the more a product costs the better it is.

These two axioms have generally limited the content of motion pictures to more expensive elaborations of what has already been presumed to please everyone. The industry's rising costs, which increase the capital risk, have always made it prudent to continue this policy of elaborate imitation. A major producer-distributing company with its staggering overhead must spend at least $1,000,000 for every one of its fifteen or twenty pictures a year. Merely breaking even is too great a risk.

The so-called "business values" partly explain the manipulation of literary property so that it will all look alike on the screen, but there is another economic cause which insures manipulation. This is the star system, which has hypnotized the entire industry: the process of publicizing actors and then building movies to exploit their box-office appeal. The star system functioned as early as 1910. It was one of the weapons used by independent producers in their battle with the licensed members of the Motion Picture Patents Company.

Carl Laemmle began the star system and Adolf Zukor amplified it, stressing certain personalities rather than motion pictures. But by having featured personalities on the pay rolls, producers then had to protect their investments with large salaries. Box-office response to the first of these stars, Florence Lawrence and King Baggott, then Mary Pickford, Charlie Chaplin, John Barrymore, Minnie Maddern Fiske and James K. Hackett, justified their inflated salaries. Justification, in each case, meant more pictures like the last. Audiences typed the stars —good or wicked, strong, tender, seductive, wistful or whatever—and these traits had to be repeated.

Type casting resulted in reassembling over and over the same limited and calculable stories to fit a star's public personality. The star system even influenced the distribution of motion pictures. When theater owners demanded more of the stars, the producer used this bargaining power to lease his other, less publicized and less costly pictures. Adolf Zukor's producing company, Famous Players, classified its releases as "A" "B" or "C" pictures, depending on cost and an estimation of box-office appeal, a rating system which became indispensable to the industry after the introduction of double-features in the 1930's.

The star system and the classification of first- and second-class merchandise affected the purchase of literary property in a particular manner. Any scenario begins from one of two sources: an "original," written to prescription; or a published work of fiction, drama, biography, or history. Originals are characteristically the source of "B" pictures, which include nearly all of the Westerns, but most "A" pictures begin with a book already published.

By Hollywood's Alice-in-Wonderland logic, anything that costs more is better. The star needs a vehicle whose notoriety will match his own. If the author's name has news value, so much the better. The announcement of an inflated sales price appears to endorse the worth of the literary property, but its worth is only its ability to attract attenion. What it becomes in the film is something else again.

The look-alike quality of the movies is never left to chance; it is a studied quality. The absolute values are the same as those in the dream-world of the slick magazines. The pursuit of happiness engages the hero and the heroine, and these tabloid characters are revealed only with regard to the particular conflict which besets their pursuit. In the resolution of this conflict everyone is paid off in kind. All that varies (with the same regularity) is how the pay-off is delivered, how the values of the hero and the heroine are vindicated.

The obvious fixtures of this dream-world have scarcely changed since they were cataloged under the auspices of the Motion Picture Research

Council twenty-five years ago. Edgar Dale's comprehensive report, *The Content of Motion Pictures* (1935), is based on the evidence, discovered by a team of researchers in 1,500 motion pictures released between 1920 and 1932. This is what they found.

Romantic love and crime were the subjects of most of these motion pictures. There were far more characters living on high income in the films than in actuality, and material well-being was what heroes and heroines wanted. As for the superficial realism of setting, the urban scene, particularly New York City, predominated. The most frequently used interior set was the bedroom, although love-making, symbolized by the kiss and embrace, occurred most commonly in the living room. Illicit love was the intent of the villains more than the heroes. (Movie villains, characteristically in their thirties, are older and more faded than heroes.) The happy ending, enforced by the star system, clearly prevailed.

This inventory gains significance, not originally intended, in view of the palling sameness of the substance. Even before the Dale report the expedience of the movies aroused indignation. At the height of the industry's independence of outside and cautious capital, when movie companies could produce whatever they wanted, John Gould Fletcher indicted producing companies for what he called *The Crisis of the Film* (1929).

"To produce something that could be understood quickly, sold quickly, repeated quickly, has been mainly their aim," Fletcher charged. "Their aim was to give the public exactly what it wanted, and if they found out that the public wanted one type of thing, to go on giving that thing with as little variation as possible." This resulted, he said, in "propaganda for the emotional monotony, the naïve morality, the sham luxury . . . the sentimental, and the acrobatic that are so common in the United States."

Only the costumes and the customs have changed with the times. The experience remains. The movies kept pace with the change in sexual mores, for instance, from the Mary Pickford vehicle, *Pollyanna* (1920), through the vamps played by Theda Bara, to the aggressive, likable, worldly woman personified by Jean Harlow, Carole Lombard, and Mae West.

The new films kept up with the fashions by mocking the mores of their predecessors. The vamp pictures mocked the behavior of the Pollyannas, and the Mae West pictures mocked the prudery with which the vamp had been characteristically defeated in her desires. But all of these films shared the same kind of moral posture. All of them reveled in the behavior assumed at that moment to be a trespass, before retributing it.

Such posturing, of course, belongs to popular entertainment. The movies have not tampered with vulgar expedience. They have simply exploited the same appeal with which Samuel Richardson's *Pamela* made its prurient plea for chastity. That book, like its heroine, sold extraordinarily well. The movies have merely rearranged the pay-off. The story of the heroine breathless from the lover's pursuit but holding out for marriage has been filmed under one title or another since the movie industry began.

Moral posturing encompasses more than chastity, as the crime pictures demonstrated after the Legion of Decency was founded in 1934. Prior to this censoring organization films presented crime without editorial comment, more or less in the guise of documenting American urban life. When the spokesmen for censoring groups had had enough of this, however, crime pictures brought the criminal to harsh justice in the last few minutes of the film, having already celebrated for an hour-and-a-quarter the criminal's *modus operandi*. Sham moralizing has also marked most of the so-called sociological films about the rights of labor, the problems of White and Negro, divorce dilemmas, juvenile delinquency, and the ethics of Big Business.

Pleasing the public has been carefully assured in the film industry. Courting pleasure—or avoiding trespass—takes the form of pre-censorship, a review conducted before a picture's release and designed to avoid costly litigation. Pre-censorship has existed since 1909, when the Motion Picture Patents Company responded to the fears of churchmen and public officials (which newspapers and magazines gleefully printed) that the movies were conducting an organized public demoralization. The Company organized a censorship board to review the productions of its member studios.

With this precedent the major film companies adopted in 1930 a list of commandments and prohibitions known as the Motion Picture Production Code. The Code is still enforced by a board of the industry's trade association—once known as the Hayes Office—nominally independent but actually a sounding board for private, vocal lobbies—political, religious, professional and civic, and comprised of the ubiquitous club woman—engaged in special pleading and in the state of public morals. The power of this official censoring group lies in its right to withhold its endorsement of any motion picture. On the basis of this awesome power it "recommends" the deletion of anything offensive to the Motion Picture Code.

The Code is notorious for its prohibition of the details of sexual intimacy in or out of marriage, whether of fruition or frustration—in fact, its taboo of all explicit references to any of the biological functions of animal or human characters. The prohibition also governs thematic treatment of these details. Love must end in marriage; divorce is forbidden. Fitting punishment must follow a display of sin or crime. There may be repentance in the motion pictures but no redemption.

Unnumbered writers—novelists, lawyers, historians, clerics and poets—have protested that this "tattered philosophy of free will" contradicts Christian ethics and the moral values the Code attempts to preserve; but to no avail. Two men peculiarly suited to the task once attempted to fix the responsibility for film censorship: Morris Ernst, this nation's most prominent attorney in censorship litigation after the *Ulysses* court case; and Pare Lorentz, producer and director of epochal documentary films. Their scrutiny, recorded in *Censored: the Private Life of the Movies* (1930), led them time and again to "the gross, vapid illusions of life contained in the ordinary movie."

Ernst and Lorentz explained the operation of the Hayes office, and discovered personal reasons for militant bigotry among dozens of individual censors; but somehow the marriage of bigotry and expedience was larger than the sum of discoverable details. Responsibility was everywhere. They concluded: "The masses made the movie. It is a nationalism; a sectionalism of thought, desire, frustration, written large."

Exploiting this desire and frustration is the business of the movies. *Hollywood: The Dream Factory* (1950) is what Hortense Powdermaker called her anthropological study of it, and the sum of all its expedience she called a taboo against mankind. "No one goes to bat for the human species; no one seems to care that mankind is presented falsely, that the majority of movie portrayals are untrue." In all the special pleas for doctors or Mexicans or ministers or Rotarians or Negroes, "no worthy organization protests that human beings are shown as passive, unfeeling robots." In a chapter called "Taboos" she continues:

Man, according to Hollywood, is either completely good, or bad. His personality is static, rarely showing any development either in growth or regression. The villain is a blackened sinner who can do no good and who cannot be saved; while the hero is a glamorous being, who can do no wrong of his own volition, and who is always rewarded.

The movies manufacture stereotypes disguised as persons. They rarely bother about complex human beings. This is a result of the manufacturer's belief that he must gratify the consumers' wishes in order to stay in business. But making profit entails more of a compromise than merely expressing certain acceptable attitudes. To visualize these attitudes on film means mutilating the literature from which they are abstracted. There is no way around it.

The film form always emphasizes the prominent features of any fiction. It simplifies the novel by caricaturing it. For the novel's system of analogies the film substitutes an immediacy which the novel does not have—the reader becomes a viewer. But the film cannot accommodate the novel's complexity. When the producer uses the film to visualize these unrealistic attitudes, therefore, he merely aggravates the film's natural distortion of the novel.

Adapting a novel to the film means more than just converting it. The first chapter of George Bluestone's *Novels into Film* (1957) concludes on this. What the "filmist" adapts "is a kind of paraphrase of the novel."

He looks not to the organic novel, whose language is inseparable from its theme, but to characters and incidents which have somehow detached themselves from language and, like the heroes of folk legends, have achieved a mythic life of their own.

One novelist has made a convincing case of this reasoning by turning the usual process around: by building a novel out of a screenplay and then explaining why. Budd Schulberg wrote the scenario for *Waterfront* (1955) about racketeering among the longshoremen of the Port of New York. Then, dissatisfied with the filmed result, he wrote a novel based on the same story.

This film had every advantage of an intelligent production. The author knew his subject and had something to say; he was allowed to control the scenario; and the direction and the acting amplified his story with sensitive understanding. It was a superb film and justly won several Motion Picture Academy awards. But the film was not enough; it told the truth of the lawless world of the waterfront, but not the whole truth. Schulberg wanted to represent the dilemma of many responsibilities for this lawlessness.

Schulberg's real subject was not the waterfront activity but the awareness of it, which he described as "the deeper truth of inconclusiveness." His article, "Why Write It When You Can't Sell It to the Pictures," in *Saturday Review* (September 3, 1955), explains why the scenario could not accommodate his subject. The film, he said, has a relentless force. It has its own tight logic which denies the ranging kind of aesthetic experiences: "A film must act, a book has time to think and wonder."

The film is an art of high points. . . . The novel is an art of high, middle, and low points. . . . The film does best when it concentrates on a single character. . . . It tends to lose itself in the ramifications. . . . It has no time for what I call the essential digressions.

By "essential" digressions Schulberg meant the exploration of complicated, contradictory characters and of their backgrounds, which only a novel can afford.

The film must go from significant episode to more significant episode in a constantly mounting pattern. . . . It cannot wander as life wanders, or pause as life always pauses to contemplate the incidental or the unexpected.

The scenario visualizes a situation. The novel comprehends it. The scenario abstracts the motion from that situation for its own subject, because motion is the distinguishing property of the film. Everything that a movie has to reveal depends on the uninterrupted movement of its story.

This property of continuous motion determines the shape of the story. Like the film on its winding spool the action must progress. Its continuity derives from successive encounters which build some large conflict whose resolution will end the film. Each encounter comprises a scene, and the average feature film has time to develop only about thirty scenes. Since each scene must advance the main conflict, there is no room in the narrative, no space in the film, to explore any peripheral subject. There is no room for what Budd Schulberg calls the deeper truth of inconclusiveness.

Abstracting motion from a novel means selecting and emphasizing a conflict. This is standard procedure in adaptation. On the subject of "Scenarios," Anita Loos's and John Emerson's *Breaking into the Movies* (1921) still speaks for scores of other screenplay manuals. "In choosing your story be sure it has the dramatic quality. It must not be rambling; and it must have an element of conflict between opposing factors. . . ." This manual describes the kind of conflict that will work: between "a man and a woman, a woman and her Destiny, or simply Good and Evil—which leads up to a crisis in which the matter is fought out and finally settled."

No mistake about this conflict. The adversaries are obvious, and they fight it out until they settle the matter. This recipe for a screenplay has no room for the simultaneous analogies which develop and appraise the subject. The screenplay reduces the novel to a single conflict which it then renders into a sequence of visible scenes.

The deliberate stages of adaptation, like reduction gears in a machine, direct the energy to another plane for more efficient use. At the first stage the screen writer abstracts from the novel a synopsis of the conflict. He then writes a present-tense narrative based on this synopsis, which develops the traits and the motives of the characters with refrence to the conflict. This is known as the "treatment," which is enough to make almost any novelist shudder.

The next draft of the screenplay manuscript is the "continuity," which translates the "treatment" into the conventions of film representation. This is the rendering of the novel. The more dramatic material is turned into scenes, encounters between the adversaries that will build the conflict. The rest of the novel is abandoned. Finally the scenario or "shooting-script" refines the "continuity," dividing the scenes into camera shots and providing transitions from one scene to another. The sequence and variation of these camera shots will accommodate the need to reveal one fact at a time, while creating suspense over facts yet to come.

But this tidy description merely theorizes. Since the organization of a film studio makes adaptation a collaborative affair, involving the writer with his unit producer, the supervising producer, usually other writers and then the director, many versions of each stage of the screenplay manuscript modify the idea with which the writer began. Even the finished scenario is not a public document but merely a set of instructions for the director, who must often make impromptu changes as he shoots the film.

This whole collaborative business diminishes the writer's jurisdiction over the story. What really cancels it is the editing, the process of organizing thousands of feet of exposed film into a narrative approximating the "continuity." Editing, or "cutting," literally establishes the point of view of the story by selecting from among the camera shots. It creates the film's presiding intelligence.

Editing can eliminate scenes, change their emphasis, or build new scenes. It can change the entire story. Because it controls all of the story's proportions, this process takes the place of the cohering presence which the author would furnish in a novel.

The process of "cutting" or editing is nearly as old as the narrative film. Two years after Georges Melies filmed *Cinderella* with a stationary camera, as though it were a stage play, Edwin S. Porter's *The Life of an American Fireman* (1902) demonstrated the vitality of "cutting" from one view of a continuous situation to another. By "cutting" Porter could show the relevance of separate but simultaneous action, such as the burning building in one place and the firemen racing toward it. And by "cross-cutting," or showing alternate shots, he could create suspense.

Porter's achievement was a triumph of production. He assembled a narrative exclusively in the "cutting-room" from film footage accumulated in other pictures. His achievement showed the advantages of "cutting" for dramatic significance. Later D. W. Griffith, the industry's greatest innovator, exploited this technique. One of his versions of the "cross-cut," the venerable convention of the chase, has been a part of nearly every feature film since Griffith's *The Birth of a Nation* (1914).

"Cutting" stresses the immediacy of conflict and breeds suspense over the outcome. At every stage it can surprise the viewer. It is a convention that exploits all the tabloid advantages of the film, and distinguishes the film from all other narrative forms. This convention is so dominating, in fact, that screenplays are normally written to accommodate it.

The scenario capitalizes on the film's capacity for suddenly establishing a new point of view. Suspense can be heightened by the sudden revelation of new facts, simply by "cutting" to another camera shot or another scene. The story itself, therefore, must exploit the unexpected turn of action, the sudden reversal, or an ironic twist. The device is known in the trade as the "switcheroo" or the "gimmick" or the "topper." If its surprise is funny the device is a "yak"; if sentimental or pathetic, it is a "bleeder."

The sudden twist of events pays off in shock value. The "gimmick" is as old as story-telling despite its new slang, but the film's natural facility for changing the point of view emphasizes the device of sudden reversal. This is how the scenario really denies the novel. The abrupt revelation becomes a disguise for the developing awareness which a novel can represent but which a film does not have time for.

The "gimmick" is a sleight-of-hand. The scenarist can plant a fact obscurely in the action and later reveal it as cause for the new turn of affairs, and if the story is twisted quickly enough the shock will

deny reasoning. The new turn of affairs may be arbitarary, even unbelievable, but the scenarist has only to remind the viewer that he has
seen the evidence before without realizing it. This is quite different,
however, from the novelist's problem of making the reader believe in
what happens.

The "gimmick" or the "switcheroo" is a way of passing off the counterfeit values of movie fiction—those lies which gratify the customers'
dreams. Because the sudden twist appears to solve a conflict so neatly
in its own terms, the device apparently justifies those terms: that people are either good or bad and that, good or bad, they are all paid off
in kind. The "switcheroo" is a dream-device which the scenario exploits.

It would be going too far to say that the scenario and the novel ex-
clude one another—but not much too far. The novel can be adapted to
the scenario only at the expense of its natural complexity. Sometimes
this is a good thing, when the novel is confused or too long for what it
has to say. The movie of James Jones's *From Here to Eternity* (1951)
was far more persuasive than the novel. But this same attenuation
causes most scenarios to denature the novels they start with.

The film cannot render conflict without visualizing the adversaries,
nor can it visualize thought except by action; and at best the "gimmick" is a very stylized action. When a novel emphasizes inaction or
the futility of action, or when a character's adversary is not another
character or even a place that can be seen, the film is bound to distort
it. Yet this is precisely the kind of "unvisual" novel that has developed
since the end of the nineteenth century.

By 1900 the doctrine of determinism had begun to influence a few
American novelists such as Crane, Norris, Dreiser and London; and by
1920 it was widespread. Toward the end of the nineteenth century the
economy of Europe and America had seemed to outgrow any individual's ability to control or even to cope with it. What seemed an irre-
vocable loss to the individual needed explaining, and the doctrine of
"scientific" determinism, as it was called, attempted to explain it.

This doctrine was based on the layman's enthusiastic misunderstanding of Darwinian biology and later of the psychology of Freud. It attempted to explain the individual human being in terms of certain in-

tangible "forces" presumed to limit or determine him. In the fiction which absorbed this irrational doctrine the individual had no efficacy. Any action was futile because he could not even define his adversary.

However irrationally it may have developed, the extraordinary influence of "scientific" determinism on contemporary fiction is a fact. Almost every American novel after 1900 in some way acknowledges it. This fact tends to make the contemporary novel intractable to any abridgment or adaptation.

When a novel's conflict involves an adversary as shapeless as the whole of society or as invisible as the hero's misguided notions of his environment, the difference between the novel and its movie is likely to be tremendous. When a novel presents an irresolvable situation, with the hero suspended in circumstance, then the film narrative (which demands the efficacy of action) actually contradicts the novel. The well-known filmed versions of two deterministic novels—Theodore Dreiser's *An American Tragedy* (1925) and Ernest Hemingway's *To Have and Have Not* (1937)—show just such distortion.

The same kind of substitution made the better novel, *An American Tragedy*, into the poorer film. This novel dramatizes the complex circumstances by which an individual's environment limits him. *An American Tragedy* tells of a young man who plots the murder of his mistress and then executes it in spite of himself. Nearly half the novel describes the murder trial, which repeats the convicting evidence so many times in so many ways that the book indicts an entire society for the youth's crime. Like almost everyone else in this society the hero has simply responded to the incentives of prosperity and social privilege. The mass of the book is the massive evidence of this implacable situation. The novel has no "gimmick"; the pay-off is exactly what the cumulating evidence promised it would be.

Dreiser's novel was first turned into a stage play, a four-act melodrama by Patrick Kearney, which concentrated primarily on the trial scene. Then a moving picture based on both the novel and the play was produced by Joseph Von Sternberg and released by Paramount in 1931. Except for the murder and the trial scenes almost no vestige of the novel remained. The problem lay in defining the youth's adversary. The mass of society was not filmable, so the producer impersonated it by law-enforcement officers. But this meant making the youth the villain.

At the outset, therefore, the film reduced the novel to the pursuit and trial of a murderer. Dreiser protested against this movie which, he said, had turned the novel into a "tabloid murder story." Arguing that the right to reproduce the novel did not convey the right to impoverish it, the author sought a court injunction to prevent a theater in New York City from exhibiting the film. The court's decision against the author added a new irony to *An American Tragedy*.

The substitution of an obvious and resolvable conflict for the determinist's view of experience distorted Hemingway's *To Have and Have Not* beyond all recognition. The novel begins with a short story (it is really a collection of short stories) about Harry Morgan, fisherman and smuggler, whose luck, as his widow says, "went bad first in Cuba. Then it kept getting right worse and worse until a Cuban killed him."

Titled "Spring," "Fall," and "Winter"—there is no "Summer" in this particular world—the stories dramatize the circumstances of Harry Morgan's losses: his fishing tackle, his arm, his boat and then his life. Dying from a bullet wound in his stomach, Morgan mutters his own realization of these circumstances: "Ain't got no hasn't got any can't really isn't any way out." The author says it took the dying man a long time to get it out and all his life to learn it.

To Have and Have Not is a series of brief glimpses at the lives of men and women living around the harbor at Key West. The analogies of these scenes suggest that somehow these have-nots all manage to help circumstances deprive them of whatever they really want in life. They all pathetically cherish some illusion of "having." A few, like Harry Morgan and his wife, discover the inadequacy of the illusion, but the rest never do. There is no other resolution.

This book denies the dream. But its author was famous—reason enough to make a film. There were a few small problems involved, however, such as inventing a new conflict with new characters in a new setting. The book's first episode, entitled "Spring," contained some useful elements; and the scenarists abandoned the rest of the episodes. Even so, this was not movie material. In this episode Morgan agrees to smuggle twelve Chinamen from Cuba to the United States, then double-crosses his employer by taking the money, murdering him, and landing the cargo back in Cuba.

This was scarcely the illusion the movies wanted to sell, so the screen writers made some changes. "Spring" became the summer of 1940, and the locale was moved from Havana to Martinique, a French possession then ruled by the Vichy government. This made Harry Morgan's trespasses acceptable. He could be hired by the French Underground to sabotage the puppet government (which would be represented, of course, by a police inspector). It remained only to change Morgan's cargo to a member of the Free French forces and to eliminate the murder.

One other improvement amended an unfortunate omission from the original episode. The scenarists wrote into the manuscript the part of an American young woman stranded on the island. Profiting by these changes, the film could easily represent an acceptable conflict: beginning with intrigue, developing into a chase, and concluding with a "switcheroo" which shifts the balance of power from the police inspector to Morgan. As Anita Loos put it: "A conflict of Good and Evil—which leads up to a crisis in which the matter is fought out and finally settled."

The scenarists—one of whom was William Faulkner—showed great ingenuity. They twisted Hemingway's story into a permissible conflict that could be abruptly resolved. The scenario ignored the book's emphasis on "why" for an easier emphasis on "how." The smuggling of human cargo, like the other episodes in the book, implies need to seek reason for an apparently unmotivated crime, but the film removes precisely this question. With the same change of emphasis the motion picture reduced *An American Tragedy* to a single narrative of pursuit and capture, omitting the complexities of why the murder had occurred.

One of the properties of the novel form is the appraisal of conflict, and both films effaced this property. But not all novels so stoutly resist the "treatment" of the scenarist. If a novel emphasizes only "what" and "how" to begin with, and if its conflict already resolves by a "switcheroo," then making a scenario is no trouble at all. One such novel, which also happens to be the story of a murder, is James M. Cain's *The Postman Always Rings Twice* (1934).

This novel tells how the passions of an itinerant bum and a married woman lead them to murder her husband, and how this passion causes the death of both murderers. The action turns on several sudden reversals. The first attempt at murder fails—fortuitously, when it develops that the man and woman were already under suspicion. After their second, and successful, attempt the clever tactics of their defense lawyer frees them. Next they are threatened by a blackmailer whom they outwit. Finally, after they are clear of the law and with all evidence destroyed, an auto accident kills the woman. This accident offers evidence enough to convict the bum of her murder, even though there was no murder.

The novel has no theme, no attitude toward its subject. It simply tells how the murderers ironically escaped until they were ironically punished. Only a few changes were needed for a screenplay that would satisfy movie values. The film built up the character of the district attorney, making him the single adversary of the murderers. It simplified the trial scenes and eliminated the guilt of insurance companies, which, in the novel, profited by letting the murderers go. It added two new scenes and new material to two others to make the heroine—played by Lana Turner—more sympathetic, and to give her an added motive for murder. It also eliminated some explicit love-making.

One reason for this faithful adaptation was that the author had already written his novel like a movie "continuity." Its sixteen chapters are comprised of scenes. Within these scenes, short units—sometimes only eight or ten lines—approximate camera shots. Thus, the book's longest description of the wife, at the end of chapter one, efficiently offers the only explanation of the mentality of her accomplice. "Except for the shape she really wasn't any raving beauty, but she had a sultry look to her, and her lips stuck out in a way that made me want to mash them in for her."

The book's point of view is a "gimmick." The first-person narrative of how the murderers go free turns out to have been written in prison, just before the narrator's execution for a crime he did not commit.

Presto! The story has been morally sound all along. In all its formal aspects *The Postman* was a scenario the moment it was published.

Cain has commented on the "legendary success" his stories have made as films, saying "I have learned a great deal from pictures, mainly technical things." By way of explaining this success, his preface to *The Butterfly* (1947) describes the similarity of all his novels. He writes of the wish that comes true, which seems to him a terrifying concept. "I think my stories have some quality of the opening of a forbidden box. . . ." The reader is carried along, he says, by the realization that the characters cannot have their wish and survive. "Thus, if I do any glancing, it is toward Pandora, the first woman, a conceit that pleases me, somehow, and often helps my thinking."

All of Cain's novels stylize the Pandora legend. The trespasser eagerly tells how he did it, then ends up lamely saying, "I see it all clearly now, but I don't know why it happened." The hero says this just as he is about to be punished. This pay-off makes everything square in the movies, but it cannot camouflage the fact that the character is only a mechanical monster.

An author's discussion of his own work is always welcome. But it is not the most reliable document in the world, especially when the work itself contradicts his own appraisal of it. For example, Cain's preface to *The Butterfly* states: "I care almost nothing for what my characters look like, being almost exclusively concerned with their insides." By "insides" Cain obviously means those inner motives and responses which make a character vital. But his characters are almost never vital. They almost never have any "insides" except the literal kind which occasionally and violently spill out.

All but one of Cain's novels are the same: a narrative without an attitude becomes a confession without a theme. All that change from one story to another are the superficial authenticity of a setting and the bewildering virtuosity of each hero's special knowledge. Be it operatic singing or distilling corn liquor or dieting or picking lemons or drilling for oil or mining silver or packaging frozen foods, each skill is relevant to the crime. In a way, these books are accurate.

Past All Dishonor (1946) has the accuracy of an absolute vacuum. It tells how a man's passion for a whore leads him to blackmail, steal and murder in order to get and keep her. The first thirteen chapters tell how he goes about it and the fourteenth tells how he gets paid off.

The chapter sequence would indicate that Cain has already given this novel the "treatment." (1) A man and woman meet and love; (2) she leaves; (3) he finds her and discovers she is a whore; (4) he sees her professionally and she challenges him to pay the price; (5) he earns money to meet the price, but loses it before payment; (6) succeeds in earning more money; (7) but gets shot in the process; (8) so she nurses him but will not accept his marriage proposal; (9) he hires himself out as a legal gunman; and (10) kills her wealthy fiancé, which (11) makes her realize how much he loves her. (12) She responds to him at the bottom of a deserted mine shaft, after which he discovers a lode of silver ore; and together they plan to steal the money to buy the mine. (13) Despite elaborate preparation their train robbery miscarries, and they become fugitives; (14) in their hideaway, ever alert for pursuers, he shoots and kills her by mistake and so ends his own life there.

Cain wrote on the dust jacket: "I have tried to put real human beings before the reader, to explain, as plausibly as I can, how a gunman got that way, what the prostitute was doing there, why the mine-owner was a bit of a heel, and so on." It is painful to think that Cain could have so condescended as to assume his readers would believe this. He must have been talking about some other book.

A novel accretes meaning by its accumulation of analogies, but the only thing *Past All Dishonor* accumulates is irrelevance. The hero kills the heroine's financé because this unfortunate man has bought her "like a prostitute"—as the hero admits she is. He joins the Union Army to escape punishment, then goes over the hill with the excuse that he is really a Confederate sympathizer. And having already decided to rob the train so that he and the heroine can live it up, he announces that his theft will keep the treasure away from the Northern Army.

These tailor-made rationalizations would fit only a robot, and the last chapter proves that they do. The hero says he has been sitting around for two days and a night: "Writing down how it came about that a boy that went to St. Anne's in Annapolis, and believed what he heard there, should turn into a traitor, a killer and a thief. I don't know why." So he begins to speculate. "Falling in love with Morina, that had something to do with it. But Virginia City had something to do with it too." Then he really gets deep.

Maybe they were wrong about the devil, maybe he didn't move out like they said he did. Maybe they just thought he did. Maybe he found a new way to conjure. Maybe he found if you give people everything they want, and nothing they ought to have, that'll wind them up in hell, too. Anyhow, for me it's all over.

Cain said the movies never bought this book because he had made the heroine a prostitute. This seems odd, since movieland can temporarily accommodate just about any heterosexual trespass so long as the trespasser will be killed anyway. The author explained himself in order to emphasize that he had never toned down a novel in order to court the favor of a motion picture producer. He must be right in his reasoning about the prostitute, since this novel is constructed exactly like every book he did sell to the movies.

They all rely on the same "switcheroo." In "Double Indemnity" (in *Three of a Kind*, 1943) an insurance claims-adjuster commits a perfect murder, and might have collected the insurance money of the deceased but for his falling in love with the victim's daughter. This dilemma he solves by suicide. Also in *Galatea* (1953) the narrator tells how his involvement with another man's wife precipitates violent death. This time the husband is the criminal, and the narrator tells of virtue rewarded as well as villainy defeated. Discovered and pursued by the husband, who is killed in his attempt to kill them, the lovers escape. But the lovers must stand trial for his murder.

The sudden reversal of *Galatea* takes place in court. Just the opposite from the trial scene in *The Postman* (where perverted evidence secures the wrong verdict), the lovers are acquitted because the inconsistencies of the truth manage to contradict the circumstantial evidence against them. This use of the "gimmick" recalls an earlier confessional, "The Embezzlers," published in *Three of a Kind*, also about

the narrator's involvement with the innocent wife of a criminal husband. In this one, however, the hero's innocence becomes so hopelessly
compromised that he must be saved by an act of author.

No matter what the twist, it always pays off in the same way. The
hero of *Serenade* (1937) has a liaison with a Mexican woman until she
kills the man who has loved him. Since the pay-off eliminates the murderer who has eliminated the pervert, the novel excuses everyone's indulgence in the lurid details along the way. This is what satisfies movie
values. The message on the paperback cover of the novel announces
that "Cain is a story-teller first and last—everything else in his work is
stripped to the basic, cinematic action."

No nonsense here about the novel's complexity. The inside blurb
of 1950 paperbond edition announces that *Serenade* "has the inevitable
toughness, the swiftness of pace, the action stripped to essentials. . . ."
But the novel belies the claim. Precisely because "the action is stripped
to essentials" there is nothing "inevitable" about it. What is "stripped"
is the subjective existence of the characters, the thought and feeling
which fashions all response and gives it significance.

It is Cain's stylization, not the Pandora legend, that fails; there is
nothing about Pandora that forbids thought and feeling. In fact, both
the best and the least of Cain's novels stylize the same legend. One is
believable and the other is not. The least of these novels, *Love's Lovely
Counterfeit* (1942), tells how a stool-pigeon uses the influence of his
mistress to double-cross the racketeer who employs him, so that he
can become a racketeer himself. Like the narrator of *Double Indemnity*
this hero gets trapped by falling in love with the right woman at the
wrong time. The irony fails because the hero is not believable anyway.

Cain later explained (in *The Butterfly* preface) that *Love's Lovely
Counterfeit* was the only novel he had written with "any expectation of
pleasing" a motion picture producer. "I thought, and still think, *Love's
Lovely Counterfeit* . . . is a slick plot for a movie, and I executed it well
enough." It is slick, all right. The novel's final "switcheroo" involves
the dying criminal's attempt to make his confession outside the jurisdiction of the law—to beat the rap but to satisfy the movies. But even
the movies would not buy this one.

What makes *The Butterfly* (1947) the best of Cain's novels is that the hero has believably fooled himself about his trespasses. Brought up in the hill country of Kentucky and West Virginia, he preaches the literal justice of the Old Testament. The deeds he performs in token of his fundamentalist faith, however, are sins by the same token. This novel is more persistently sordid than any of the others, involving multiple possibilities of incest, bastardy, cuckolding and murder. But when this hero dies, with the usual confession, he is believable because he has agonized all along over his impossible compromise with God.

The only one of Cain's novels which explicitly preaches the justification of its hero is also the most immoral. This is *The Moth* (1948), which tells of the hero's twenty-three-year exile from home. During these wanderings he has committed armed robbery and escaped unpunished; but this is only the half of it. He had originally left home under the accusation of seducing his fiancée's little sister. As it turns out, however, his innocence of the seduction somehow countenances the unpunished crime which he later did commit.

The last four chapters of this novel which go through the motions of trial and sentence would pass for a parody of expedience. They are also a good blueprint of Cain's fiction. The prodigal son and his father agree on a plan whereby the son will write down his experiences, which the father will then edit and evaluate. "I've no gift for words, Dad," says the hero, "I'd tell the what and leave out the why."—which the book has already done for twenty-six chapters.

Then the father pronounces a long judgment, the heart of which is: "What, after all, has loused you, as you put it? Me? Yourself? Circumstances? All three to some extent. But mostly the time in which you lived—a calendar."—whatever that means. But the author gets away with this double-talk because it excuses one crime on the strength of the hero's innocence of another. As in so many of Cain's novels the moralizing is an accessory after the fact—the real fact having been an unbelievable character in the first place.

It seems incredible that Cain could write: "I care almost nothing for what my characters look like, being almost exclusively concerned with their insides." And from his preface to *The Butterfly* it is apparent that he thought he had not sold out to the movies. His novels, however, do not support his opinions.

Perhaps Cain is like most writers who have learned how to satisfy the movies and have convinced themselves that the film is really more persuasive than the novel. This has fooled a good many novelists before him. Back in the early days when Hollywood was beginning to buy novels, Jack London mouthed this prejudice. "Visualization is everything for the teacher," he was quoted as saying in *Moving Picture World* (January 31, 1914). "I love to teach, to transmit to others the ideas and impressions in my own consciousness."

So far so good. London had just seen the movie of his novel *The Sea-Wolf* (1904). But even as London explained himself, he lost out. "I am a realist and essentially a picture writer. In writing a story I always keep in mind these two motives; first, I want to make the details so plain that he who runs may read, and then there is the deeper underlying psychological motive."

Notice the afterthought. This is just what James M. Cain's last chapters unwittingly burlesque. As for the priority of motives, "that he who runs may read" determines the filmed adaptation of most novels.

Ever since Jack London's opinion, some forty years ago, the scenario method of fiction has continually proved the congeniality of novel and film—at the novel's cost. The movie reduces the complexities of a novel to a conflict, then counterfeits the complexities by visual tricks. When these tricks are used to justify the expedient morals of popular amusement, then the novel becomes something else again; it becomes just another story.

Chapter VI

Instant Fiction

INEXPENSIVE paperbound books, or "paperbacks," now comprise the largest share of the book trade's retail volume. Even in a business notoriously built on exceptions and contradictions, the paperback stands out. The presentation of the inexpensive paperback customarily contradicts the book itself; it negates the distribution system which delivers the book to the buyer; and it impugns the very claims it makes to the purchaser. Even the marketing of the paperback novel denies the reading process; in fact, the publishers have made it possible to *not* read almost every paperback novel they print.

They have achieved this extraordinary feat by means of the package itself, which has created a startling image of American fiction during the past twenty years. This image is easy to see. I find it, for instance, in the packaging of several hundred novels—302 to be exact—published in soft covers during the last twenty years. This is about seven per cent of the more than 4,000 fiction titles now in paperback editions.

There is nothing scientistic about this shelf-list of books (or even scientific); it is no controlled sample from specified retail outlets. It contains merely the novels I have bought from time to time with small change. But it does happen to represent ninety-seven American writers, whose works were originally published during the last hundred years; and it includes the imprints of twelve major American publishers of inexpensive paperback books: Ace, Avon, Ballantine, Bantam, Crest, Dell, Gold Medal, Permabooks, Pocket Books, Popular Library, Pyramid and Signet. It is a fair representation of contemporary American fiction.

The image created by these paperbacks is primarily on their covers, conveyed by a kind of "outside idiom" which comes across in a hurry for efficient non-reading. Just seventy-one adjectives describe all of these books, but by a declining ratio. There are forty-nine adjectives on the first hundred covers (arranged alphabetically by author), seventeen new ones on the next hundred, and only five new adjectives on the covers of the rest.

A frequency list of the words is even more revealing. Twenty-three adjectives are repeated more than five times, and a dozen words are so insistent that the image of this fiction is incontestable. These novels are "moving," "brilliant," "dynamic" and "compelling." They are "gripping," "graphic" and "fascinating." They are "emotion-charged" and "blood-stirring," and occasionally "drum-tight." But more than anything else they are "poignant" and "powerful." They are about equally "compassionate" and "brutal"; and some—often the less expensive ones—are both.

These adjectives keep company with picturesque verbs. These novels were not written, for instance—by and large they were "carved." They were "carved from the frontier," they were carved "from the city" and "from the past," they were "carved from the human heart." These carvings are about persons "caught in a web"—usually a "web of destiny," occasionally a web of "stark destiny." Moreover, these novels "score." They score by being "merciless," "stinging," "biting" or "fearless." And they "speak out" too. But for every "outspoken" novel, seventeen are "frank" and three are "utterly frank." The subject of this candor is variously "bawdy," "daring," "intimate," "racy," "stark" and "unnatural." Searching for a new sensation, one publisher has even labeled the contents of his book as "TURGID!"—which is certainly being "utterly frank."

What one discovers about these "emotion-packed," "action-charged" books—by Mark Twain, Herman Melville, Mickey Spillane, Frank Norris, Theodore Dreiser, Erle Stanley Gardner, Thomas Wolfe, John Marquand, William Faulkner and ninety-one others—is that they are apparently all the same: a fact, were it true, which would save everyone a great deal of time. How all these novels suddenly got to be the same in the last twenty years is something of a mystery, until you begin to inspect the economics of paperback publishing. Then it all becomes clear—along with the fact that the reader's good faith and the book trade's ultimate good intentions have been contradicted in the paperbacks more efficiently than ever before.

These inexpensive editions are the latest version of an old publishing idea: cheap books in large volume. This newest version dates from 1939, when Robert DeGraff began the Pocket Books series with thirty-four titles whose sales totaled five hundred thousand copies in the first year. After World War II the market for cheap books increased in every way: in new titles, in gross sales, and in the number of authors and publishers represented. After the notoriety of a Congressional investigation of pornography in 1952, the steadily increasing sales of the paperbacks made good news copy.

In 1953, when some twenty publishers sold more than two hundred and fifty million copies of more than one thousand titles, the nation's press began to acknowledge what everyone called the revolution in books. Whether one pointed with pride or viewed with alarm, it became fashionable to talk about books as a mass medium, and to ponder the "cultural gain"—or loss—which resulted from it. In 1955 current titles were first cataloged. There are now more than six thousand paperback titles in print. As early as 1956 the best estimates of the size of this revolution placed the cumulative sales at two billion copies of more than twelve thousand titles. The bookkeeping has not yet caught up with the facts.

Only a few facts are needed, however, to assess the effect of the paperbacks on the novel and its readers. At first these editions were reprints, particularly of fiction. For the first fifteen years of this revolution nine out of every ten paperbacks were novels and more than half of them still are. During this same period the number of novels issued in trade editions, compared to the total number of trade books, has proportionately decreased. To all intents, therefore, the paperbacks furnish the fiction market.

But as long ago as 1950 the shrinking supply of novels in the public domain or on publishers' backlists forced the reprinters to search for other sources of supply. They began to publish non-fiction; they published volumes of short stories (a product with which trade publishers had never succeeded); and by a variety of schemes involving both trade publishers and film companies, the reprinters began to publish original manuscripts. By some lapse of reasoning, however, the publishers disguised the appearance of these various products in such a way that each new book began to look like every other.

Contemporary publishers have not wholly intended this, any more than their predecessors, seventy-five or a hundred years ago, intended to ruin the markets which even then existed for cheap books. In the 1840's inexpensive reprints disguised as subscription items became so flagrant that Congress adjusted the postal laws and put an end to profiteering through low mailing rates. Again in the 1870's cheap books abounded, but with benefit of piracy. For nearly twenty years, until Congress passed the International Copyright Act of 1891, the paperbound reprints increased to a point where they totaled one-third of all the books produced in the United States. But cheap books miscarried again. Even before the copyright legislation, competition had forced reprinters to issue such shoddy products that they lost their market.

This current revival of cheap books exploits some old economic conditions in a new way. The paperbacks are distributed not as books but as magazines. They are produced consequently like magazines and retailed like magazines. They even look like magazines, and the new readers they have found are generally the people who used to read magazines instead of books. The decline of the pulp magazines after the onset of the paperbacks is one symptom of this new readership. Another symptom is the high sale, in paperback editions, of novels which had never sold very well in the bookstores.

The most convincing claim of discovering a new audience can be made by Erskine Caldwell's paperback publisher. Of the forty million copies of Caldwell's books sold to date, thirty-five million have been paperbacks; and most of the rest—including hard-cover reprints and foreign editions—were sold subsequent to the paperbound edition (1946) of *God's Little Acre* (1933; 1946). This appeared thirteen years after its original trade edition (1933), and the reprint sales now total more than seven million copies. By means of paperback editions Caldwell has sold more copies of more novels than any other writer in the world.

This makes books a big business—or Caldwell's books, at any rate. But how many millions make a mass audience? Judging by magazine sales, for instance, the paperback reprints have not yet arrived. More than six million people buy one issue of *Life* or *Reader's Digest*—nearly as many as have bought *God's Little Acre* in the past fourteen years. In television, sponsors have canceled programs which have reached as many as twenty-five million viewers at once. Gross income is another way of estimating the mass market, and by this standard the average paperback novel is a tiny venture compared to the average Hollywood film.

For every book a trade publisher sells, nevertheless, the reprinter sells twelve or fifteen. By book trade standards—whether by cost, sales revenue, or number of purchasers—the paperbound books are on their way to a mass market. Making books for millions instead of thousands has forced publishers to face the vexing problem of preserving the book's individuality. It is the problem of resisting the compromise of mere public acceptance, the compromise of conformity and therefore mediocrity.

The economic organization of paperback publishing creates great pressures toward the conformity of individual books. Reprinting is basically a distributing operation, and the distribution of paperbacks depends crucially on middlemen who can afford no interest in literature except as a commodity. The system really limits the reprint publisher.

The reprinter stands between the trade publisher and the national distributor who sells to wholesalers. His contract with the trade publisher gives him the right to reprint a title and to sell it in certain markets for a limited time at a specified price. For this privilege he pays royalties. On a book retailing for fifty cents the reprinter usually pays two cents each for the first one hundred and fifty thousand copies and a cent-and-a-half thereafter. To secure this contract in the the first place he has had to guarantee a larger advance against royalties than any of his competitors has offered.

The reprinter begins, therefore, by assuming some of the trade publisher's risk. He prints his own edition, realizing that no matter what his break-even figure, he must sell at least thirty thousand copies a year in order to make up the expense of distributing the book. He then consigns the book to wholesalers who warehouse the book and distribute it to retail stores. From the sale of a hypothetical twenty-five-cent book the reprint publisher will ultimately receive fifteen or sixteen cents. Since his cost (for manufacturing, overhead, royalties and shipping) runs to twelve cents a copy, he can count on a net profit of three or four cents—but only after absorbing the cost of unsold copies; and this cost is exorbitant. It takes the profit from eight sales to recover the cost of one return. The cost of over-sales has put dozens of houses out of business.

Everyone who handles the book, from publisher to retailer, works on a narrow margin and depends for his profit on a high volume of sales; but the risk belongs only to the reprint publisher. This curious state of affairs stems from the marriage of convenience which reprint publishers and local wholesalers made during the early years of the present revival of the paperbacks. The reprinter could not afford to distribute his books by mail; and magazine wholesalers, during the War, were short of magazines and needed something to sell. Each needed the other, but the method of wholesaling magazines had been established long before the reprinter came along. The wholesalers did not buy the books, any more than he would buy magazines. He would merely perform for a fee the service of distributing them.

The system is even more limiting to the reprinter. Magazines go out of date; new issues replace old ones. To the wholesalers nothing is quite so dead as the magazine he distributed last week—or the book, for that matter. If last week's book is still in the retailer's rack when he makes his next call, the wholesaler withdraws it in favor of another title, possibly issued by some other reprinter. The publisher must therefore continually issue new titles to replace slow sellers. This system puts a high premium on predictable books. Each new book must offer—or appear to offer—what the last book offered, only more of it. This fact conditions the editorial policy of all paperback publishers.

Each book must appear to have the salable qualities of its predecessors. Since the book must compete for attention with magazine covers as well as with other books, it must also advertise itself on the retailer's racks. The advertising is therefore calculated to make the book stand out—but conventionally. It must demonstrate the same appeal but more blatantly, which explains those few frenetic adjectives on all the eyecatching covers, haranguing the customer like a sideshow barker. The aim is to shock, but shock is only a symptom of the affliction.

The real disorder in the paperback venture is the steady demise of the publisher's editorial prerogative. (The quality paperbacks, on the other hand, retailed as books and not as magazines—for thousands instead of millions of readers—are a different matter.) What has happened to the inexpensive paperbacks—whether they cost twenty-five cents or seventy-five cents—is that the means of distributing a new book now determines what the book shall be. It is of no use to exhort the reprinter to study the needs and tastes of his readers, if, in order to stay solvent, he must continue to produce books which imitate other books with a proven sales value.

You can sense how much the editorial responsibility has been vitiated, by recalling the trade publisher's part in this venture. As originally conceived, the inexpensive reprint business repackaged and redistributed books already published. The trade publisher had already taken editorial responsibility for the book, and his part of the deal consisted merely of assigning certain rights to the reprinter offering the highest down payment. Reprinters still consider it worth while to maintain the appearance of this arrangement, but the nature of the transaction has changed to the point where the trade publisher (desperately needing subsidiary income) now offers a service to the reprinter. The trade publisher knows what kind of books the wholesaler can and cannot sell; if his present list does not include such fare his next list probably will.

Ways and means vary. Before accepting a first novel a publisher customarily solicits bids from reprinters, attempting to find a partner in the venture. With an author's second novel the publisher will certainly consult the house which reprinted the first one. Literary agents play it both ways: offering a manuscript to the trade publisher, having first arranged for the reprint rights; or selling it to the reprinter, who then finds a trade house who will bring it out—or, in trade talk, "famous it up." For the sake of appearances you can argue either way about this and be right. On the one hand, the trade publisher occasionally gets desirable manuscripts he would not otherwise have had. On the other hand, short of a veto, he wields no editorial influence. In fact, the trade publisher becomes the reprinter.

Appearances aside, it makes sense to share the printing cost of a book's several editions, particularly when the cost can be measurably reduced by first printing the pages of the paperback, photo-enlarging them for the pages of the hard-cover edition, and then printing the trade edition by offset. This saves the cost of a second set of printing plates. Although stored and later distributed as a reprint, under this common arrangement the paperback is literally the original.

This confusion of traditional distinctions, and therefore of editorial responsibility, has been further blurred by the economic organization of reprinting firms. In some cases the paperback reprinter is actually a magazine company, and this company's distributing organization handles what its subsidiary "publishes." Fawcett Publications, a magazine house, owns Gold Medal books. Reprints bearing the "Popular Library" imprint are published by the subsidiary of Pines Publications, a producer of magazines and comic books.

Sometimes the imprint of a book bears the title not of the publisher but of the distributing organization, as with Dell books; but the editorial responsibility in this case actually belongs to the manufacturer, Western Printing and Lithography Company, which primarily prints magazines and comic books. The control of another firm, Bantam Books, is even more complicated. This house was organized in 1945 by Grosset and Dunlap, a hard-cover reprinter, and by the Curtis Publishing Company, the magazine publisher which distributes the Bantam products. But one of the partners, Grosset and Dunlap, was already jointly owned by four trade publishers and the Book-of-the-Month Club.

No matter what his auspices, the reprinter has had to deal more and more in original manuscripts. The wholesaler's replacement of old titles every few weeks creates a continual need for new ones. The supply of published novels can no longer meet these needs. Backlists have been depleted and the competition for current wares has driven the prices up; so, to cut costs and to gain some measure of control, the reprinter publishes original manuscripts. "Originals," in fact, now represent a third of the titles published by reprint houses, and this percentage will increase.

This situation offers certain advantages to the author. He gets a better contract from the reprint publisher, retaining all rights but those to the paperbound edition. He keeps all the royalties too, for there is no trade publisher to share them. It also aids the unknown writer, whose first novel might not otherwise have been published. A writer without a reputation is often a liability to the trade publisher but no problem to the reprinter, whose customers are not impressed by reputations anyway.

The reprinter has more control over his product when his product is an "original." He customarily offers an advance on a fragmentary manuscript—several chapters and an outline—reserving final payment until its completion. This is one way of prescribing fiction, although publishers never relish discussing this delicate subject. They prefer to point out merely that writing novels to order rarely proves to be commercially successful. "We don't actually commission fiction," says one reprint publisher, "because writers are better than we are at spotting trends."

Say it however you wish, the author of the paperback original must cut his cloth to fit the pattern. The theory of bulk sales with narrow margins of profit dictates the need for novels which will sell quickly. There are specifications for this, and they are fundamentally like the requisites of magazine fiction. This is no mere coincidence. By design both products sell quickly, by the same means, and to large numbers of customers.

Like magazine fiction, the paperback novel should offer strong story quality, with a prominent conflict and a plot which resolves this conflict by some surprising twist. Also in the manner of the magazines, the paperback must avoid offending recognized political, religious or civic groups; it must avoid esoteric or learned references, and what publishers condescendingly call "literary" style. Without the sponsorship of advertising the paperback can indulge the reader more explicitly in violence and sexual activity, although this is often only superficial to the novel. The appeal of the paperback, as one reprinter puts it, is "basic approach to *basic* problems."

Regardless of the book, this is what the reprinter promises the customer. All over its covers, and inside as well, he strains to show the book's extravagance. What he accomplishes by this is the limitation of each title to the mean level of all the others. The lie is terribly damaging to the book and to the reader. The random sample of 302 American novels, which launched this discussion, raises the question of a monolithic literature. When a novel succeeds on the retailer's racks its cover copy accurately prescribes the specifications for its successors.

This inflated "outside idiom" actually limits what it describes. The language celebrates excess for its own sake. What other message is there except the glut of excess on the paper cover of Meyer Levin's novel, *Compulsion* (1956; 1958)? This copy promises "increasing horror and suspense" about "the crime of the century"; it proclaims the novel and its subject "sensational," "best-selling," "spellbinding," "entertaining," "shocking" (twice), "enlightening," "fascinating," "graphic," "absorbing," "gripping," "provocative" and "startling." "Stunning"—which does not appear—describes the total effect.

There is yet more to the matter. The publishers themselves have raised the question of literary excellence by plastering testimonies to that effect all over their books. Carefully quoted, these claims are attributed to "critics," which is what a publisher calls book reviewers whose testimony happens to suit him. This testimony appears in the language of qualified superlatives. "Masterpiece" and "Classic" perform heavy duty, carefully hedged by disclaimers such as "one of the greatest" or "among the greatest," "perhaps the greatest of all time," or "in the nation" or "in the century." So-and-so, an unknown author who cannot yet qualify for greatness of this magnitude appears instead as a "master story teller" or merely "at his best."

What palls is the utter misrepresentation of a book's contents. The paperback edition of Ernest Hemingway's novel *Across the River and into the Trees* (1950; 1950) is really a collector's item. It carries Tennessee William's affidavit that this is "the best . . . the finest thing that Hemingway has done." But this laughably bad judgment is a mere amateur's try compared to John O'Hara's absurd statement, also quoted on the cover, that Hemingway is "the outstanding author out of the millions who have lived since 1616." When it comes to handing out literary credentials no publisher has yet matched this package, but they are all trying.

The affidavit of literary association on the cover is used to excuse or to justify the book. It also braces up the reader; it is that little extra something which helps the tourist pretend he is traveling first class. The reprint package of Frederic Wakeman's *Shore Leave* (1944; 1948) typically flouts such big-time literary talk. This book has "some of the wise-cracking wit of Hemingway's *The Sun Also Rises*." "It's like an almond-bitter *Farewell to Arms*; a more desperate Hemingway in a more tragic age." About the hero: "All by himself he made up a lost generation."

The blurb in the paperback edition of Erskine Caldwell's *God's Little Acre* likens the hero's lusting after his daughter-in-law to the "Song of Solomon." We are told of *Tobacco Road* (1932; 1947ff) that Jeeter Lester is "heroic in his ineradicable love of the soil, his refusal to leave it for the superior living conditions of the town and its industrial civilization." Something has suddenly happened to the concept of the hero after several thousand years. Every notion of heroism which the modern world has inherited involves awesome power, size or glory; and Jeeter Lester violates every one of these qualities. The blurb accompanying *Georgia Boy* (1943; 1950) similarly patronizes its predecessors. This is asserted to be a classic of American boyhood which will stand beside Hemingway's "My Old Man" and Mark Twain's *Huckleberry Finn*. But the fact that *Georgia Boy* has nothing to do with the juvenile character who tells the stories dismisses the book from this particular hall of fame.

The book publisher has an impeccable answer to this sort of caviling. After all, he did not write these critical claims, he merely displays them. They are all carefully quoted. Nor is there anything new about the extravagance of book reviewing. He is right, of course.

The low state of book reviewing in America has always been attacked by writers, even by reviewers themselves. Nearly 150 years ago John Neal interrupted his novels to sermonize on this subject. E. A. Poe made capital—and good copy—of incompetence and knavery in book reviewing. The whole matter of literary exploitation so bothered Henry Thoreau that in editing the recollections of his Concord River journey he inserted the note that "books are for the most part willfully and hastily written, as parts of a system, to supply a want real or imagined." This sounds like the disdainful comments of Edmund Wilson, Irving

Babbitt, and O. H. Cheney. Testimonial advertising always attempts to manufacture masterpieces where none exist.

The contemporary reprinter, however, has contributed something new to this malpractice—an entire tabloid package which distorts more efficiently than ever before. Comparison by superlative soon exhausts its subject. When such comparison involves two billion packages, more or less, then who can tell from these packages what the contents of any one of them might be? How shall the reader know his purchase? All of these novels look the same—a new kind of instant fiction packaged in two billion compelling sequels to one another.

The reprint publisher concentrates on a quick sale to the customer. The book must sell itself, must catch the attention and lead it rapidly into the story. Its whole presentation builds the habit of buying on impulse, and one way to do this is to promise quick sensation. In this way the reprinter has achieved a large volume of sales, but not necessarily large numbers of customers. As every trade publisher knows, sensation can always be sold to a constant fringe-market, no matter what the subject of the book. Despite this, publishers usually find it better business to slant books toward the wider market of persons who feel more comfortable with the accepted mores. It is just possible, however, that the reprint packages which sell sensation only are purchased by this same fringe of buyers over and over again.

Even assuming that they know their customers, the reprinters (like the trade publishers) have missed the distinction between book buyers and book readers. They have successfully exploited the truism that shallow books catch on quickly, or not at all. But by selling all their novels as instant fiction, they penalize those books which have some complexity. It takes more time to read the novel which demands some reasoning collaboration; therefore, it takes such a novel more time to be talked about and to sell. But the paperback's entire presentation denies this fact. It does so by always encouraging the buyer to expect entertainment without effort.

The presentation usually makes this indiscriminate promise by abridging the contents of the novel into a preview, usually printed on the book's first page but sometimes on the back cover. This preview tells the reader what to look for. It stresses the "becoming" movement of the novel, stating a conflict and raising the question of how the novel will resolve it. The preview insists on some unique excess within this conflict which makes it different from everyday experience and gives it news value.

The preview is journalistic. Like the news story, which telegraphs its climax, the preview keeps the reader going. It even looks like a news story, from the headline and the lead sentence featuring the uniqueness, to the narrative of events, and finally to the occasional details. This newsworthy preview ideally fits those novels which have nothing more to offer than the resolution of a unique series of events.

The preview in the paperback edition (1953) of John O'Hara's *Appointment in Samarra* (1934; 1953), for instance, gives a faithful account of this novel. After a 24-point headline which proclaims a "Fatal Flaw," the lead sentence identifies the hero who passionately loves his wife, but whose character is "flawed by a destructive weakness." Three sentences then paraphrase the action:

In the brief three-day span of this tense ironic novel, Julian's life moves swiftly to its inevitable tragic climax. His downfall begins at a country club dance when he throws a highball in the face of Gibbsville's wealthiest, most powerful man. A drunken encounter with a nightclub singer in a gangster's roadhouse lends its swift momentum, and from a disgraceful brawl in a fashionable men's club through a final, bitter quarrel with his wife, Julian's life spirals downward with dizzying speed.

Another sentence informs the reader how quickly it all happens. And a final statement testifies that the novel is a "modern classic." From beginning to end this preview expands its facts like a news story.

The newsworthy résumé stresses the action and disallows its implications. But because novels differ from one another precisely by these implications, the monolithic preview usually distorts a novel. The paperbound edition (1954) of Walter Van Tilburg Clark's novel, *The Ox-Bow Incident* (1940; 1954), for example, distorts by default. In the customary sequence of headline, lead sentence, synopsis and "expert" literary testimony, it clarifies the story's news value. This is "a powerful novel of the American West"; it is "an unforgettable tale that blazes with the strength and vigor of its setting"; and it is "a searing and exciting story of honest men of action who let their mistaken fury lead them to violence and injustice."

This generality scarcely suggests the novel's real subject, which is the inadequacy of mere virtue in the world. At a kangaroo court, a posse of ranchers has tried and executed three innocent men. Following the "shocking outdoor trial"—where the preview of the narrative stops— the man who has clearly tried to prevent the execution now astonishingly takes the responsibility for it. Convinced of the suspect's innocence, he argues, he has nevertheless joined the posse unarmed, purposely to avoid a showdown with its leader. With this confession the novel then focuses on the other men who have given their frightened consent, as they become aware of their own irresponsible righteousness. These implications of the execution, which the novel is all about, are not even whispered in the preview.

The paperback presentation of Robert Penn Warren's *All the King's Men* (1946; 1951)—"A GREAT NOVEL . . . about great corruption" —similarly overlooks what that novel is all about. The preview features the unscrupulous politics of Willie Stark, who forces one of his employees to double-cross a personal friend. From the moment he does so, "the story moves steadily to its tremendous climax." In this way the preview alludes to Stark's assassination. But the novel's real subject is the pathology of Willie Stark's power, and it is dramatized through the self-realization of a few well-meaning people who, for convincing personal reasons, have sold out to this man.

Self-comprehension is what a novel can best represent, but this is just what the previews omit. Any fiction appraises experience simply by resolving a conflict, but the tremendous possibility of the novel lies in the breadth it has in which to make analogies to this conflict, such as the shared problems of the various ranchers and their victims in *The Ox-Bow Incident*, or of the several employees of Willie Stark in *All the King's Men*. The previews commonly emphasize the action for its own sake, but this merely advertises a book's similarity to all others.

If a preview were to emphasize the action with regard to its particular implications, on the other hand, it would advertise the book's individuality. The difference would be more than a matter of altering words here and there; it would mean changing the preview's point of view to accommodate the book itself instead of the reader's assumed tastes. And this is all the difference in the world.

See how obviously the reprinter limits what the novelist offers in the first paperback edition of Nathanael West's *Miss Lonelyhearts* (1933). After a screaming headline ("Dear Miss Lonelyhearts, HELP ME . . ./ HELP ME . . ./ HELP ME, PLEASE!!!") the preview informs the reader that this is the lovelorn column of a big city newspaper, "and when 'Miss Lonelyhearts' turns out to be a *man*—the result is bound to be both explosive and shocking." But the shock and explosiveness have nothing to do with the gender in the title; the novel's opening sentence settles that. The point of the book is not that Miss Lonely-hearts "turns out to be a man," but that he turns out to be a man with a Christ-complex, whose inability to cope with human misery out-rages and destroys him. The novel so far exceeds the reprinter's dis-torted promise that the preview might better be placed between the covers of another book. In any case, it has been dropped from the later printings of this one.

This limiting journalism of the reprinters even extends to tabloid reading-guides on the cover itself, to help the reader make up his mind. Thus, the retitled paper edition *The Night Before Dying* (1955) of Robert M. Coates's *Wisteria Cottage* (1948; 1955), saves the reader time:

Louisa—haughty, love-hungry with claws of steel/ Elinor—warm, allur-ing, and very, very soft/ Florence—shrewd, calculating, and too fond of young men/ THESE THREE:/ caught up in the web of rage and contempt spun by the twisted mind of Richard Baurie, the youth who deceived them all and then, step by terrifying step, directed their lives down the path to explosive violence.

What more do we need? One more step and we can get through a book without reading it. The paper edition (1952) of J. P. Marquand's *Point of No Return* (1949; 1952) admirably performs this final chore in a paragraph of illuminated writing, with pictures punctuating the prose.

Here is Charles Gray, (   ) still dreaming his dreams of his lost, lovely Jessica, (   ) living out his life in quiet desperation, with his nice wife, (   ) and their two kids, (   ) (   ) in their Connecticut home. (   ) The boundaries of Charley's life are home, the country club (   ) where he plays golf, the bank (   ) where he works.

Another paragraph states—but without informing—what the hero's universal problem really is:

Here is the poignant story of a man imprisoned in the grip of circumstances beyond his control—a man caught in the net of his own daily life. POINT OF NO RETURN is a beautiful, powerful and universal novel, by one of America's greatest writers—(   ) JOHN P. MARQUAND.

This nonsense is the result of economic cause. The present revival of inexpensive paperbacks owes its existence to a particular method of distribution, and the books themselves have been tailored to accommodate it. This method of bookselling has caused remarkable changes in the form of the novel itself but more obviously in the representation of the whole idea of literature. The latter consequence deserves a close look, for the reprinter has become a taste-maker.

Put yourself in his shoes. In order to tell the reader what to look for and to condition him for more of the same, you must ignore or misrepresent the relative worth of the individual book. This is true even if you are publishing the works of a single novelist, particularly if he happens to be a best seller. Once committed to an author, once started on this market-building program, the publisher cannot countenance the difference between artistic success and failure, even though this difference may be vast. He must press all these works into the same shape and appearance.

The collected reprints of Erskine Caldwell decisively illustrate this. More copies of his books have been sold than of any other novelist. Caldwell is one of the monoliths of the reprint business; even by its own standards his gross sales are extraordinary. Since 1946 his twenty-five paperbound novels and short-story volumes have so far sold thirty-five million copies. In addition to the seven million copies of *God's Little Acre* four of his other novels have each sold between three million and five million copies; the sales of two others are approaching three million; and five more of his titles have sold over a million.

Caldwell can explain this sales record in his own obtuse way. "My grandfather, who had the reputation for telling the biggest whoppers ever heard in Sycamore County, Georgia, used to tell me that his stories were actually no better than hundreds told by others, but that he had learned how to raise interest to the point where people would begin nudging one another in anticipation when they saw him coming down the street." The advertising copy on his own books has the same effect.

The blurbs in his reprinted novels and short stories make interesting reading. They repeatedly claim for their various contents nothing less than the entire aesthetic range at the same time. One novel achieves "a matchless gift for portraying comedy and tragedy"; another, "the matchless blend of comedy and tragedy"; still another is "funny, earthy, tragic." His first book, *Tobacco Road*, offers "humor, tragedy, horror and pathos," and *Episode in Palmetto* (1950; 1953), published twenty-five years later, is a "moving mixture of the comedy and tragedy of everyday life." *Ths Sure Hand of God* (1947; 1949) is a "riotous, bawdy, and sometimes tragic story"; and the episodes in *Gulf Coast Stories* (1957) "range from bawdy comedy to quiet tragedy."

The impression is inescapable that this author offers all things to all readers. In fact, this is just what the preview in *God's Little Acre* asserts. "What accounts for the extraordinary appeal of this book?" the copy writer candidly wonders. "The answer, the critics say, lies in its humanity which offers every reader the kind of reading experience he prefers." Everybody wins a prize. "If it's laughter you like, it's here in abundance; if it's social significance, you'll find that too; if you seek insight into the lives of people who may seem very different to you, it's here. And if you're looking for good writing, Erskine Caldwell is one of the best literary craftsmen of our generation."

If you sense the splendid equivocation in this marketese you are on the right track. In fact, the copy writers are not alone in their puzzlement over Caldwell's fiction. Its tone is undeniably ambiguous. The author disdains public comment about it, by himself or by anyone else; and there is no substantial appraisal of it. No one has yet contradicted these claims.

There is reason for this reticence. Caldwell's autobiography, *Call It Experience* (1951; 1956), says nothing significant about his writing, although his comments in another volume do get to the point. For the trade edition of a collection of short stories, called *Jackpot* (1940), his publisher prevailed upon him to write a series of prefaces, and Caldwell wrote seventy-five statements ranging from a sentence to a paragraph—including that one about his grandfather—which parody the art of prefacing. In its entirety one of these prefaces reads: "If Professor Perkins would relax, he might at least get a little fun out of some of these stories." And later: "If Professor Horatio Perkins is still leafing through these pages, I hope he will not become discouraged and give up. Even if he does not succeed in discovering the secret of writing fiction, at least he will find comfort in the knowledge that the author himself is up a similar tree."

In one of these prefaces Caldwell explains how he parries polite questions about his work. Once a year he jots down ten or fifteen titles, and every three or four weeks he writes a story for one of them. It saves the trouble of looking around for titles afterward. As this straight-faced lie might indicate, Caldwell likes shaggy-dog stories. His fiction is just as shaggy.

This sort of remark, like his fiction, puts the critic off. Despite generous reviewing, Caldwell's fiction has received only scant critical attention, for two good reasons. His fiction has made a great deal of money, which tends to embarrass academic criticism; and it is often funny—terribly funny—but without any obvious significance. His stories are not satires; they encourage no social program; and such undirected humor embarrasses academic spokesmen. Caldwell has even affected dismay over the interpretation of his writing as humorous, thereby adding another hair to the shaggy dog.

Erskine Caldwell writes fantasies about improbable people. He writes about grotesques who understand one another but who are out of touch with the rest of the world, like the crackers and the hillbillies he grew up knowing. They are incongruous characters: they take irrelevant matters seriously, and they take the momentous for granted. They somewhat resemble the characters in medieval *fabliaux*, such as those Chaucer's Reeve and Miller and Summoner tell about, or the rogues in Fielding's or Smollett's novels. But Caldwell's fiction has more of an animus, like the tall tale which insults the listener, such as Mark Twain learned from his newspaper colleagues.

Caldwell caricatures these peculiar people. Except for a few bold details the reader must complete them for himself and make his own assessment. The author merely tells anecdotes about them. He discloses, without developing, a situation. He writes in *Journeyman* (1935; 1947), of the man who bets his father-in-law's watch in a crap game, covers it with his automobile, then his wife—and loses them all. He writes of a father, in *Tragic Ground* (1944; 1948), who calls at a brothel to take his daughter home, forgets his errand, and stays the night. He tells of the fun-loving widow, in *The Sure Hand of God* (1947; 1949), who entertains her gentlemen callers with a hypo of what she believes to be vitamins. The implications of these anecdotes, however, become the reader's responsibility.

These are typical anecdotes, bizarre and toneless. The quality of every one of his novels depends on the extent to which such anecdotes become analogies, or to which they develop the implications of one another. In one of his prefaces to *Jackpot* Caldwell writes, "I have a great respect for my grandfather's method of criticism. To him a story was either a humdinger or God-awful." And these are precisely the alternatives of Caldwell's own novels.

The least of his novels are merely literal repetitions of anecdotes. In the best of them, however, the anecdotes variously enforce one another and evolve a meaning beyond any one of them. By literal repetition Caldwell's improbable people become impossible, inert characters. But when the episodes vary, they suggest a whole world in which these improbable people come alive. This distinction marks Caldwell's novels far more fundamentally than the superficialities of subject matter on which the copy writers continually harp.

Trouble in July (1940; 1945) is Caldwell's finest novel; *This Very Earth* (1948; 1951) is one of his worst. Their subjects are utterly different. But you would never guess these differences from the paperback blurbs. The news-story preview of each novel promises the display of some sociological problem: one of race hatred and the other of juvenile delinquency. The prose of both blurbs is charged with hormones. One teaser features the dishonesty of "an over-sexed, promiscuous girl," and the other features a girl's vexing hunger for a man, "to keep from being lonely." The advertising marvelously disguises the facts.

Trouble in July tells of a man-hunt which ends in two murders. One is the lynching of an innocent Negro accused of raping a white girl. The other is the execution of this girl who has wrongfully accused the Negro. The lynchers stone her to death. The horror of this story is its believability. These obsessed characters do come alive, as the novel reveals a state of mind that prevails in their world. Their awesome stupidity is incongruous with any outside sense of values; but the wild, fanciful anecdotes which comprise the novel have so diversified brutish irresponsibility that these characters seem capable of anything.

The anecdotes complement one another. The irrelevant indulgences of the characters can be ludicrous and laughable or terrible, depending on the circumstances. The fat sheriff "wants to keep the lynching politically clean" to avoid publicly declaring himself for this Negro against the white men whose votes he will need. But he also wants to keep up appearances, so he locks himself in jail on the fatal evening to make it seem as though the lynchers had forced him out of action. It develops, however, that in the dark he has locked himself in the wrong cell, with a mulatto woman in whose company his wife and the lynching party later discover him.

Another episode concerns the argument between the village barber and Shep Barlowe, the girl's father, over how to conduct the lynching. They start to fight with knives, and when an old man tries to restore the peace they knock him down and presumably kill him. The old man's fate is not clear, however, since no further mention is made of him. Still another episode recalls how Shep Barlowe behaved when his wife died. She disappeared one day, upsetting his whole routine, and his temper lasted a week before he set out to find her. When he finally did discover her corpse at the bottom of the well, he threw all his cordwood down after her.

No editorializing accompanies these anecdotes, but they complement one another. They develop the conviction of a kind of mass mind that can hang or stone—or bury in cordwood—anyone who opposes it. Even so, the Negro might have escaped had he not stopped to feed his rabbits; and the girl wishes she could bring herself to tell the men about her mistake. Thus, the novel cumulates the sense of monstrous incongruity peculiar to a lynching.

The sadism in *This Very Earth* is no more costly, no more horrible. It is just not believable. The reason is that this novel's anecdotes literally and categorically repeat one another, and nothing relieves the constant extremity. In this book a man named Chism Crockett has resigned his life to the indulgence of his own passion, which includes the exploitation and the torture of his children. He gets his eleven-year-old son drunk and makes the boy watch him fornicate. He blackmails one of his daughters and tries to exploit a love affair of the other. The man has no more motive than the white girl has in *Trouble in July*. But this novel lacks the various disclosure that might imply a cause.

Chism Crockett merely and literally repeats himself throughout *This Very Earth*, and so do the other characters. Chism's son-in-law is seen almost exclusively in the act of beating his wife (the only development being that he finally beats her to death). Chism's son and Chism's father are also caricatures; they also exist without living. One repeatedly tries to reason with Chism and the other repeatedly harangues him. All the characters affect concern over whether Chism should stay in the city or move back to the country so that his children can have a wholesome life—as though this had anything to do with his behavior. These characters exist only by the author's assertion, and each one compounds the felony by imitating himself. There is no cause or consequence in their actions, and no reason in the novel.

By insisting on the sensations of one of Chism's daughters—the "Bad Girl" who is "too free and easy . . . to keep out of trouble"—the preview in the paperback edition of *This Very Earth* suggests a rationale the novel does not have. This is true of the presentation of most of Caldwell's novels. The advertising insists on the vitality of sex or sin, but the novels disclose no such vitality. The fiction contains characters who literally repeat their own excesses, and this goes unassessed by any other behavior. The fault is not in the sexuality but in the unbelievable self-sameness.

Once, long ago, Caldwell did build a convincing novel about this goatish concupiscence. In *God's Little Acre* the members of Ty Ty Walden's family live and die by lust. The beautiful Griselda inspires Ty Ty's embarrassingly funny rhetoric, her brother-in-law's animalism, an absurdly futile pursuit by another in-law, and a murder by her jealous husband. These irregularities cause Ty Ty continually to lament God's unfortunate error in creating animal and human in the same being, and Ty Ty's laments reveal the shrewd stupidity by which these people justify themselves.

Ty Ty's denial of his tithe, by moving God's Little Acre expediently out of the way of each prospective gold mine on his property, dramatizes the fallibility of these characters. He has so often violated the Third Commandment that when the murder happens to occur on God's Little Acre, lately removed from the site of the newest dig, the coincidence becomes a retribution. By their various distortions these ludicrous anecdotes develop an idea about the rationalization of hate and desire which can put an end to everything.

· But this was many years and many novels ago, and as each new reprint reminds the purchaser that it is written "by the author of *God's Little Acre*," the irony in the gross implication becomes more painfully obvious. The case of Erskine Caldwell is typical. Every reprinter promises more of the same, no matter who the author or what the book happens to be.

There is an old joke in the book trade about the person who asks, "Why should I buy a book? I already have one." But this turns out to be a pretty expensive joke. The reprinters' distortion of their products has encouraged just this sort of inertia. With the narrow margin of profit, every reprinter understands the vast effect of a small change. A half cent a copy, even for one printing, can mean the difference of thousands of dollars. The reprinter is used to this kind of arithmetic and to the need for precision, but he overlooks the comparable effect of small changes in the literary quality of his product. This is a curious oversight, since he himself makes such pretension of displaying a book's literary credentials.

It is irrelevant to ask why the reprinter does not publish better books. He publishes the best he can find, commensurate with the risks of a large-volume business. In this particular matter of conscience he can probably sleep better at night than the trade publisher. But by marketing his wares all as the same product he distorts the books he does publish. Every novel is the extension of its author—it is individual. The value of a novel lies in this significant difference, within the experience everyone shares. But the reprinter denies this.

The parrot-like salesmanship of the reprint business contradicts itself. It denies the possibilities of the distribution system. Since the basis of the business is the rapid turnover of many titles—with very little display room in which to sell—the reprinter must attract attention to each book. To this purpose the individuality of a book is naturally congenial. It is even strategic in finding new readers. But by ignoring or disguising this individuality the reprinter encourages the reader to limit every book that he does buy to what the reprinter says it is.

Meanwhile the image grows of a literature so parochial that all its books render the same experience, that all are equally "poignant" and "powerful," "brutal" and "compassionate," and that one can do the job as well as another.

Chapter VII

After Marquand, the Deluge

IF A NOVEL convinces readers of what they want to believe anyway, chances are it will succeed commercially. If it informs or instructs the reader at the same time then it can be readily excused for being fiction and for being successful. This takes some doing.

The image of such fiction—of an entire literature of such fiction, in fact—is what the inexpensive paperbacks attempt to sell. But paperback advertising merely extends to more books the implication of qualities magazine fiction and movie fiction actually possess. The magazines and the movies have stylized the novel form to make it serve acceptable attitudes without seeming to.

The fiction in both these media stresses a sharp, definable conflict which will surprisingly resolve in a favorable manner. To help disguise this fortuity, to make it seem convincing, this fiction offers a superficial authenticity of costumes, setting, speech and manners. More important, such fiction contains no analogies which would test or evaluate the conflict. A single encounter exists by itself, solved or "proven" in its own terms, with all the absolute value of a cat's-cradle.

These are permanent qualities of the stylized fiction of the magazines and the movies. Making the illusion convincing is a matter of making the conflict localize some large, public, and usually urgent difference of opinion; and there are as many ways of doing this as there are writers. But there is usually a similarity in ways and means from one fiction to another.

This is a sore point with all writers. Although there is always a continuity of ideas and techniques in any art form (no writer can achieve what he does without others who have gone before him), any author resents it when his work is made into some facile equation with the work of others. In his preface to *The Butterfly* James M. Cain spoke for the majority of writers when he said, "Schools don't help the novelist, but they do help the critic; using as the mucilage the simplifications that the school hypothesis affords him, he can paste labels wherever convenience is served by pasting labels. . . ." Cain straightened out the critics, "these strange surrogates for God," in this elemental matter. "You're really being a little naïve, you know. We don't do it that way. We don't say to ourselves that some lucky fellow did it a certain way, so we'll do it that way too, and cut in on the sugar. We have to do it our way, each for himself, or there isn't any sugar."

The novelist writes as he is, no doubt. But that is only half the story. His work is published under auspices which deny this spirited principle of individuality. "Imitation by publishers has become an increasingly frequent cause of intensified competition," O. H. Cheney's *Survey* informed the trade in 1931. In a chapter entitled "The Book, The Buyer, and The Critic," Cheney wrote of this compulsive publishing which causes disastrous overstocks: "two or three simultaneous books on some English poet or French beauty, seven simultaneous biographies of a football coach, hordes of books on Russia. Even if everyone of the books were good, what good would it be?"

This is not just a problem of quantity. By a calculated imitation the book trade sells books by disguising whatever individuality they have. Publishers think of books in categories and exploit any association they can. A book's entire presentation is usually aimed at cashing-in on some previous success. This is almost a matter of superstition among publishers. It even extends to the titling of books.

When Alfred Knopf published Kurt W. Marek's exciting study of archeology (under the pseudonym of C. W. Ceram) and entitled it *Gods, Graves, and Scholars* (1951), it sold startlingly well. When they were sure of its success other publishers moved in. Knopf had apparently uncovered more of a cache than his archeologist had. The University of Oklahoma Press happened to release a study by Joseph L. Smith, entitled *Tombs, Temples & Ancient Art* (1956). But the three-decker alliterative title had already been rediscovered in Leo Gurko's *Heroes, Highbrows and the Popular Mind* (Bobbs-Merrill, 1953) and Paul Wellman's *Glory, God, and Gold* (Doubleday, 1954).

"God" was a frequent partner in this multitude of success stories. Henry Armstrong's autobiography, *Gloves, Glory, and God* (F. H. Revell, 1956) was followed by Howard E. Kershner's *God, Gold, and Government* (Prentice-Hall, 1957); by George Ashbaugh's story of the Mormons, *Gods, Sex, and Saints* (Augustana, 1957), and by W. H. D. Rouse's *Gods, Heroes and Men of Ancient Greece* (New American Library, 1957). Prentice-Hall was still at it with the title of William E. Hulme's book, *God, Sex & Youth* (1959).

If a three decker title cannot accommodate "God," then the next best thing is alliteration. *Rogues, Royalty, and Reporters* (Houghton Mifflin, 1956), by William B. Ewald, appeared in the same year as *Zoomies, Subs, and Zeros* (Greenberg), by Charles A. Lockwood and Hans C. Adamson, and *Magic, Myth, and Medicine* (World), by Donald T. Atkinson. An anthology of crime, *Murder, Mayhem and Mystery* (Barnes, 1958), edited by Alan Hynd, followed them to market, along with *Blondes, Brunettes, and Bullets* (McKay, 1957), by Nils T. Granlund.

Even if publishers could not work in "God" or alliteration, there was still the magic trinity of *Gods, Graves, and Scholars*. Louis Paul's *Heroes, Kings, and Men* (Dial, 1955) and Grillot De Givry's *Witchcraft, Magic and Alchemy* (Books, 1958), attest to this. And if one trinity is not enough there is always the sub-title, as demonstrated by William Irvine's *Apes, Angels, and Victorians; The Story of Darwin, Huxley, and Evolution* (McGraw-Hill, 1955). Real originality frightens most publishers, to the detriment of their books. There is more than just the reassuring likeness of these titles. Most of the books ended up being hawked for a few cents in the mail catalogues of the "remainder" houses.

This is the way publishers herd their products. When a book does find a market it will surely be followed by others like it—or as nearly like it as their publishers can make them seem. This explains the domestic novels which clustered after Susan Warner's *The Wide, Wide World* (1850), the novels of ethical religion which flocked after *Rob-*

ert Elsmere (1888), or the vogue in fat historical novels which *Anthony Adverse* (1933) and *Gone with the Wind* (1936) revived. But these are merely some obvious cases of what goes on all the time.

Whether an author belongs to any "school" does not much matter —his publisher will enroll him in one. A successful book has always created a market for more like it, and there are always writers willing to gratify the demand. The evidence of these clustered books is always the same; their mannerism deteriorates the original appeal. They caricature those qualities in the original which were presumed to make it sell in the first place. Sometimes the mannered imitations even caricature one another.

There are different ways to describe this syndrome. Alfred Knopf has described it in terms of the difficulty of publishing the works of new authors. "One of the reasons . . . is that they have to compete dollar for dollar in retail price with works of a similar kind and length by the best-established authors." (Knopf printed this in *The Borzoi Quarterly*, Second Quarter, 1957.) As he put it, it is a case of the reader buying a sure thing or buying a risk. "In other words you can buy five or six hundred pages of a new novel by John P. Marquand and know just exactly what you are going to get, or pay the same price for a book of the same length by someone you never read and have never heard of, which book may utterly disappoint you after fifty pages." One expedient remedy, of course, is to minimize the risk, to make the new novel sound like one of John Marquand's. This would be mannerism.

Wherever you find fiction directed toward a timely subject you will find mannered novels. A good bet for a timely subject is business and the businessman; and most business novels display obsequious mannerism. For the past ten or twelve years the magazines have given business novels devoted attention. Every few months pedants gather, sort, and classify attitudes in novels to discover whether or not the author really approves of his hero. The polls have nothing really to say about fiction, since fictional attitudes cannot be classified as though they were actual. Only rarely can readers agree on thematic niceties in any competent and reasonably complex novel. Aside from what they attempt to prove, however, the polls do reflect a lively interest in the business novel.

It is not a new but a continuing interest. American business novels began to appear after the Civil War, when it looked as though industrial capitalism would destroy the ideology of an inherited democratic and agrarian way of life. Machines, technological unemployment, and the pressures that heavy capital could exert apparently threatened to annihilate free enterprise. Some novels dramatized the moral problems of making money; some exposed business malpractices; a few worried over the threat of a powerful proletariat; most of them localized the love-and-duty conflict in a business setting and steered clear of ideas. But right from the start American business novels capitalized on the public sense of urgency about their subject.

By 1900 novelists could count on the widespread distrust of business, particularly of Big Business. The many-sided transactions of financial capitalism had presented new opportunities for fees, confused the notion of profits, and increased the suspicion that the middleman was growing disproportionately rich. The Congressional investigation of the money trust, in 1912 and 1913, consequent to J. P. Morgan's organization of the General Electric, United States Steel and International Harvester companies, reflected the popular suspicion of Big Business. Almost continuously investigated by state legislatures, after its organization in 1870, the Standard Oil Corporation was already a national scapegoat by 1902, when Ida M. Tarbell's exposés of it began to appear in *McClure's Magazine*.

Muckraking journalism increased the market for economic fiction. Novelists could represent business transactions with the assurance of both knowledgeable and partisan readers. Fiction and journalism were often scarcely distinguishable. Upton Sinclair insisted that *The Jungle* (1906), his novel about the meat-packing industry, had the validity of a sociological study. The economic novels of Robert Herrick, Frank Norris and Theodore Dreiser were just as stoutly documented.

Publishers worked the appeal both ways. Charles Edward Russell, a New York reporter, published a factual report on the meat-packing industry, *The Greatest Trust in the World* (1905). It was a series of magazine articles documented by maps, tables and graphs, and reproductions of forged trade bills. But aware of readers' wishes, the publisher advertised the book as a "tragic romance of modern business life."

The methods of newspaper reporting and a strong editorial legacy account for the distinctive qualities of American business novels. Their subject is always timely, and their tone is urgent. In both respects they have kept pace with the vast transformations in the business world since the end of the nineteenth century. New industries with new products for new markets have helped revolutionize financing, distribution and selling, as well as manufacture. Through all these changes the economic novel has kept tabs on the businessman's response to business.

Business novels still worry over the fact that business swallows up the individual, but they have updated the subject. In the timely versions of this plight the individual's impotence is inevitable. Being swallowed up, in fact, is the only way to succeed in business. Keeping up with the times, therefore, contemporary business novels are devoted to the pathology of success.

Mannerism begins to show up in the novels over the attitudes they urge toward this presumed inevitability of success. Popular fiction always turns out to have gratified people's wishes in an apparently convincing way. Popular fiction in America has always been in the peculiar position of having to justify success. The business novel is a persistent, local instance of this.

Success can be indiscriminately applauded, which is easy to do; it can be rationalized as inevitable and therefore right, which is a little more involved; or it can be explained, which is still more complex. Among contemporary business novels, the first which gained any popularity by trying to explain this inevitability was John Marquand's *Point of No Return* (1949). The present pathology of success in business novels really began with this book, which made a great many, and many different, audiences aware of a situation; and it made a singular impression on the book trade. In the flood of business novels which deluged the market after *Point of No Return* even the waves had waves.

After appearing in abridged form in the *Atlantic* and then as a five-part serial in *Ladies' Home Journal* the novel was published in 1949. During the summer of that year the Book-of-the-Month Club offered it as a dividend. Grosset & Dunlap then published two editions of *Point of No Return;* and by the time Bantam's first paperbound edition appeared in 1952 well over a half-million copies had already been sold through trade, book-club, and reprint distribution. Later in 1952 the book was adapted to the stage and began a year's run on Broadway.

The success of Marquand's business novel gave point to Alfred Knopf's remark (which he originally made in 1951) about buying a sure thing when you buy Marquand's books. Although not sensational, the book's sales were high, and they reflected the steady buying of distinctly different markets. The fact that eight different publishers have since anthologized parts of the novel indicates its appeal to a variety of tastes and judgments. Also, it had created this appeal at a time of a rising market for novels in paperbound editions. Mannerism was one obvious result. Clusters of business novels thematically similar to *Point of No Return* began to appear in the early fifties.

Point of No Return provided a point of departure for most of its successors. It dramatized a situation many novels have subsequently caricatured by exaggerating and simplifying it. But Marquand took a satirical—not a popular—view of his subject, and the mannerists, avoiding this view, have ended up with attitudes which do not fit the situation.

Marquand's novel dramatizes Charles Gray's career in the Stuyvesant Bank to that climactic point when he learns whether he or Roger Blakesley is to become the bank's newest vice-president. The job will ultimately lead to the presidency, and each man has committed himself and his family to a war of attrition for a prize which only one of them can have. It would seem so simple: Gray has an adversary competing with him for the favor of the bank's president, Tony Burton, yet this exhaustive personal conflict turns out to be irrelevant.

Gray realizes he cannot reduce the bank to any manageable or satisfying terms. "The Stuyvesant was the aggregate of the character of many individuals, who merged a part of their personal strivings and ambitions into a common effort." Gray conjures up metaphors to explain the bank to himself. "It was like a head of living coral rising above the surf, a small outcropping of a greater reef." And all of its individuals, from the doorman to the directors, "were . . . asses following their bundles of hay." "They were all on an assembly line, but you could not blame the line. It was too cumbersome, too inhumanely human for anyone to blame."

A few pages before the end of the novel, Gray is still trying to appraise it all. He and his wife have been invited to dine at Burton's home, obviously to be told the fate of his career. After a few more hours of attrition for the Grays, in social small talk with the boss and his wife, the gentlemen retire to the library, and Gray concentrates on the imminent disaster. In that short walk across the hall, "he was actually walking . . . over the road of his career, a feeble little human track like the progress of a sea creature in the sand."

Having seen his own tiny image, Gray begins to adjust to it. His career is as good as over, and he must retreat to a new position. He and his wife will sell their suburban house and move into a smaller place; they will give up their plans for the more exclusive country club and for private schools. He begins to realize how tired he has been. He will never have to try so hard again, or be so cautious or obsequious. Then a deep sense of relief overcomes him. " 'It's over,' he said to himself as he walked across the hall. 'Thank God, it's over.' It was the first time he had felt really free." But the shocking news of success explodes this peace.

Gray suddenly learns that he has won the job, in a manner that stuns him. Burton casually announces the fact, then shows surprise that there should even be any doubt. There has been no conflict between Gray and Blakesley as far as the Bank is concerned. "You never thought any of us were considering Blakesley seriously, did you?" Blakesley was just not the right material; and as for the vice-presidency, says Burton, "it never occurred to me that you'd have any doubts about it."

It paralyzes Gray to learn that he has never had any control of the situation, that he has no more power to refuse the honor than he had in winning it. He feels dull and very tired. He foresees a new professional friendship with his employer, and transactions for a larger house, a new car, a more exclusive country club. Even before the end of the conversation he realizes he has never left the treadmill.

Gray has made no decision. His success, already decided for him, is analogous to his entire life. He cannot even discover where the point of no return occurred. There has been no point at all, but a line stretching back into his past, across which he could never step.

Growing up in a small New England village, Charles Gray has always known the primitive rituals of the caste system. But "system" means more in this book than merely social stratification. To Gray's father, for instance, it has meant the arrangement of one's whole economic existence. "The system is not fluid and it is very hard to beat," he says. "What system?" Charles asks. "Why, the system under which we live. . . . The order. There's always some sort of order."

The hero's father has cultivated an independence in social matters which has made him an eccentric to the rest of the community, as if he were trying to beat the system by scorning it; then, following the loss of an inherited fortune on the stock market, he proves his point by suicide. The son absorbs the lesson; as he later explains to his wife: "There's no use getting mad at the system. We're part of a system where there's always someone waiting to kick you in the teeth in a nice way." Gray solves the system by acceding to it, and the plot of the novel bears him out.

Charles Gray's debilitating success dramatizes the peculiar course of literary naturalism in America. You can see how small the businessman has shrunk when you measure Gray by another hero, Silas Lapham, about whom William Dean Howells wrote, sixty-four years earlier. The comparison is useful. The Rise of Silas Lapham (1885) presents a hero with a moral problem, involving financial success or failure, which he resolves by himself. Howells idealizes the individual's control of affairs, and thereby hangs another tale.

Silas Lapham manufactures a paint whose excellence has made him wealthy, and he determines to use this wealth to improve his family's social position. But Lapham has made a costly compromise with his conscience, having forced out of partnership the man whose money he once needed. When this partner returns and asks for help, Lapham's wife prevails on her husband to pay off his conscience. The ex-partner is dishonest, but Lapham pointedly ignores the bad risk and loans him large amounts just before his paint business begins to fail.

The hero must capitalize his business or go bankrupt, but he has loaned his capital and spent his credit. At this point the ex-partner reappears, having found some purchasers for the land Lapham holds as collateral on the loans, and which both men know to be worthless. The hero's dilemma is clear: to sell the land and recover his loss, or to refuse to sell and save the other party, and the author subjects him to all the tortures of righteousness.

Lapham spends the night pacing his room, and Howells likens his struggle to Jacob wrestling with the angel. Like Jacob, following the struggle, Lapham finds peace. He has victoriously decided to go bankrupt. Virtue triumphs. He loses the battle to win the great moral war.

The picture of this Victorian businessman wrestling with the angel apparently gratified the women who read the novel and dreamed of what a virtuous world it would be if their husbands would only listen to them. The fun of justifying success consisted in deciding the terms on which one would accept it. But what made the dream convincing was the assumption, which Howells shared with his readers, that man was a free agent in the first place.

Marquand and his readers share no such luxury. Within the literary history which contains both novels the fact of "scientific" determinism separates them. Toward the end of the nineteenth century, this doctrine became incorporated in a theory of composition known as literary naturalism, which aimed to document determinism in copious and authentic detail. With the illusion of complete objectivity, according to this theory, the novelist would prove that the individual man is a small and limited creature, determined by heredity or by the social or economic forces of his environment.

No one has yet written the novel which could perfectly conform to Emile Zola's definition of this theory—not even Zola. Because naturalism denies any special significance to human beings, it therefore denies the vitality of fiction. Nevertheless, the prestige of literary naturalism in Germany and France, the translation of Zola's literary criticism into English, and American fiction's affair with journalism have so influenced writers that virtually every economic novel in America after 1900 at least implies some reference to naturalism.

This theory reflects the change in the businessman from an active hero to a passive one, from a Silas Lapham to a Charles Gray. Business history records substantial cause for the extinction of a Silas Lapham from the business world. Lapham was an entrepreneur, owner and manager. During the twentieth century, however, business organization outgrew his kind. With the development of the great public corporations, even before World War I, ownership and control began to separate and to offer disparate images to the public mind.

During the thirties the concept of ownership changed as Big Business strenuously publicized the notion of a people's capitalism, dependent on many small stockholders. As for control, people gradually heard about a new kind of businessman, called the administrator. Here was a new image of the businessman. The image was anticipated by Adolphe A. Berle and Gardiner C. Means in their epochal study, *The Modern Corporation and Private Property* (1932). They discovered that some two hundred non-banking corporations dominated the national economy and that the control of these corporations lay not in their legal owners, the stockholders, but in their executive managers.

Manuals of business management sold briskly as early as the 1920's. By the time of World War II, James Burnham's *The Managerial Revolution* (1941) dramatized the new apotheosis of business administrators. The nation, said Burnham, must now acknowledge business managers as a new social group. This new professional manager actually controlled the instruments of production. But even the manager was only an employee. He had no function by himself. He was only a unit of the great business society.

No wonder Charles Gray sees himself as a small sea animal and the Stuyvesant Bank as the outcropping of a reef. *Point of No Return* uniquely represents its times, as Howells' novel once did. But in Marquand's view Charles Gray's promotion to the Bank's vice-presidency is distressing. This is where Marquand's successors part company with him. But they don't part very straight.

These mannerists exaggerate the plight of the businessman overcome by success, but they avoid any honest dilemma over it. Instead, they celebrate it. Their main problem, therefore, is to make it look as though there were a problem in the first place between the businessman and this benevolent business system. The best way to see this mannerism at work is to compare some of the caricatures of the passive businessman which followed *Point of No Return* to market.

Between 1952 and 1956, the five years during which the first paper-bound edition of Marquand's novel remained in print, the most commercially successful business novels were Cameron Hawley's *Executive Suite* (1952) and *Cash McCall* (1954), Howard Swiggett's *The Power and the Prize* (1954), and Sloan Wilson's *The Man in the Gray Flannel Suit* (1955). All of these books appeared in paperbound editions, two of them had additional book-club sales, and all of them were adapted to motion pictures. Each earned more for its author than John Marquand's novel had earned.

These books variously emphasize the most recognizable qualities of *Point of No Return*. A fifth novel, published during this period, is George DeMare's *The Empire—and Martin Brill* (1956). This novel amplifies the qualities of *Point of No Return* as well as those in its four other predecessors. But all of these latter novels are eclectic; they are all stylized.

The narratives differ. In all of them, however, a particular business enterprise becomes both the emblem and index of "the system." And most of them have inflated the net assets and size of the business and its control over the individual. The change from "company" to "corporation" and then to "empire" suggests their magnification of the system. Even Howard Swiggett's *The Power and the Prize*, the most apparently humanistic of them all, insinuates a benevolent determinism by a board of directors.

Swiggett's novel tells about Cleves Barwick, the executive officer of Allied Metals Corporation, and his endeavor to form an international company that will revolutionize the world production of nonferrous metals. But Barwick falls in love with a woman of whom the chairman of the board cannot approve. A refugee from Central Europe and a suspected Communist sympathizer, she would presumably become a liability to the Corporation. The chairman discredits Barwick's choice in such a way as to jeopardize the negotiations for the new company. Clearly, Barwick must choose between the woman and the company.

His defense of his fiancée rests solely on her denial of having been a Communist, and apparently he can reconcile the conflict only by lying.

The Corporation's directors give him a chance to declare that he has already investigated her political past, thereby clearing the Corporation of any guilt which may befall her. Barwick refuses to lie, but an old movie "gimmick" saves him. The directors were merely testing his integrity. They know he has not investigated his fiancée, so instead of firing him for his testimony they promote him to the chairmanship of the board. With this endorsement he completes negotiations for the new company before embarking on his honeymoon.

Here is the old-fashioned conflict between love and duty, but Swiggett has updated it. The hero with a choice to make is not really a free agent. Although Barwick has maintained his right not to explain anything, the circumstances has been rigged. He is on trial before a jury which already possesses the facts and which conducts the prosecution. At the moment of his triumph Barwick is less the protagonist than he appeared. As with Charles Gray the system has acted benevolently, but in this novel nobody worries about it.

One might miss this subtle downgrading of the hero in an exalted system had not Howard Swiggett literally repeated himself in his next and final novel, *The Durable Fire* (1957). In this latter version of the same story the hero argues with his uninformed and hypocritical boss, and the case goes before the directors of the Corporation. It turns out, however, that these representatives of the benevolent system already know the facts and merely wish the hero to justify their decision in his behalf.

Business enterprise even more thoroughly pre-empts the individual in Cameron Hawley's *Cash McCall*; and by another round of inflation the presiding force of this business world appears even further removed from the company employees. This Olympian force is itself a business: the purchase and sale of corporations, sustained by the federal tax law's provision for capital gains. In this new world the oldtime religion of company loyalty loses favor, and the novel's apparent conflict proceeds from this fact.

Ownership has become a commodity. Brokers manipulate companies, often fraudulently for profit, denying the permanent value of a business and its service to the community. So it seems to Gil Clark, a young man dedicated to managing the Suffolk Moulding Company, which will apparently be sacrificed to this sort of manipulation. Gil finally meets his adversary, Cash McCall, the symbol of this system, the manipulator whose name has become legend.

But this Croesus confounds all expectations. He operates legally. "I don't make the rules, Gil. I only play the game. I never thought much of making the kick-for-point after touchdown, either, but as long as it's in the rule book, that's the way the game is played." What could be more American? Or more unassailably moral? "There's only one way I can get a wallop out of a deal like this, Gil. And that's by way of knowing that I haven't dug money out of another man's hide."

McCall is downright benign, as any magazine reader could tell in an instant: he is in his "late thirties, possibly forty . . . more like a professional athlete than a businessman." He also has impeccable manners, and although he owns unbelievable wealth (he smiles with a "purse-string puckering around the eyes") the name "Cash," rumors notwithstanding, he has legitimately inherited from his mother's family. Some more of his heritage conveniently explains his motives: through his father's futile wage-slavery Cash has learned to disdain company worship.

Having given him necessary credentials, the author enhances the hero with a kind of parental authority. He owns most of the corporations in sight, including the one which has currently employed Gil Clark. McCall has, in fact, secretly maneuvered that young man's career into his own orbit. As for Suffolk Moulding, the company whose disposition he presently controls, Cash McCall has only the most responsible intention. It turns out that young Gil Clark did not have any problem at all. He only thought he did.

McCall merges Suffolk Moulding with two other properties he has dramatically acquired, saving the stockholders—including a medical research foundation—from ruin, and so demonstrates his superiority to lesser-minded company men. His supra-business really nurtures what it seems to prey on. The benign force comfortably ruling the economic world, which depressed John Marquand's hero, has here become a happy inevitability.

This novel celebrates earned income—large amounts of it—for its own sake. Cash McCall even delivers a lay sermon, scolding Americans for their public discomfort over wealth. But faced with precisely this discomfort in the public mind and wishing to justify profit, the novelist trafficks in attitudes. The sanctioning doctrine of Good Works has been at hand ever since Benjamin Franklin canonized the Arminian Heresy. So Cash McCall, like his patron saint, does well by doing good.

The happy doctrine of profit through Good Works also explains Cameron Hawley's earlier novel, *Executive Suite*, a splendid suspense story with a little something for everyone. This book deifies the materialist, but so covertly that the reader is never offended by his own appetite. The sudden death of Avery Bullard precipitates a crisis in the furniture business. Which of the five vice-presidents of the Corporation will succeed the late Mr. Bullard to the presidency? The leading contender is the controller, Loren Shaw, a relentless and aggressive man dedicated to company profits.

Shaw is a money grubber, a conniving materialist, and the book makes a heavy case against him, casting suspicion on all his motives. The movement in the company to stop Loren Shaw quickly settles on MacDonald Walling, the youngest of the vice-presidents. The erosive battle between these two recalls the earlier, mannered contest between Charles Gray and the man he thought he had to beat. In this one, however, Don Walling triumphs much more theatrically. He wins the directors' votes at a show-down with Shaw by an impassioned speech which states the theme of the novel—or seems to.

Walling's convictions are not at first entirely clear. He damns Mammon, specifically Loren Shaw's priority of stock dividends, he applauds high-quality products and recognizes the employees as human, and he promises new and greater growth for the Company. These comforting attitudes seem safe enough. But the rhetoric of Mr. Walling disguises some fortuitous illogic. Speaking in anger, he excoriates Avery Bullard, who had had an eye on the profits, who had "been so busy building a great production machine that he . . . lost sight of why he was building it." Yet Walling earns the vote, after some talk of making newer and better furniture, by promising to build an even bigger company.

This young man surely offers the directors the image of his predecessor. But at the time the author throws the switch, after Walling's rhetoric, the directors scarcely realize that a vote for Walling is a vote for Shaw. This fact becomes magnificently clear when the visionary Walling appoints Shaw, the money-man, to the new executive vice-presidency, explaining: "I'll need somebody to help me keep my feet on the ground."

Further evidence of this union of purpose—presumably too complex —never reached the movies. In the film Loren Shaw bitterly concedes defeat, but not in the novel. Perceiving that Walling's presidency will be the best for Tredway and for its dividends, Shaw is among the first of the voters to throw his support to the young man. All's well with the company. The new president has sold a bill of goods. Unlike his adversary he has managed to present his materialism not merely as a matter of profit but as a mission to be celebrated. What counts with the directors is the moral hocus-pocus which disguises the materialism in the first place.

Slick fiction, John Marquand's included, contrives to make it easy for the hero to take what is coming to him. What comes is material well-being. But these later novels differ from their predecessor by renouncing the uncomfortable sense of compromise and by presenting instead some justification for the hero's happy retribution. The most striking example of such expedience is Sloan Wilson's *The Man in the Gray Flannel Suit*.

Like *Point of No Return* this tale begins in authenticity, telling the problems of a pleasant young man with his attractive wife and their average children, living in a normal, hectic world. Tom Rath has two problems, professional and private, which equally urge him on to self-discovery. Professionally, he must decide whether or not to be a businessman—to commit himself to executive endeavors in the communications industry—or to find a less demanding job which will offer dignity and spare time. Privately, he must decide whether or not to tell his wife about his paternity of an illegitimate child in Italy during the war. In the manner of a morality tale, each problem offers the hero neat and exclusive alternatives.

And he decides: professionally, to abandon the chance to be a gladiator and to accept the lesser job; privately, to tell his wife about his illegitimate son, and to secure her blessings in settling an annuity upon the lad. But as it turns out, the hero has had no problem at all, because he could afford, in each case, to make the morally preferable decision. In the novel's most revealing sentence, Tom Rath perceives that "money is the root of all order." Since he has inherited his grandmother's estate before having to decide his problems, his choices have none of the moral significance proclaimed for them. The hero has merely had to wait for circumstances to make it easy.

In this parody of Virtue Rewarded the reward comes first, and the author's contrivance makes a caricature of the benevolent society. When Tom Rath's legacy appears doubtful because of a counter-claim, for instance, a probate judge goes out of his way to investigate the other claimant and to discover his dishonesty. The villagers, in effect, endorse a drastic exception to the zoning laws, allowing Tom the opportuity to turn his inherited land into a profitable development. Finally, when the hero denies the business opportunity offered him, even chastising his boss in the process, that unbelievably tolerant benefactor obtains for the hero a life-time sinecure.

It is all so appallingly easy. The novel scarcely honors its publisher's claim that it speaks for a whole generation. On the contrary, this hero's endowments are so special and his society's dispensations so tailored to his needs, that his gray flannel suit would not fit anyone else.

Stylization exaggerates gestures and attitudes. Each of these novels offers a comparative, and some a superlative, to what John Marquand has set down. Competition for the top job is more erosive, more obviously dramatic in *Executive Suite*; the hero is more willfully passive in Sloan Wilson's novel; and the company more specifically paternal in *The Power and the Prize*, yet dwarfed in *Cash McCall* by an economic force above and beyond even the corporation. In short, whatever the problem, it is more urgent in these eclectic novels.

These stylized attitudes are rendered by stylized conventions. The author's chore is to dispose satisfactorily of the hero's problem; or the other way around, to make it seem for awhile as though the hero has a problem. It is the same either way. Some evidence need only be planted early in the story, which the climax can then recall in reversing the situation. This is the "gimmick" in the magazines and the movies.

John Marquand plants his evidence for the climax of Charles Gray's struggle in a long, detailed flashback. This is Marquand's most prominent convention. The hero's past is the majority of the novel, and the whole of it is the evidence for the way things suddenly turn out. These latter novels by the other authors, however, stylize the effect of sudden reversal by leaving out the past which precedes it. The climax is more sensational that way, less mundane and more dream-like.

In *Point of No Return* the hero's success is decided for him because this is the way it has been all his life. The sequence of events accounts for this apparently incontestable logic. Marquand introduces the problem in the narrative present, then suspends it for a thorough and painstaking exploration of Charles Gray's past, during which the hero is seen time and again abiding by accepted conventions of behavior.

Growing up in a small town, Gray conducts a courtship across the tracks and then dutifully abandons it. He conforms to the accepted image of a young man in a brokerage house, even playing the stock market conservatively in an era of wild speculation. He repeatedly contemplates the joys of unconventional behavior, yet keeps his thoughts to himself. Tempering his private observations with public good sense, he earns the complaisance and benediction of friends and employers. This pattern repeats itself so often, throughout the middle half of the novel, that when Marquand resumes the problem of the vice-presidency, he has already and repeatedly signaled its resolution.

The narrative past has determined the narrative present. Charles Gray's conservative honesty in deference to the system is bound to win the system's approval. Once you know the past, granting a consistent character, there is no present problem. What at first appeared problematic turns out to be merely a foregone conclusion. So it is with II. M. Pulham and George Apley, in fact with most of Marquand's heroes.

Marquand manages a convincing surprise by making the evidence so obvious that the reader takes it for granted. The problem has apparently solved itself; it is a kind of optical illusion. This surprise by illusion is precisely the quality in Marquand's narrative method which succeeding novels have exaggerated. By a kind of fictional shorthand they have abridged the past tense, which in Marquand's novels solves the present problem.

None of these latter heroes has a past in the sense of a history already resolved. Except for fragmentary flashbacks identifying the characters, these novels remain continuously in the present. They have abridged that part of the narrative which accomplishes the solution, but they must still fulfill the fictional requirement of a conflict solved. They must come out even at the end. So instead of solving the problem they dissolve it.

This tour de force is like the solution to a puzzle, and just about as significant. Sloan Wilson's hero did not have to work at a distasteful job in order to support two families; he only thought he did, until his inheritance made everything dreadfully easy. Gil Clark, in Cameron Hawley's novel, merely thought the brokerage of corporations was malevolent, until Cash McCall revealed the truth. Don Walling never challenged the primacy of company dividends, in *Executive Suite*; it just took a little time for him to reveal himself as a more imaginative money-man than his adversary. And was there ever any doubt that the directors would endorse Cleve Barwick's high-principled courtship? Only by assertion.

The difference between John Marquand's patently logical solution of a problem and the mere illusion of the problem in the first place also makes the difference between an attitude and the commercial exploitation of it. These latter books all say less than they seem to. By dismissing the problems they have posed they disqualify the attitudes these problems seem to have produced. The greater the exaggeration in the first place, therefore, the more obvious the fake. In the extreme this affliction reduces a novel to saying nothing of its own.

The fifth and most recent in this cluster of business novels, George DeMare's *The Empire—and Martin Brill*, reaches this point of oblivion. It tells of five employees in the public-relations department of a vast and anonymous organization. This nameless corporation, which sells an unknown product, is called merely "the Company," "the System," or "the Empire."

During World War II, the time of the story, the Empire's public-relations problem is to broadcast its vital importance to the national war effort. Its headquarters occupy a skyscraper in a large Eastern city, and the nerve center of these headquarters is on the top floor. The reader catches a glimpse of two vice-presidents, one floor below, mysteriously referring to the "Old Man," but that is as close as anyone gets to the soul of this system. According to the blurb on the paperbound edition (1957), "it might be called the story of the successful 'company man.' But it is also the story of hundreds of thousands of 'big company' employees whose dreams are never fulfilled, who find themselves imprisoned in a treadmill of frustration."

Of the novel's five case histories, one man commits suicide because his mistress denies him. The second becomes an alcoholic, loses his job, and tramps the streets. The careers of numbers three and four contradict each other. Number three stands firm on a moral matter (like Cleves Barwick in *The Power and The Prize*), gets promoted when events turn out to justify his position, and passes from view to the upper stories of the skyscraper.

Number four, who is morally dishonest, seeks preferment at the expense of his colleagues. When his connivance is discovered, the Empire awards him a horizontal promotion, and he passes from view among the lower stories of the skyscraper. The fifth man, Martin Brill, is the hero only by deference of the novel's title. He is kicked around the Empire and finally promoted to the chair of the man who first hired him. But on the way to this promotion he has suffered battle fatigue.

This schematization of the five characters accommodates the anonymity of the Empire. The only ruling force in the System is the irony of denial. The successful executive kills himself, the dedicated companyman gets fired. The employee who renounces preferment wins, and the one who puts it before all else loses. Martin Brill, the man alleged to have great expectations in the Empire, gets unaccountably shuffled off into a minor job and exiled from headquarters. Then, having given up, he unaccountably wins.

The anonymity, the irony, the lack of any cipherable plan, and the boss nobody ever sees are all symptoms of literary naturalism. Moreover, signs of earlier naturalists mark the final impression of this book.

There in the misty afterglow of the fading light, it towered like a huge and shadowy fortress, heavy and sinister, rising out of the sea. It was the Building—the great, shadowy Building. It seemed to him, as he stood there gazing at it from the distance, as if it were a symbol of the whole vast Empire—the granite stronghold of the mysterious powers of the age—fabulous, immense, and strange.

If you recall the static symbol of the Chicago Board of Trade Building, with which Frank Norris concluded *The Pit* (1903), you might marvel at the coincidence.

But this eclectic novel has also absorbed and exaggerated more recent determinism. It capitalizes the "System" and in great detail inflates the concept of its benignity. "It was only an impersonal, cold conglomeration of hundreds of thousands of unsentimental, commonplace people, machines and buildings, tracks and towers, lights and voices; but somehow it was a solid thing, and it was there to stay." The individuals within it are as nothing,

. . . but the Company which would see thousands like them come and go, rise and fall, would endure, would remain there forever, substantial, unchanging, powerful, enjoying a species of immortality, not as humans but as humanity itself, a monument to the creative force and endurance of collective men, no matter how mediocre—and to the power of human need.

Marquand's metaphor of the Stuyvesant Bank, the "head of living coral rising above the surf, a small outcropping of a greater reef," offers a comparable realization, but it is simpler and more dynamic. The comparison between one man's metaphor and another man's catalog suggests the entire relationship between these two novels.

Perhaps there were more salable attitudes for this latter novel to absorb. The "system" in it is more pervasive than in *Point of No Return* and more impersonal than in *Cash McCall*. The retributions of the Empire recall the rewards and penalties of the board of directors in *The Power and The Prize*, although retribution no longer has any sense of necessity. *The Empire—and Martin Brill* attempts to show the *modus operandi* of the big company. But the anonymity defeats this, and the machinations degenerate instead into office politics, like those in *Executive Suite*.

The Empire—and Martin Brill is no copy. It is an original artifact. The author's personal experience in just such an actual business corporation, in fact, inspired his convictions. But he represented these convictions by literary conventions which served other needs in other novels. His compendium consequently attracts no central or compelling idea to his particular subject. Reading it is like wandering through a hall of mirrors, seeing only the distorted reflection of other books.

This particular cluster of economic novels is a small symptom of a general condition in the book trade. The fiction of business has got thoroughly mixed up with the business of fiction. Most other "professional" novels, as they are called—about doctors or lawyers or policemen, about Madison Avenue or Hollywood—tell the same story. The overproduction of fiction follows the elemental fact that a successful book attracts more like it. Each new stylization is more like it than the last.

There is no end to this subject, but what happens to the novel form must be obvious. It deteriorates until some writer conceives of a novel out of his own experience and organizes the actual chaos of things into an ordered, complex whole which appraises the way of the world. He is an artist. If he can write well enough and if he has unaccountable good luck, people will talk about his book and even buy it.

On the strength of this, publishers will spot a "trend." Then the whole dreary process will start again. A cluster of new novels will begin to appear: packaged, advertised, some of them even written to exploit and exaggerate the characteristics of the original book, but always contrived to attenuate it. This is all so terribly calculable, except for the artist in the first place, thank God.

Chapter VIII

Arms and the Manner

THE human ideal of goodness has always had a hard time of it, which explains why the triumph of virtue makes the headlines and why fiction is so necessary. Conflict is a constant in fiction, but its local metaphor changes, keeping up with the times. By mid-century in America the most persistent local metaphor of the novel's conflict was warfare—for an obvious reason. So far in the twentieth century warfare has been the most compelling denial of the idea of human efficacy in God's world.

Contemporary book publishing has reflected this notoriety. In 1948 *Publishers' Weekly* counted some 270 American novels whose subjects involved World War II, many of them published before the war had ended. While the total number of published novels was steadily shrinking after V-J Day, the number of war novels began to increase; 1948 was a crucial year for war books. The large sales of Dwight Eisenhower's *Crusade in Europe*, Winston Churchill's *The Gathering Storm*, and the early volumes of official military histories reflected widespread interest. The fiction market throve on Norman Mailer's sensational first novel, *The Naked and The Dead*.

Mailer's novel profited by an extraordinary advertising campaign. A series of teaser ads in trade and review journals stimulated interest many months before publication. Advance sales were high, and the novel continued to sell: 137,000 copies through the trade in eight months. The Book-of-the-Month Club distributed 100,000 copies and the Book Find Club another 64,000; and still the trade sales prospered, totaling over 200,000 by January 1951, when the novel appeared in a paperbound edition.

Later in 1948 Irwin Shaw's novel, *The Young Lions*, made almost as much of an impression. It was distributed by the Fiction Book Club, and the Post Hall Syndicate and Omnibook both purchased second-serial rights. The significant fact in the sales of both novels was their stamina in the market. It was three years before *The Naked and the Dead* went into a paperback edition, and during this time 200,000 copies of the trade edition were sold. The sales of each novel in paperback now total more than 15,000,000 copies, and are still increasing.

In 1951, a few months after the publication of the paperbound edition of *The Naked and the Dead*, two other war novels appeared, with even more conspicuous success. *The Caine Mutiny* (1951; 1954), by Herman Wouk, sold over 200,000 copies through the trade in its first nine months, and by the end of 1952 it had nearly doubled that total. Its book-club distribution (by Book-of-the-Month Club, Literary Guild, Peoples' Book Club, and Doubleday Dollar Book Club) was unprecedented. *The Caine Mutiny* was also condensed for the Reader's Digest Book Club, serialized in some forty-five newspapers, and adapted to the stage for both Broadway and road-company productions; and like Shaw's and Mailer's novels it was filmed in the grand manner. The other novel of 1951, James Jones's *From Here to Eternity*, has sold more than 2,500,000 copies in reprint form. It was the first of these four novels to be filmed, and on the strength of its film it has achieved the largest sale of all of them in the shortest time.

For nearly ten years, beginning with the publication of Mailer's novel, the new market steadily increased. There were all sorts of reasons for it. Millions of Americans home from the war wanted to read about themselves. The crisis of Berlin and the American airlift, and then the police action in Korea made warfare imminent again. Even more imminent was the film industry's capitulation to television, until Hollywood successfully gambled on the wide screen in 1954. This last-gasp invention created an urgent need for spectacular story material. The war novel satisfied all of these interests.

One dissonant note occurred in this chorus of war novels, but at the time it was not very loud. Ira Wolfert's *An Act of Love* (1948; 1955) had been published along with *The Naked and the Dead* and *The Young Lions*. It was promoted as a "Big" war novel like the others, but it did not share in their riches. The success of the other books had apparently no effect on its sales. Ten times as many copies of Mailer's novel were sold in eight months as were ever sold of Wolfert's novel. Wolfert's trouble was that he saw the war as a problem in ethics by believing in the efficacy of his hero; and the relatively poor showing of his book was prophetic.

But the four famous novels had tremendous effect. Even before Hollywood's wide screen raised the profit in war fiction, the influence of these four books became apparent on the lists of reprint publishers. Reprinters began purchasing the rights to novels published before the campaign of '48 and still in trade editions. The publishing dates of the trade and reprint editions of Frederic Wakeman's *Shore Leave* (1944; 1948) represent a familiar pattern, and the pattern was still evident ten years later with the belated reprinting of Lawrence Kahn's *Able One Four* (1952) as *The Tank Destroyers* (1958). These two reprints were not among the very few which rescued novels worth saving, such as Harry Brown's *A Walk in the Sun* (1944; 1957) or *The Gallery* (1947; 1950), by John Horne Burns.

The search for newly salable material reached even to the fiction of World War I: Ernest Hemingway's *A Farewell to Arms* (1929; 1949) for instance, *Soldier's Pay* (1926; 1951) by William Faulkner, William March's *Company K* (1933; 1958), and Eric Remarque's *All Quiet on the Western Front* (1929; 1958). By suggesting to book buyers a continuing tradition of war fiction these reissues of old titles made useful advertising copy for the newer fiction of World War II and the Korean conflict. Thus, the paperbound package of a Korean-War novel by J. D. Hollands entitled *Able Company* (1956; 1958) explains in reviewers' jargon, that this " 'Great War Novel' . . . should rank with Remarque's *All Quiet on the Western Front*," a claim which stretches a coincidence of subject matter beyond all reason.

The claim made for Hollands' novel is ludicrous. The only similarity between the two books lies in the kind of war each represents. The war in Korea, as in France more than thirty years before, was a war of position, and the ground fighting in both became an erosive stalemate. But two novels about war could scarcely differ more than these do. Remarque's novel is selective and suggestive; Hollands' novel is a fulsome encyclopedia of dreary details. This difference, however, did not keep Hollands' reprinter from claiming fame by association.

This is a typical trick, especially when one reprinter has published both of the novels on which the claim is based. The reprinter proclaims Lionel Shapiro's *The Sixth of June* (1955; 1956) to be "The greatest story of love and war since Hemingway's A *Farewell to Arms"*— which he also reprinted. Sometimes this little device is even laughable. According to its paperback cover, Kenneth Dodson's *Away All Boats* (1954; 1956) is "The mightiest novel of men at war since *Battle Cry,"* which was originally published the same year. How could false inflation be more modest than this?

Inflation is customary in this sort of claimed esteem. *Battle Cry* (1953; 1954), by Leon Uris, "shares the greatness of *From Here to Eternity* and *The Caine Mutiny."* Wirt Williams' novel, *The Enemy* (1951; 1956), "Takes its place . . . beside *The Caine Mutiny,* and the stories of Conrad and O'Neill." These likenesses belong to the advertising, not the book.

War and Peace is claimed among the credentials of *The Sixth of June,* which is about like comparing *The Origin of the Species* with *Peter Rabbit.* The borrowed esteem on the paper cover of Ross Carter's actual account of paratroopers in Europe, *Those Devils in Baggy Pants* (1951; 1952)—"Not since *The Naked and the Dead—Mr. Roberts—* or *South Pacific*—has there been a book like this!"—patently denies the facts. The cover-claim of Lonnie Coleman's *Ship's Company* (1955) blandly contradicts itself: "Action, danger and high passion in a book that ranks with *Mister Roberts."* It is the old promotional device of trying to cash in on someone else's best seller. These false claims might be dismissed were they not symptoms of the reason so many books are published in the first place.

When the reprinter informs the customer that Robert Bowen's *Bamboo* (1953; 1955) is "Compared to *From Here to Eternity,"* he is misrepresenting a literary idea. *Bamboo* is a short novel about a thirty-day leave which a regular-Navy sailor spends in the shacks and bars of Manila: drinking and brawling with his shipmates, living with a Filipino girl, and repenting his drunken brutalities. Glandular functions and vague remorse entirely comprise this character, of whom the author makes no consequence. The only grounds for comparison with Jones's novel are the excesses of a thirty-year man on peacetime duty in the Pacific. Excess has some significance in Jones's novel, in the claustrophobic lives of a dozen characters, but it leads to nothing in *Bamboo* except the pale recollection of *From Here to Eternity*.

Mannerism in war fiction extends beyond the advertising to the contents of the novels themselves. Most of the novels published after those four which built the current market are startlingly similar to one another, but they are similar in ways which their publishers would rather not mention. Like all other books which swarm after a best seller, these war novels exaggerate conventions which their predecessors developed. As a result the book trade recognizes a conglomerate product, published from time to time, which could be called the "normal" novel.

For the past ten or twelve years the normal war novel has been the most familiar species of contemporary American fiction. Its properties and the way they evolved, moreover, illustrate how the publishing industry hastens and formalizes the degeneration of a species. This degeneration is similar to what has occurred in those clustered business novels whose authors followed John Marquand to market. But there are more factors involved in the degeneration of war novels.

The "normal" war novel is partly the result of a widespread obsession for authenticity which the subject itself inspires, and partly the result of the stylizing of certain fictional conventions. This conglomerate product so obviously denies the possibilities of the novel form that it bears looking into. Its gross authenticity prevents fictional development and disqualifies the whole subject of moral choice; this can be seen first by observing the characteristics of some normal novels. Then it will be useful to notice the derivation of these characteristics, to inspect the conventions of earlier war novels which the normal novels expediently distort.

First, to the characteristics themselves. The normal novel is a "Big Book." It bulks large, it is heavily populated, and its subject is sensational. It involves timely attitudes about emotional disturbance, sexual difficulties and racial problems. Nearly everything about its subject is excessive; even its manner is excessively ponderous. In the mistaken attempt to be "brutally honest," as the ads say, it is excessively literal.

The normal war novel is the saga of a group of private citizens assembled for military training and gradually built into a fighting unit, imbued with camaraderie, and embarked for combat. When this group finally meets the enemy, the citizen-soldiers test themselves at terrible cost, and the whole erosive experience yields only a muted hope for the few survivors. Most of the soldier-writers have the same significant story to tell, with the same claim to authenticity and with the same compulsion.

The first narrator in William March's *Company K*, one of the revived novels about World War I, speaks for all soldier-authors. "I wish there were some way to take these stories and pin them to a huge wheel," he says, "each story hung on a different peg until the circle was completed. Then I would like to spin the wheel, faster and faster, until the things of which I have written took life and were re-created, and became part of the wheel, flowing toward each other, into each other; blurring, and then blending together into a composite whole, an unending circle of pain. . . ." He is obsessed with making a picture and a sound of war which encompasses everything else.

This is the way it was, the author says. He was there and cannot be contradicted. Both the strength and the failure of the normal war novel proceed from this fact. The military units and the campaigns which involved them are matters of public knowledge and give a certain signal value to the book. But the disadvantages of authenticity are crippling. The immediacy of the author's subject can overwhelm him, to the detriment of fiction. When the subject of war—the denial of human efficacy—overwhelms the author, his novel has a hard time convincing anyone. He can write only of determinism, and this contradicts the nature of the novel.

The novel is a humanistic form. By simplifying chaos into conflict it poses alternatives for its characters; it presents the possibility of choice and turns action into consequence. This does not limit the author to any particular attitude, happy or unhappy, but it does assume that the individual has a hand in the vast circumstances of cause and effect. There is no such thing as a convincing deterministic novel. A novel may argue determinism, which is quite another matter, but an author overwhelmed by warfare can record only events without human cause, which is just what happens in the normal war novel.

Authenticity cripples this stylized war fiction. It presupposes certain kinds of characters, it dwarfs them in their setting, and it dictates a set of attitudes conditioned by shock. These arbitrary conditions usually make the characters unbelievable. The soldier-author came to know the personnel and operations of some basic military unit: a squad, a bomber crew, or a watch-section aboard ship; but he also met many different kinds of men, far more than in any normal circumstances. He feels the obligation to make his story universal, and so one way or another he tries to confine his extensive, actual acquaintance to the fictional version of the military unit he knows.

The actual citizen-soldiers have come from everywhere, representing every human quality, sharing only their amateur status. Some belonged to racial minorities, others were racists. Some grew splendidly, others remained weak and ineffectual. Some were bestial, some ignorant, and a few had quick, disciplined minds. They represented all regions and every social class. William March's narrator states his case—and, unwittingly, the problem. "This book started out to be a record of my own company, but I do not want it to be that, now. I want it to be a record of every company in every army."

How do you achieve a fiction which represents this actual range of human involvement in war? William March introduced 113 members of Company K, each with his own story to tell. His novel is a congregation of small voices, a succession of brief intimacies which leave only the impression of bewildering sameness. With the same war but with radically different proportions, John Dos Passos invested three fictional soldiers with heavy symbolic value; so symbolic that they rarely become individuals.

Somewhere between these extremes the normal novel of World War II settles on a platoon cosmology. Some small, definable military unit contains a few permanent tenants and a great many transients. Four or five principal characters are carefully differentiated and then surrounded by a dozen or two dozen caricatures. The normal result is a crowded procession of strangers: the brave officer or the cowardly officer, the shagbark sergeant with a deep sense of commitment, the Jew who becomes a better soldier than his Gentile persecutors, the bully and the bigot and the poet, the sensitive chaplain, and the cynical doctor.

This is the cosmology in Leon Uris' novel, *Battle Cry*. The book is an encyclopedic record of a radio company in the second Division of the Sixth Marines: from civilian life, through boot camp and further training, to combat in the Pacific War and the climactic battle in the landings on Saipan, then back to civilian life. Despite the accumulation of day-to-day details the characters never develop or change. In a remarkable variety of circumstances each new disclosure merely manages to reveal more of the same. The reader knows these individuals no better than the author once knew their actual counterparts.

These characters demonstrate the sentimental assumption that human beings are good (with the author's solicitous attention most of them decide in favor of chastity or marriage). Beyond this, however, one can judge them merely as soldiers; excellent Marines, to be sure, but nothing more. When some of them die, terribly and violently, the fact has nothing to do with their individuality, but only with where they happen to be when the enemy shell explodes. Because the reader never knows them, he must respond to death or survival in merely quantitative terms. Life and death in this novel evoke about as much emotion as the lyric to "Ten Little Indians."

The same cosmology marks another normal novel: Kenneth Dodson's *Away All Boats* ("The mightiest novel of men and war since *Battle Cry*"). This novel tells of a war vessel, an attack transport, in the Pacific theater. Through the small-boat officer and his crew the novel introduces the rest of the ship's personnel: on the bridge, in the ward room, by the landing net and on the beachhead. The confusion and stress and misdirected energy of a landing operation are effectively amplified by the dozens of walk-ons and extras engaged in haste and violence, a fact congenial to the filming of the story in Vistavision.

The persons on this seascape are forever appearing about their business and disappearing again, but they have no consequence. The ship's

Captain Hawkes becomes eccentric as the pressure mounts. He keeps a pet monkey, for which he reserves all his intimate disclosures. He commands his ship-fitter to build a sail boat, and scavenges the fleet for red ink to dye its sails. His obsession for sunsets periodically paralyzes him, and when he conns his ship in such a trance he nearly sinks it. Hawkes is no character in his own right, but he is a pale reflection of Herman Wouk's Captain Queeg. As in *The Caine Mutiny* much is made of this eccentric man jeopardizing the entire command. Then suddenly the narrative denies the conflict it has elaborately built up; Hawkes sustains a brain concussion and dies in his bunk.

Executive Officer Quigley is another Queeg-like character who turns out to be an anti-climax. He has made a career of evading responsibility. His deftness at this threatens to involve some of the junior officers in a crisis with the captain, but in the events of the ship's last campaign somehow nothing comes of it. Then, there is an ensign aboard who schemes for favors at the expense of his colleagues, but after several dark hints about his malevolence, the author excuses him from the novel. These truncated characters all come to nothing. Events outgrow them, and they have no cause and no effect.

The characters are casualties of the novel's limiting authenticity. This book only pretends to be about human beings, while it makes them merely components of a military unit. Its only necessity comes from the chronology of military events, the sequence of landing operations from Makin to Okinawa; it stops only when the Navy has run out of beachheads. Like *Battle Cry* (which was temporarily "the mightiest novel of men at war") Dodson's book wages a war of attrition on its characters.

The details of these books concenter events, not characters. This explains the pervasive but unlocalized setting of the normal war novel. All the training camps and ultimately all the beachheads are indistinguishable because events are reconstructed in terms of that great common denominator, military procedure: the officially prescribed method of carrying out any operation. Procedure constitutes the setting of these narratives regardless of their location.

Just as procedure prescribes the action of a soldier's life and all the methods of his trade, so in these novels it guides the reader in the tech-

nicalities of soldiering. Procedure is the basis of all military communication, the means by which the individual remains a part of his unit
and his unit a part of the entire organization. Military crises can best
be understood in the terms of procedure, particularly procedure gone
wrong, which is why it becomes such an insistent metaphor in these
novels.

Sometimes this metaphor accomplishes wonders. *The Good Shepherd* (1955), by C. S. Forester, tells the story of seventy-two hours in
an Atlantic convoy, sometime in 1942; it dramatizes the convoy's continuous battle with a pack of German submarines, seen from the bridge
of a destroyer. Details of the battle are refracted through the Captain's
mind: incessant trigonometry problems which jostle his recollections
of Ecclesiastes and Job, and earlier moments in the Captain's own life.
An interior monologue punctuates the narrative which advances by the
sequence of orders on the bridge and by conversations between vessels
on the TBS radio circuit. The counterpoint (of procedural information and one man's recollections) makes a convincing picture, but
Forester's achievement was unusual.

The enabling metaphor of procedure more often interferes with the
characters, and burdens the story with irrelevance. The final episode
in Dodson's *Away All Boats*, after the ship has been hit by kamikazes,
necessarily becomes an urgent problem in damage control, but by then
it is too late to salvage the story. Too many earlier episodes have merely
demonstrated procedure for its own sake. Long before its climax the
novel has become an instruction manual.

Occasionally a novel, like Wirt Williams' *The Enemy* (1951; 1956),
exists exclusively in terms of procedure. This tells of the cruise of a
destroyer in a task group ordered to hunt Nazi submarines in the Atlantic prior to the invasion of Normandy. It enlarges on the irony of
cruising 20,000 miles to achieve only an oil slick on the ocean—the
only evidence of the enemy. But the fiction appears to exist merely for
the sake of demonstrating shipboard routine and the procedure of anti-
submarine warfare.

This demonstration specifies the details of a watch schedule, the
prescribed methods of steaming in formation and communicating between ships, relieving the watch and taking the conn, the mechanics

of a search plan for an enemy submarine, the operation of the sonar stack, and the arming and launching of depth charges. Everyone mouths the same esoteric vocabulary of compass readings, commands to the wheel, code names in the security procedure, and all of the conversational short-cuts between crew members. In his fascination with these magic terms the author even stops to define the accepted kenning for a bologna sandwich.

The Enemy thoroughly demonstrates the mechanics of bearing and range without measuring anything human. Beyond their procedural vocabulary the characters have no existence, but this is not even an issue in the novel. First acquaintance establishes several facts: that the executive officer has a wife and prefers merely to drink while on liberty, that the captain is capable and has red hair, that the gunnery officer likes jazz and gunnery problems, and that the cohabitations of another officer become a public joke. This is all. Even the officer who hides in the depth-charge locker and sucks his thumb is merely a more insistent caricature than the others.

The paperbound edition of *The Enemy* quotes Ernest Hemingway as saying, "A first-rate novel of the way it really was." That about sums it up. The urgency to explain "the way it really was" can overpower a fiction. It can dismiss cause and effect in favor of merely how it happened. Presumably the urgency in these ponderous narratives is the imminence of death, but even here they contradict themselves.

Death in the normal novel convinces more than life does. The details of dying receive loving attention. The suppurating corpse and the still-warm body punctured by a single bullet are meant to suggest the range of horror, just as the typical characters are meant to suggest the range of commitment, but the novels achieve only shock and contradiction. The soldiers with the most to live for die. They suffer death by irony; and by this insistent fact these novels imply some force which disqualifies moral being.

Occasionally a war novel that is not quite normal will make a point of moral judgment. Fred Majdalany's *Patrol* (1953) demonstrates the awful discrepancy between the terrors of the isolated few who are actually committed to battle and the many hangers-on behind the line. It tells of a hazardous and unnecessary reconnaisance, ordered in effect by the headquarters mess officer who was anxious to please a general. Among the patrol's casualties, the company's commander has fought on the lines so long and so continuously that his body simply wears out, unable to sustain a superficial leg wound. He dies by irony.

Ned Calmer's *The Strange Land* (1950; 1951) insists on the same ugly comparison between the values of the combat soldier and the values of the spectator. This novel describes an Allied attack upon the Siegfried Line, launched under the worst possible conditions merely to gratify a major general's personal and professional advancement. The higher the rank and the farther away from the enemy, the more criminally irresponsible men become.

A comparable but different crisis of morals occurs in Francis Irby Gwaltney's *The Day the Century Ended* (1955; *Between Heaven and Hell*, 1956). On the titled day, somewhere in the Philippine jungle, the hero realizes the inadequacy of the chivalric ideal which his National Guard commander has taught him. He has also learned to hate the brutish cruelty of the American army and the prison company to which he has been summarily transferred. The book makes no choice between confused ardor and organized hatred, but disqualifies them both in the hero's singularly moral concern over human behavior.

Still another narrowly defined case against warfare is Walt Sheldon's *Troubling of a Star* (1953; 1954), about the American Air Force in Korea. By the actions of three of its characters, two pilots and their commanding officer, this novel evaluates the public concept of heroism and finds it fraudulent. The brave pilot commits an act of compassion for which he is grounded and branded a coward. The cowardly pilot hides his own ineptness by commiting suicide in a dive attack on an enemy tank—by public standards an act of heroism. Their commanding officer, who has sought preferment with napalm bombs and public relations, badly mistakes the courage of one pilot and the cowardice of the other. Having seen enemy soldiers burning up after one of his unit's missions, this colonel retires himself from service and accepts a job with the church—after first punishing the compassionate pilot.

The novels of Sheldon, Gwaltney, Calmer and Majdalany are all humanistic, having jettisoned the equipment of the normal war novel.

They all happen to be negative in attitude, but that is beside the point. Gwaltney's is the best of them, although each one, in its narrow didactic version of human failure, has abandoned the chance for analogy, for development. Ideally, the normal novel should be able to develop its platoon-organization into a convincing system of analogies, but this is a rare achievement.

Anton Myrer accomplished it in *The Big War* (1957; 1958). This novel carries the usual full pack: members of a squad in a marine company assigned to a landing operation on a Pacific island; episodes in the lives of three of these soldiers, from their terminal leaves in the United States, during their passage across the Pacific, through their beach-head landing to the final days of the battle on the island. Yet Myrer has achieved something different from the mere shock and denial of the normal war novel. The experiences of his three main characters dramatize a growing perception of moral man and the cost of morality.

In *The Big War* the son of a Greek millhand, an ebullient Irishman, and a proper Bostonian reveal disparities in the presumed New England conscience. The moral man is Danny Kantaylis, the millhand's son. This Greek has gone over the hill to marry a girl who carries his child and the burden of her mother's neurotic hatred of him. He has already refused a veteran's privilege of retiring to an easy duty with war-bond rallies, and he returns to camp to suffer imprisonment and beatings for his absence-without-leave so that he can rejoin his squad to go overseas.

Outward bound on a spaceless, impressionistic voyage across the Pacific, the men in this squad begin to emerge, refracted through the disdainful consciousness of the Bostonian, Alan Newcombe. Broken in rank Kantaylis will nevertheless lead the men; and his over-developed, uncompromising, and ultimately fatal sense of responsibility begins to dawn on Newcombe. The refraction of this through Newcombe's mind is the burden of the book. As this young patrician gropes toward some understanding of Kantaylis' excessive commitment, he begins a confessional to the girl he took to bed for one night and never saw again: letters written but not mailed, composed but not written—a painful, ludicrous spectacle by which Newcombe grows a capacity to feel and to love.

The narrative bears out Newcombe's struggle over the terms of the complicity between man and God. The battle repays the soldiers in kind. With the squad cut off in the jungle, Kantaylis leads an impossible counter-offensive against an enemy tank, which he destroys even as it destroys him. Newcombe's final perception of this act of compassion precedes his own violent death. Among the squad's survivors, along with the bestial mortals whose ignorance of compassion has insured their safety, are several slow but educable men and Jay O'Neill, who perceives instinctively what Newcombe had to struggle to learn.

Back home, in *The Big War*, the next-of-kin offer the same bewildered motley of response to the fact which governs this fictional world: that the moral man's commitment kills him. Compassion saves the world, yet it cannot preserve itself against what it saves. As in Kantaylis' death and in the birth of his natural child, compassion begets life then dies in the birthing. Like any war novel, *The Big War* acknowledges the ironies of death and life, but it also assumes the complicity of the individual in the scheme of things. Its appraisal of the consequence of moral man, in a world at war or not, very nearly explains the ironies it poses.

Most normal novels deny the participation *The Big War* demands. They show sequence without consequence, violent death by merely external means. Their characters demonstrate humanitarianism and a capacity for misdemeanors, but none of the passion or the pride or the purpose that cause tragedy. Most of them conclude, long before the end, that human responsibility does not exist and that moral struggle is irrelevant in the face of the implacable force of war. And worse, they take inefficacy for granted.

These all are signs of mannerism. The normal war novel evolves by the borrowing of literary conventions from previous novels. These conventions can make a book superficially similar to a predecessor—enough for advertising purposes—but they make no sense by themselves; the argument which would validate them has been left out. The enabling dialectic of these mannered novels exists not in themselves but in earlier books. Most contemporary soldier-authors have thoroughly accepted their predecessors' tentative conclusions, and what were once thematic characteristics have become ornamental.

Tracing back along this line of descent is not very difficult. Most normal war novels stylize the books which created the contemporary market: *The Naked and the Dead*, *The Young Lions*, and *From Here to Eternity*. Each of these earlier books has a dialectic. Each searches out the cause of inefficacy and argues determinism. These books, in turn, develop an argument which already existed in John Dos Passos' novel, *Three Soldiers*, which is the archetype of most contemporary war novels.

Military organization grinds Dos Passos' three soldiers to extinction without regard for their defiance or their futile self-indulgence. All three have joined the AEF's crusade to France in the Great War. But the war ends halfway through the book, and the Army which preceded the war and which remains after it is the force which crushes them. One soldier remarks of their common plight, "It's part of the system. You've got to turn men into beasts. . . ."

The force categorically denies their ambition to be persons. The soldier who merely wants to make corporal and to lead a squad against the enemy contracts a venereal infection; he is court-martialed, sentenced to a labor battalion, and assigned to permanent KP. Another soldier wants to distinguish between his obligation to the Army and his right to deny the sadism of its petty officials. But the system goads him into murdering his immediate adversary, and he spends the rest of his short life as a fugitive. The third soldier responds to the system's organized pieties ("which glorify personal greed and fear and hatred") by deserting ("to join the forlorn men, to throw himself into enviable defeat, to live life as he saw it in spite of everything"). He is hunted down and consigned to a brutal and permanent captivity.

The novel specifies each individual's complicity in his own downfall. Each soldier in his way realizes his partnership with circumstance. But the action is refracted successively through the minds of these victims, so the most obvious impression is the blame of the system. The Army's arbitrary denial is so consistent, and chance is so prevalent, that the individual's plight seems utterly insecure.

Contradiction rules this particular world. Warfare itself is inconclusive, and death by combat is ironically incidental. The only deaths made much of in the book are a murder, a suicide, and a heart failure (suffered by a recruit who dies in bed, having refused to answer muster). The military enemy is scarcely seen, but the omnipresent enemy is the Army. When a company clerk, a Jew named Eisenstein, says as much—about the system's need to turn men into beasts—he is court-martialed for his disloyalty. He has already been tried by the rest of his outfit and found guilty of being a Jew, a contributing factor to his later indictment.

The normal war novels of the present generation have updated the irony of *Three Soldiers* in a peculiar way. They insist on a similar denial of the individual, but they ironically overlook the fact that each of Dos Passos' three soldiers complies in his own downfall while blaming the system. They faithfully exaggerate the details but ignore the reason in them. Thereby they contradict the whole contention of *Three Soldiers* that the individual is the agent of his own dereliction.

This has happened by stages. The best sellers which established the contemporary market—*The Naked and the Dead* and *The Young Lions*—exaggerated certain features in *Three Soldiers*. All three novels document events which defeat the individual, but Mailer and Shaw make a deterministic theory of it; and both create a dialectic about the individual and the sovereignty of the system. Their dialectics are so ponderous, however, that later novels have merely exaggerated the symbols and the narrative details and left out the thesis. What has happened, therefore, is determinism by default.

The Naked and the Dead and *The Young Lions* are the most doctrinaire of all contemporary war novels. The determinism of *The Naked and the Dead* is primarily secular. This novel tells of the invasion of a Japanese-held island; its principal characters are a general, a lieutenant, and the members of an intelligence-and-reconnaisance platoon. For each character the author has thematically joined past and present by a device he calls "The Time Machine": ten impressionistic biographies (in the present tense) which punctuate the narrative (rendered in the past). The war merely intensifies whatever it is that has already limited each individual. From this unpleasant past each character brings to the war a kind of undirected dislike which grows under new pressures into casual hatred.

But the accumulated past is only a secondary cause of dehumanization. Something called "the medium" is the prime cause—and the subject of the most speculation. The lieutenant sees his own analogy in the floating seaweed, the giant, rootless kelp which absorbs its nourishment from the medium around it. The general tries to find a metaphor of life and death in the trajectory of an artillery shell—the asymmetrical parabola, rising gradually and abruptly falling. The "resistance of the medium"—the atmospheric pressure—causes the suddenness of the fall. But the general tries to apply this metaphor to all of experience: the resistance of the medium causes an abrupt descent analogous to the "tragic curve." Whatever "the medium" is it cannot be controlled.

At this point the unresolved speculation drifts back into the narrative, which "proves" the general's analogy. Nothing that happens to end the campaign—or the lives of the characters—has anything to do with human cause. A fatal patrol action turns out to have been unnecessary in view of a victorious frontal attack, but the attack itself has succeeded because an ignorant staff officer has mistakenly deployed his troops. This particular military operation has merely intensified the denial of one's own efforts; it has merely sharpened all of the unfocused groupings without relieving or changing a thing.

The Young Lions also insists on an unknowable determining force. The book is less oracular than Mailer's, but it obviously contradicts itself. Shaw invokes a vindictive statement from the Old Testament book of Nahum, in which God promises to devour the young lions, the war makers of the earth. But the execution of this promise in the novel denies the justice of the Old Testament God.

The divine prophecy involves five young lions in particular: three Germans and two Americans. One idealistic German becomes a capable soldier and then a predatory animal; he is finally shot to death without ceremony. Another German, a professional killer, loses his face in an explosion and dies by suicide. The attrition of war itself apparently validates God's prophecy and accounts for these two deaths. But the story of the other young lions strangely qualifies the prophecy. One of these is an American Jew assigned to an infantry company of Southern Whites; he must fight even to live, let alone to find acceptance. Then, having won his struggle at enormous cost, even as he celebrates the compassion of another human being, he too is killed.

This soldier is shot in the midst of his eulogy to "the human beings" who will conquer the animals in the world. This is the novel's final impression; it is no casual irony. Halfway through the book a German soldier has similarly been murdered in the midst of his plan for peace and his plea for humanity. "We have to show the world that there are still human beings in Germany, not only animals," he says just before a crazy series of events snuff him out. This illogic defies the God of Nahum. The technicality of being a young lion apparently prevails over the humanism of these two soldiers.

The only principal character left standing at the novel's conclusion, in fact, has apparently escaped God's promise by his own ineptness. He is like the uncommitted, ineffectual majority of men. He has enlisted in the army to support a vague ideal and conveniently to escape his domestic entanglements. Failing to become an officer, he has arranged a transfer from hazardous duty, and his entire career is a record of aimless irresponsibility.

The scheme by which this man lives and the others die is impenetrable. If the author intended this soldier to represent the Old Testament man divinely ordered to witness and believe, then he has burdened the God of Nahum with unbelievable subtlety. This inept soldier, by the structure of the novel, does not even know of the life and death of most of the others. Some system of value based on chance or implacable denial rules this fictional world. Like the unresolved musings of the general—Mailer's spokesman—in *The Naked and the Dead*, the contradiction of *The Young Lions* focuses attention on some nameless determining force.

James Jones's deterministic novel published three years later, contains some vestiges of a dialectic. The agents of faceless force are the generals who see "all men as masses, as numerical groups of Infantry, Artillery, and mortars that could be added and subtracted and understood on paper." So says the sergeant who contentedly regards himself as "the instrument of a laughing Providence." Another soldier, a private named Prewitt who has denied the Army's total claims upon him, tries to formulate the reason for his persecution: ". . . it was the system that was at fault, blame the sysem. But he could not even blame the system, because the system was not anything, it was only a kind of accumulation, of everybody, and you could not blame everybody, not unless you wanted the blame to become diluted into a meaningless term, a just nothing."

As in Dos Passos' novel, this hard-headed private of James Jones has complied in the events which bring him down and finally kill him; and so have all the other characters: a soldier who gives up and resigns from the system by accepting the charge of insanity; the sergeant who exploits the system for his own ends; the company commander who tries to make a prudent show of conformity and fails. But the novel abandons this humanistic premise, and buries it under a massive accumulation of events which overtake the characters. The inefficacy of these soldiers is just as much the subject of Jones's novel as it is of Mailer's or of Shaw's, although Jones's Private Prewitt is more sophisticated than the others, more informed about what will happen to him and more willfully compliant, less enraged or bewildered. This reflects the fact that Jones, unlike the other citizen-soldiers, belonged to the regular Army.

The economic importance of these three contemporary books anticipated the similarities of the normal novels that followed them. *Battle Cry, The Enemy, Away All Boats, Able Company*, and dozens like them all packed the same equipment without the reason for it: the reportage, the heavy documentation of setting, the maze of procedure which confines large numbers of small human beings—as though details were intrinsically worthwhile. These stylized novels report the facts of warfare without the heat of thought. They have no antagonism; they fail to search out the design of things because they have abandoned any notion that the complicity between events and the individual might work both ways.

The war novel has calcified about as much as it can in Lawrence Kahn's *Able One Four*. This book abridges the normal novels so efficiently that it reads like an index. According to its paper cover it celebrates "an unheralded and heroic branch" of the service, as almost all of them do. Its characters are the crew of an armored vehicle engaged in the Allied advance across Germany. After a glimpse at the crew members, the author briefs the reader on the procedure of waging war in a tank destroyer, then gets right to the climactic battle. It is all very orderly.

Procedure rules this handbook and confines what passes for characters. Procedure is the insistent setting of the tank destroyer itself: "Elevation—six-four-eight," "left one-two-seven," "fire for effect," "up five hundred"; "Super wants you at oboe time. Repeat, oboe time. Over."; watchword and countersign, H.E. and A.P. shells; "TOT starts at zero five four five"; K-rations and "five-in-ones," and "bedcheck Charlie"; "Wilco, out."

There is not much else to say about the five enlisted men and their lieutenant. The college graduate suffers from battle fatigue, has bad dreams, and obsessively writes letters to his wife. A more well-adjusted member of the crew has no wife and did not go to college. As for the others, the lieutenant is overworked, the coward is unpleasant, and the "tight-lipped" sergeant benignly rules the crew. The last man is a replacement, an "innocent kid" who diligently learns his new job as gun loader. When the tank destroyer finally gets shelled, there is a characteristic irony about the destinies of its crew: the college man goes into shock, the coward gets off with a flesh wound, and the innocent youngster violently dies; his corpse on the road beside the tangled vehicle—the book's final impression—literally fulfills the epigraph on its paper cover: "Blood . . . guts . . . and hot steel!"

Able One Four is legion on publishers' lists. This abridgement of the normal novel is about ciphers, not people; it is an extremity of literary naturalism, but not the only one. This tyrannous fashion even subjugates novels which start out to be humanistic. *The Good Shepherd*, by C. S. Forester, is typical of the contradiction. This is the book which makes procedure so convincing, but it ends up with some unassimilated second thoughts which deny the narrative itself.

The problem of getting the convoy through, in *The Good Shepherd*, lies with the escort commander; the narrative makes this clear. His skill and training and sense of responsibility oppose a formidable yet equally human enemy. Although the issue is in doubt, the terms of the battle are finite, even professional. This scarcely fits the attitude which has sold so many war novels, but Forester's conclusion makes amends. At the end of the convoy the captain throws himself on his bunk while his exhausted mind sums it all up: "Chance—the chance that elevated a paranoiac to supreme power in Germany and a military clique to power in Japan—dictated that when it was too late he should receive the coveted promotion to commander, if it can be called chance." No ending could deny its narrative more arbitrarily than this one does. "Chance had made him an orphan; chance had brought about the senator's nomination. Chance had put him in command of the convoy escort. Chance had made him the man he was and had given that man the duty he had to carry out."

Stylizing has caused the scarcity of humanistic war novels—even unconvincing ones. Putting characters into situations for the sake of situations deprives the characters of cause and effect; it forfeits their responsibility in what happens to them. The more a given novel is concerned with human complexity, therefore, the more its caricature is likely to deny it.

The most influential of the war novels posing an ethical problem has been Herman Wouk's *The Caine Mutiny*. It so happens that Wouk's novel also disqualifies the ethical problem he poses. He built a shrewd combination of acceptable attitudes, more adroitly than C. S. Forester later did, but *The Caine Mutiny* is at least based on the human capability of causing or avoiding a particular crisis. Because of its tremendous commercial success it was later caricatured just as strenuously as were the novels of Mailer and Shaw and Jones. And the stylizations of Wouk's ethical novel were just as deterministic as the normal war novels turned out to be.

Despite all the books unreasonably likened to *The Caine Mutiny* one obvious choice has gone begging. This is Martin Dibner's novel, *The Deep Six* (1953; 1954). The same publisher issued both books a year apart. Dibner's book is an obvious case of total recall, and the publisher must have felt he could not serve the sales of either novel by advertising this fact. Superficially, Dibner's book is more like *The Caine Mutiny* than *The Caine Mutiny* is. It exaggerates every predominant characteristic of its predecessor and therefore arrives at a totally different state: it is a gross caricature of mechanical men.

The Caine Mutiny offers a case history of Commander Queeg, a ship's captain burdened by bad luck, incompetence, and the symptoms of mental illness. His officers build their grievances into a convincing case for relieving him of his command. After the executive officer has accomplished this legal mutiny he is acquitted in a court of law through the shrewd tactics of his defense attorney. Then the novel suddenly turns on itself.

The defense attorney indicts the ship's officers for their moral trespass, but for reasons irrelevant to the trial or to the narrative. The defense attorney is a Jew with grievances against the Nazis, who boiled his mother into soap. He ignores Queeg's pathology for his own. He applauds all the Queegs, all of the professional soldiers who stood guard against the Nazis while these reserve officers were leading a fat, happy life.

Wouk's spokesman indicts the mutineers on the ground that they are accountable for their irresponsibility—a condition from which he pardons Queeg at the same time. Either his pardon or his indictment is illogical. Actually, the author has shuffled his attitudes so that nearly everybody wins. All of the major characters get an endorsement and a reprimand. The novel's only major casualty is the enlisted man whom Queeg has driven insane.

Certain situations in the narrative of this ethical problem have undergone an obvious sea change in *The Deep Six*. They have become bloated. Instead of an ancient destroyer, the ship in the latter book is an ancient cruiser; it floats more incompetence, more sadism, and more tyranny than the destroyer. A curious thing happens to the demonic qualities. The cowardice, the vindictive cruelty, the mental illness and moral trespasses implied of Queeg are multiplied in the latter novel; they become explicit in the persons of four different officers in Dibner's book.

The captain of this cruiser has no concept of his own command, and like Queeg he is suspected of incompetence by his superiors. The gunnery officer, like Queeg, is an outright coward. The executive officer is a psychopathic hater; like Queeg he issues degrading commands for the sake of personal reprisal, and like Queeg he is relieved of his duties. The malevolence which Queeg's character implies becomes a fact in the character of an ensign aboard the latter ship.

Violence is always threatened aboard the *Caine*, but it explodes aboard the cruiser. Racism is only a belated topic in Wouk's novel, merely asserted after the mutiny and left undeveloped, but the persecution of a Negro become a major factor in Dibner's book. Homosexuality is insinuated in *The Caine Mutiny*, in Queeg's persecution of his helmsman; Wouk used it to establish the complexity of Queeg's paranoia. But in *The Deep Six* homosexuality is a blatant fact; an officer's trespass upon an emotionally disturbed enlisted man embellishes that novel's climax.

The exaggerations multiply wherever you look. Wouk tells a separate story in the love affair of the junior officer who survives the court-martial to become the *Caine*'s last captain. To satisfy his mother he has forsaken a girl whom he later decides he loves. This story measures the man's growing up.

The love story in *The Caine Mutiny* is a way of giving the character credentials, for it is his reflections on the mutiny which are allowed to stand. But the love story in *The Deep Six*, also involving a girl from across the tracks, exists merely for itself. Her body is simply one of the many temptations in the way of virtue. The junior officer is also a painter who is tempted by the financial gain of drawing cheap illustrations, and he is a Quaker deeply involved in the hatred aboard ship. But he has already made up his mind before the novel starts: he stands resolutely for painting, marriage and good will. It is ever so easy and unconvincing.

All of these exaggerations lose point in the second novel. *The Caine Mutiny* is concerned with the nature of its central character, and it presents a crisis of moral responsibility. But *The Deep Six* merely demonstrates a number of moral felonies. To be sure, Wouk resolved a crisis to everyone's advantage, but Dibner merely shocks; he offers nothing to resolve. The gross irony of *The Deep Six* is that it has nothing to fathom.

Dibner's stylization of *The Caine Mutiny* is on a par with Robert Bowen's stylization of *From Here to Eternity*, in his novel called *Bamboo*. Both Bowen's and Dibner's novels negate cause and effect; they offer separate sensations but no sensational analogies of a conflict. They negate the very properties by which a novel can appraise experience. There is only an academic difference between these books and

(no heading)

Lawrence Kahn's *Able One Four*. Preceded by so many normal war novels, Kahn's book employs conventions which were clichés to begin with. But there is no point in comparing degrees of unbelievability.

Most normal novels exploit shock and denial, but do not develop it to any avail. These novels offer sequence without consequence. For that illusion of necessity which all fiction must have they depend merely on details of actual experience and on the conventions of other novels. Because they fail to make convincing characters they disqualify the whole system of moral choice—without which, why fiction?

All of these authors of normal war novels offer passive, abhuman characters—the better if passive, because if they act on their own they are not human enough to make it believable. This particular species of fiction shows no evolution of form. "Devolution" would suit it better. The normal war novels, for the most part, breed abhuman characters in an abhuman world.

Chapter IX

Just Deserts

THE BOOK TRADE denatures novels in an effort to sell more of them, and publishers excuse themselves on the grounds that they cannot give the people "better" than the people want. Publishers simplify their wares, invest them with palatable attitudes, and make them easily digestible; then they advertise them as vital and life-giving. But they cannot have it both ways; a novel's vitality lies in its being complex enough to approximate life.

Most contemporary business novels and war novels commit this fraudulent simplism. They are not the only offenders, but they are representative. The normal war novel burdens the characters with consequences they did not cause and cannot change. Because of the incapacity of these characters nothing much is at stake. The system prevails. With the metaphor of business instead of warfare, denatured novels resolve the conflict more pleasantly but just as irrevocably in favor of the system. The businessman is confined by the great corporation which employs him, but it is all for the best. The benevolent system will take care of him.

Under the book trade's auspices these novels add witless authority to such determinism. They create characters for ready-made situations dictated by the success of previous books—like the narratives, the characters have been denatured. But there is even more to this denial of moral struggle. The aim to gratify quickly makes a novel serve an attitude. Thinned down to a narrative which must be resolved, the denatured novel is susceptible to any attitude. It becomes contrived, yet this is what commercialism has forced upon writers.

The peculiar task of the denatured novel is to furnish some expedient reciprocity for all the excesses it contains in the first place. It is "moral," as the publishers say, because every character gets his just deserts. This reciprocity masquerades as justice, which it is not; but like most ingenious devices it will satisfy anyone who takes it for granted. The device approximates an eye for an eye, but it exploits an astigmatism in this old and tested retribution. What happens is more nearly an eye for a tooth, which is something else again.

Expedient reciprocity, for example, is what makes *The Caine Mutiny* come out even. Almost every character gets what is coming to him —even a little more for good measure, which is immediately satisfying. The trick is to balance a character's debits and credits from all sources and to pay him appropriately in a lump sum. This seems so obviously tidy, and it avoids tedious delays of the sort actual people have to encounter.

Wouk's novel excuses Queeg for his trespasses on the grounds that he is sick; it even applauds him for being a sick man who has stayed on duty (although it only implies that the sickness was service-induced). The book also indicts Lieutenant Keefer who has interpreted Queeg's irresponsibility to the rest of the officers and managed the charges of mental illness against the captain. Keefer might be sick too (he is certainly obsessed with Queeg), but Keefer is held responsible as an individual and Queeg is pardoned.

The book obscures this moral lapse by making punishment and reward seem reciprocal. During the trial the defense attorney, Greenwald, has just destroyed whatever esteem Queeg had, so in a fit of remorse he publicly does the same for Queeg's tormentor. He insults Keefer by throwing a drink in his face and blaming him for the affair. This insult does not justify Queeg any more than Queeg's defeat has justified Keefer, but it gratifies the wish that everyone should get his just deserts.

In order to make this reciprocity stick (and it does stick; Keefer is overcome by a sense of defeat), the author must validate Greenwald in some way. He invents a past for Greenwald (which has nothing to do with Keefer) to justify Greenwald's insulting somebody or other. His Jewish mother in Germany was killed by the Nazis, so he trades on this deserved compassion by throwing a drink at the tormentor of one of the men who opposed the Nazis. This all happens so quickly that it hides the illogic, and the reader settles accounts at a tooth for an eye.

This sort of pay-off never works in actuality, which is why it is so satisfying in fiction. When a character accrues a large balance of credit he can squander it all, if the author likes, in some violent attack upon some other character; the more violent the pay-off the more satisfying. In this way an author can excuse one excess by another and still maintain the pretense of being moral. But excess is the real subject.

Virtually every war novel trades on its subject; *The Caine Mutiny* is conservative in this respect. War itself licenses dishonesty, violence, and trespass. The novelist can declare himself impeccable simply by claiming that this is the way it was; he is merely calling a spade a spade. Peacetime mores are often irrelevant in wartime, so when he heeds the call of the spade he can dig deeper in the dirt and get away with it. Or so he rationalizes.

War does cauterize the routine experiences into which it cuts; no doubt it is to be judged differently. But this does not relieve the novelist of the need to make his situation believable. If anything it limits the bounds of probability, but most war novelists do not see it this way. Walt Sheldon's novel, *Troubling of a Star,* for example, obviously exceeds its license. This is a novel about the cowardly pilot and the brave pilot and their commanding officer in Korea. It is pointedly didactic, but this does not hide its indulgence. Of the five other characters in the novel, two of the women are nymphomaniacs and the third is pleasingly amoral. One of the men (the only enlisted man) is a homosexual, and the other is a black marketeer who keeps one of these imperious women.

There is plenty of violent reciprocity among these trespassers. The homosexual is ground up and spit out of an airplane propeller; one nymphomaniac murders her keeper and the other speeds the cowardly pilot to his flaming death. The expedient violence evens out the debits and credits, which clearly exist for the sake of the violence. This does not even begin to convince, because the novel's selectivity is so obviously contrived. The world is simply not populated in this way.

Excess is not limited to felony and perversion. Even chastity can be too much. In Francis Gwaltney's war novel, *The Day the Century Ended,* the soldier-hero indulges in a long recollection of his honeymoon, of the consummation of his marriage, and of subsequent achievements of this union. This soldier's preoccupation is understandable, but it does not happen to concern the action; it is gratuitous—which is one thing love ought not to be. Chaste or unchaste, any situation which exists for its own sake is an extravagance no fiction can afford; it destroys the whole proportion. From the total impression of any novel, nothing secedes like excess.

The war novels have no monopoly on excess. That ultimate business novel, *The Empire—and Martin Brill,* by George DeMare, presents the same sort of crapulence. This is the book in which the anonymous corporation rules all of its employees. The blurb on its back paper cover asserts there is another story in this novel, in the "heart and knowledge of Martin Brill," "fascinating, sardonic and perverse." This is an account of Brill's sexual experience with the "lovely April who could give him her body but withhold her heart."

This marketese refers to the hero's frustrations over a woman who would lie with him even as she reminded him of her charity. But the "lovely April" has no other function. The flesh larded into this narrative has no cause and shows no necessity. The "lovely April" is a paperbound heroine imposed on the story, and one reason why the book is so scattered. She is unbelievable, which is her only connection with the rest of the novel.

In the flood of business novels which deluged the market after Marquand's *Point of No Return,* Cameron Hawley's *Cash McCall* gave a special notoriety to the conflicts in buying and selling companies. This subject in turn begat more derivative books, including some which were not business novels at all but merely disguised to look like them. John MacDonald's paperback original, *Man of Affairs* (1957), for example, is incidentally about a raid on a company for the sake of manipulating its stocks, but the book's real subject is a violent house party in the Bahamas at which the scoundrel tries to secure some signed proxies.

The extravagance of *Man of Affairs* includes bribery, blackmail, fornication and violent death, all tricked up to seem as wholesome as a

Girl Scout cookie. The excess is rationalized by expedient reciprocity. The narrative keeps tabs on what every character has coming to him, so that each excess apparently justifies another. For example, one unpleasant character gets ripped apart by a barracuda; and worse, he is eaten up as a bonus for being beaten up by the hero.

It takes some India-rubber logic to justify this sadism, particularly since his only misdemeanors were insulting his wife and then the hero. But the extravagant pay-off is arranged in easy stages. This unpleasant character wanted to embarrass the hero after that stalwart had beaten him up so he went skin diving with the barracuda; he had been beaten up because he had picked the fight; and he had picked the fight in the first place to justify his having insulted the hero (this was his real mistake—committing two misdemeanors in a row, without letting the hero have his turn).

This travesty on retribution typifies the paperback violence on sale in every cigar store. It is a peculiar derivative of journalism and slick magazine fiction sold in the same store. Journalism is a point of view as well as a technique of writing. It is a kind of selectivity. The reporter chooses a timely subject; more important, he stresses whatever is unusual about it—he finds an angle. It is the exception to the routine which makes the news story, and millions of readers are used to it.

The exceptional slant is also a legitimate fictional device, particularly if the intended readers also read newspapers. But the journalistic point of view in fiction has its hazards; fiction does not have the authenticity of fact—it cannot take consent for granted. Instead, it must provide its own justification; the invention must convince. The more a fiction exploits the unusual, therefore, the more patently it must justify it. The more excessive the action, the more difficult this feat becomes.

The feat in journalistic fiction is to present an action with its rationalization already in the narrative but not immediately apparent. In fact, it is characteristic of such fiction that it jumps off feat first. This, of course, is the magazine technique. The slick writer's trick is to present some apparently unsolvable conflict and then dissolve it through the sudden emphasis on some latent factor which has been present all along. He merely corrects a misunderstanding he has allowed to exist. The happy ending of most magazine stories is built in to begin with.

Whether the extravagance is a happy ending for a magazine or a violent sensation for a paperback, the sleight-of-hand is about the same, and the greater the shock the greater the satisfaction. There are many euphemisms for the technique of making an action acceptable. Magazines refer to "editorial values," playwrights call them laws of dramatic action, and professors of literature refer to conventions, but they are still the tricks of the trade. The trick in writing paperback fiction is to excite the reader with excess in such a way as to placate or elude his judgment which would otherwise condemn it.

Paperback novels are aimed at particular kinds of retail outlets: drugstores, newsstands and cigar-and-candy stores. With these outlets it is natural that novels—particularly original paperbacks—should exploit the techniques of the newspapers and the magazines with which they compete for attention. What is interesting is that technique in all of these media is so much like the gimmick in the movies: the sudden reversal which pays off every character in kind. The appeal of this fiction is the moral posture which excuses itself without stooping to do so.

It is no coincidence that so many of James M. Cain's novels became movies and appeared in paperback. Cain just happens to represent this fiction whose declarative subject does not much matter and whose real subject is violence. The eclectic war novel or business novel—or medical novel or hillbilly novel or whatever—are merely more extreme versions. These denatured novels merely detour their narratives into one sensation after another, with an expedient sham and the pretense of being moral.

Sham and expedience are considerably older than the novel, but their authority has been increased in this particular form of writing by two recent developments in American literary history. One development, of course, concerns the new and various auspices of·subsidiary markets. The magazines, the films, and the paperbacks have all increased the efficiency of rationalizing the reader's indulgence. But another development, which is literary, has made this new efficiency possible. In fact, the change in the novel form since the end of the nineteenth century has become utterly congenial to the denaturing process. It has made the novel more easily exploitable.

This major change in the form of the English novel has occurred within the past hundred years, accelerating in the American novel during the past thirty. It is the author's withdrawal from his own fiction: abdicating from the position of the moral observer and leaving such commentary to the characters. The novel has gradually changed from a dramatically illustrated essay to a dramatic presentation of a limited point of view.

The crucial stage of this large development is commonly credited to Henry James, who learned to build a story around a character's attempt to define his predicament. For James the process of the character's discovery constituted the entire story. No sooner had James developed the convention of refracting incidents through the mind of a single character, however, than other novelists began to popularize it. There were different ways to appropriate the limited point of view, but the great popularizing movement was actually a retreat from James's subject of the mind itself.

Reading James's novels is hard work; but the fiction of Edith Wharton, Anne Sedgwick and Ellen Glasgow simplified the involvements and the emotions by describing them. These writers had learned a lesson from the master, and more people were able to read (and buy) what they wrote. This particular stylization, however, of substituting description for the dramatic illusion, has continued to the point of utter boredom. Herman Wouk's *Marjorie Morningstar* (1955) is a fair sample of the extremity.

But other American writers developed the dramatic point of view in other ways. James had argued, in his famous essay on "The Art of Fiction," that art is a personal, direct impression of life. Impressionism was already a fact when James wrote this, and the development of impressions instead of commentary was another way of removing the author from the scene. After awhile the overseer of the fictional world was no longer even a character. This is the narrative fashion which so much popular fiction has caricatured during the last thirty years, clearly under the influence of Ernest Hemingway.

Hemingway was a style-maker long before he won the Nobel Prize in 1954, before the Swedish Academy cited him "for his powerful style-forming mastery of the art of modern narration." He has said that "style" is the way you got something done; it is the simplest and therefore the best way of doing it. His fiction demonstrates it. Hemingway's stories are apparently irreducible. The narratives are simple and explicit, but so understated that their signficance is always a matter of implication.

The characters rarely testify about the encounter which makes a story, and the events themselves stop short of resolving it. Hemingway's short stories usually end just at the point where the conflict becomes explicit, or where the character realizes the conflict. The importance of this moment in the life of a character had been the particular interest of Sherwood Anderson, from whom Hemingway absorbed a great deal.

Anderson's interest was introspective; he attempted to show some past crisis in the character's life which would account for his present nature. He built his story according to what he called the "history of moments." This critical "moment" is also the subject of most of Hemingway's short stories, but with a difference. For Hemingway the story is the process of making this moment finally explicit.

Indirection and understatement mark Hemingway's fiction; they emphasize the irony which is usually his subject. These devices are also what the stylizations of Hemingway exploit and exaggerate, and the result is usually empty and pretentious. The cohering principle of Hemingway's stories is the realization of the way things are. The end is implicit in the beginning; it merely and finally becomes explicit. There is no other resolution. But caricature can destroy this principle.

Hemingway explained his purpose and its hazards in his autobiographical essay, *Death in the Afternoon* (1932). This primer on bullfighting is also an essay on style. Hemingway began by saying that he "wanted to put down what really happened in action; what the actual things were which produced the emotion that you experienced." He wanted to show the "how" of things so exactly that the "why" would be apparent. "The real thing," he said, was "the sequence of motion and fact which made the emotion," and which with luck would endure. In this "sequence of motion and fact" his stories cohere.

The sequence omits emotion. By stressing the physical sensations which accompany emotion, however, Hemingway renders the moment of crisis by impressions of inconsequential things. When Frederic

Henry leaves the hospital, in A *Farewell to Arms*, his child dead and his lover dying, his mind records the precise facts about a plate of ham and eggs. In *The Sun Also Rises*, when Lady Brett discusses her generosity toward another man with Jake, the sexual cripple she would rather have had, Jake orders a martini. The man dying of blood poisoning in "The Snows of Kilimanjaro" tries to appraise the fatal turn of his misspent life, and he recalls the details of the picture he was trying to take with his camera when he fatally scratched himself.

By this process the dying man finally gets the picture of his life, which is what Hemingway's fiction is all about. A few characters get the picture with distorted clarity; and others never get it at all. Nothing is resolved, but the clarity of "the actual things . . . which produced the emotion that you experienced" gradually emerges. It emerges by incongruity: by the omission of what you might expect to find.

In *Death in the Afternoon* Hemingway wrote "The dignity of the movement of an iceberg is due to only one-eighth of it being above water." To define the submerged mass he plots what he can see. He is like the painter who sees the "negative" space around the object it configures. As the chasm dramatizes the cliff, the silence completes the experience. "If a writer of prose knows enough about what he is writing . . . he may omit things that he knows," Hemingway declares; "and the reader, if the writer is writing truly enough, will have a feeling of those things as strongly as though the writer had stated them."

But this is where stylization fails to convince. Hemingway himself anticipated it: "A writer who omits things because he does not know them only makes hollow places in his writing." Whether there are "hollow places" or pregnant ones, in this style of indirection, depends on whether sensations exist for their own sake or to serve the narrative. Exaggerating the ironic understatement or incongruous omission denatures the novel form, because it leaves no overseer in the fictional world: no presence to preside, no scheme or pattern to explain itself.

Sensation for its own sake can destroy the indirection of fiction. In the extreme it even denies the complex nature of human experience, as the narratives of Paul Bowles illustrate. Bowles describes predicaments which arise out of nowhere and lead violently to nothing. *The Sheltering Sky* (1949) is about a white woman in the Sahara desert who is raped to the point of insanity. *Let It Come Down* (1952) is about an American who hammers a nail into the ear of his Arab victim for no apparent reason. That is all there is to these narratives.

"The Distant Episode," a short story in *The Delicate Prey* (1950), weighs just as much as any one of Bowles's novels and fairly summarizes all of his fiction. In this story a nameless professor is attacked by Arabs who cut out his tongue, throw him into a saddle bag, and keep him as a pet; they dress him in tin plates and teach him obscene dances. After a year or so they sell him, and at this point the professor recovers sufficiently from his stupor to break away and run out into the desert by himself. There is nothing else.

This is the end of the line. Experience becomes merely inexplicable sensation. Paul Bowles's mindlessness is not worth considering, except that it shows the absolute vacuum which an author's exit from his fiction can accomplish. Into this sort of vacuum, in the absence of any cohering scheme, some slick variation of tit for tat can be made to pass for moral judgment. This is where journalism becomes relevant to the novel, along with commercially sponsored sham and expedience.

Publishers add the pretense of morality to fiction that is already mindless. When they piously say they must give the people what they want, they mean that people want sensation for its own sake, along with some face-saving device for indulging in it. As both an editor and an advertiser, therefore, the publisher who makes the pious disclaimer usually encourages the point of view which justifies one sensation by another.

The reprinter's advertising of Erskine Caldwell's mindless fiction is one example of this; so is the advertising of James M. Cain's. The difference between these two writers is that Cain himself exploits the moral pretense; he has misused the sort of narrative indirection which Hemingway developed. But even Cain is modest compared to the lumbering distortions of John O'Hara.

O'Hara is a self-conscious legatee of Hemingway's "style-forming mastery of the art of modern narration." He has eulogized Hemingway as "the outstanding author out of the millions of writers who have lived since 1616"; and he has acknowledged his own indebtedness to Hemingway. His short stories, like Hemingway's, advance to an explicit disclosure of the conflict and then stop. But they are more obvious and more insistently ironic than Hemingway's, and more limited in subject. They usually clarify the inept rationalization of a weak, unpleasant character; and they manage a precise twist at the end, in the manner of the short short story. O'Hara excels in this form. He is so adept, in fact, that he conforms all his novels to it.

John O'Hara writes the longest short short stories in the literature. His first and best book, *Appointment in Samarra*, is usually praised for its brevity and efficiency. The book dramatizes the events which precede a suicide. It is a terrifying story, no doubt of it; but mostly because it never explains itself. It lacks that novelistic quality of appraising as it represents its subject.

Appointment in Samarra chronicles events during the last three days in the life of a suburban businessman: his social trespasses which embarrass or insult his peers, and which presumably cause him to kill himself. Each trespass is credible, but the author's problem is to make them seem like a chain of events. In this he fails, for they do not reveal why the hero did what he did. Instead, the book offers the expedient reciprocity: the churl gets his just deserts, and the ending says, "I told you so."

A short story and a novel satisfy differently. A single incident can end convincingly in one of many ways; but when a series of incidents substantially repeat one another, as in a novel, each is bound to help explain the rest, and the number of convincing resolutions decreases. The simple shrug of irony will not do for a novel. This hero kills himself after his self-esteem has suddenly caved in. His trespasses are symptoms of this fact, but why or how they are connected with his appalling inability to stay alive the author ignores.

O'Hara even obscures the question with a series of flashbacks which have no relevance to events in the present. For example, the hero's grandfather embezzled a lot of money and then blew his head all over the hayloft; but neither embezzlement nor suicide is hereditary. As a boy the hero had once stolen a flashlight from a store and been caught; but this scarcely justifies his suicide over money matters. The hero's faithful wife once had some unpleasant sexular adventures before she met the hero, but they are obviously irrelvant to his problem.

None of these alarums and excursions show cause; but they do interrupt the narrative and confuse the sequence of "fatal" events enough to obscure its illogic. For this reason the story succeeds as well as it does.

O'Hara keeps telling the same story that E. A. Robinson superbly told, of "Richard Cory" who put a bullet through his head for no known reason. O'Hara adds nothing but words. His most celebrated novel, *Ten North Frederick* (1955), tells of another suicide, with two important changes: it is longer and more pretentious than his first novel. It tells about a well-born, capable citizen who drinks himself to death. All the circumstances of this character's erosion are explicit, yet the novel invalidates all of the lengthy reasons that might have caused it.

The hero's wife despises him after realizing she cannot ever own him; but the hero is scarcely aware of this. He loses two million dollars in the stock market; but he has one million dollars left. He sustains a broken leg and a concussion; but they heal in plenty of time for him to begin drinking himself to death. Much is made of his frustrated political ambitions; but he shows every resolve to regain his self-confidence, and says as much.

The book minimizes the only uncontradicted reason why this hero might prefer cirrhosis of the liver. He despatches his daughter's marriage by annulment and abortion. He does so in the space of three sentences: about seventy words of the novel's 140,000. Despite the novel's exhaustive testimony about his love for his daughter and his sense of responsibility in general, there is not a word about the soul-agony this experience might have caused him. In one sentence, fifty pages after the event, the hero tells his lover (his daughter's roommate) that he thinks he might not have done the right thing. This is the sort of "hollow place" Hemingway warned about. In O'Hara's case it is a vast emptiness which completely begs the character.

O'Hara's other major efforts are equally pretentious. *A Rage to Live* (1949) amplifies the sexual instinct in its heroine. The first half of this inordinately long book sounds like a mating manual, as it trains the heroine for marriage, and the second half demonstrates the unconvincing foolishness of this assertedly shrewd woman. In tedious detail it describes her just deserts and how she earns them, but why she earns them is no concern of O'Hara's. His latest book, *From the Terrace* (1958), is even more fulsome and more evasive. It is a complete statistical record of irrelevant details in the life of an investment banker and his community. This pompous exhibition even includes footnotes, yet it completely shuns the responsibility of making a believable fiction.

O'Hara's endless narratives are monuments to moral pretense. They fake the novel's complexity with the simplism of total recall. All fiction distorts, and a novel's genuine complexity can make distortion into a commentary on more than itself. But a novel's only justification is its relevance to actuality; if it is not believable in this sense, it is worthless. The trouble with most denatured novels like O'Hara's is that they are unbelievable, so whatever pretense they make is gross.

The ideal of a mindless pretense to morality is what the marketese of the book trade tries to create. Because fiction has always been considered a luxury in this nation, it has nearly always been sold in a buyer's market and disguised as a useful instrument. The economic history of the trade since the 1890's, and particularly since the 1930's, has merely aggravated the difference between what seems and what is.

The distinguishing fact about most of our national fiction is that it is published for non-readers. This nation now has more literate citizens who do not read than any nation in the world. All publishers know this, which is why most of them are afraid to take a chance. The best way to stay solvent is to satisfy the customer. But the customer is rarely a reader; he is merely a consumer.

In every retail industry the consumer is king. He is the "average man" who is sought after and gratified. This is relevant to the economic organization of the book trade. The major changes in the publishing industry since the end of the nineteenth century have all been changes in marketing methods, and they reflect the demise of the entrepreneur. The publisher is no longer in control. Much of his editorial function has been appropriated by the so-called "subsidiary" distributors of fiction via magazines, films, book clubs and cheap reprints; and these distributors are committed to the mythical "average man."

Book publishing always has been inefficient; the trade publisher has never really been in touch with the readers who buy novels. The book industry knows no such thing as that ideal of total communication which market researchers lovingly idealize; in their jargon the publisher has no efficient "feedback" from book buyers. This is so because his real customers are not book buyers but marketers.

When the bookstores return his "best sellers" by the carload, the publisher looks around for some signals. He gets them from the advertising of the book club which has turned down his last twenty books; from the reprinter who in turn responds to the magazine wholesaler; from the movie studio which takes its orders from film distributors and theater owners. In short, the trade publisher gets his signals from merchandisers and from the owners of entertainment properties who use fiction as a by-product.

At this point the old antithesis between art and entertainment dissolves into a synthesis called manufacture. From his marketers, the publisher derives an image of the tired housewife or the traveling businessman or the stenographer waiting for her home permanent to set: consumers, who will pay to be gratified by fiction. Then, if the artifact happens to please, the publisher will search for others which reproduce it without seeming to. He manufactures reproductions. He also rationalizes—in public—that he cannot give people any "better" than they want. But this is specious. The publisher does not know about the consumers of the subsidiary products any more than he might know about his readers.

Although the publisher has become a frightened man, he still has a few vestiges of editorial authority. At least he has not yet reached the absurd predicament of the automobile manufacturer who lets his public relations staff design his products. The publisher has not yet choked on his own "feedback" because the trade is so badly organized (blessed are the disorganized). It has never been so centralized as the automobile industry—or any other industry in the national economy. The diffusion of influence in the book trade has obstructed communications and delayed the tyranny of the consumer.

In the present confusion the trade publisher still has a chance. At least he is the only one who can do anything about it. Now, as ever, his individual decision of whether to publish a given book or how to publish it, many times repeated, defines the quality of the literature. Literature may be no concern of the publisher, but it *is* his business. It so happens that the individuality of a book serves both literature and business. If the publisher can convince his marketers that the peculiar difference of every book is its most salable quality, there might yet be a revolution in the book trade which would give the reader his just deserts.

Index